# Todd Haynes: Interviews

Conversations with Filmmakers Series
Gerald Peary, General Editor

# Todd Haynes
# INTERVIEWS

Edited by Julia Leyda

University Press of Mississippi / Jackson

www.upress.state.ms.us

The University Press of Mississippi is a member of the Association
of American University Presses.

Copyright © 2014 by University Press of Mississippi
All rights reserved
Manufactured in the United States of America

First printing 2014

∞

Library of Congress Cataloging-in-Publication Data

Haynes, Todd.
  Todd Haynes: interviews / edited by Julia Leyda.
    pages cm. — (Conversations with filmmakers series)
  Includes bibliographical references and index.
  Includes filmography.
  ISBN 978-1-61703-983-6 (cloth: alk. paper) — ISBN 978-1-61703-984-3 (ebook)  1.
Haynes, Todd—Interviews. 2. Motion picture producers and directors—United
States—Interviews. I. Leyda, Julia editor of compilation. II. Title.
  PN1998.3.H385A3 2014
  791.4302'33092—dc23

                    2014001978

British Library Cataloging-in-Publication Data available

# Contents

# Introduction

One thing becomes strikingly clear in reading this collection of interviews: Todd Haynes likes to talk. From the beginning he has been generous with his time, making himself available to interviewers of every stripe without discriminating: famous film critics, academics, bloggers, and writers for local and niche publications, all get a crack at him. Given his extensive influences and interests—experimental cinema, melodrama, celebrity and stardom, feminist and queer theory, and serial television, to name a few—it comes as no surprise that he comfortably moves among such different discourses. In assembling this collection, I have tried to include a representative sample of this range of sources and contexts.

In my correspondence with these writers in my capacity as editor of this volume, I was impressed by the number of contributors who remarked on what a pleasure it was to conduct these interviews. When I had the opportunity to do my own interview with him, I immediately understood. Haynes is not only whip-smart and extremely knowledgeable about film, politics, theory, and popular culture, he also comes to the interview ready to rethink and reconsider his own films, engaging enthusiastically with even the most obscure questions.

These interviews also trace several important and recurring issues in his body of work: the tension between formalism and emotional engagement, social ostracism of non-normative behaviors or identities, and the centrality of popular culture in contemporary life. Interviewers pursue these and other threads throughout his career as they ask him questions about his latest release as well as previous works, giving readers of this book a chance to observe the development and sedimentation of various perspectives and retrospectives.

Todd Haynes first attracted attention for his 1987 film *Superstar: The Karen Carpenter Story*, a short biopic of the pop singer performed by dolls and presented in the mode of a television disease movie. The clever underground allure of the film conceals its stealth mission: it seduces the viewer, expecting camp or irony, into a powerful emotional encounter with the character of Karen. *Superstar* thus marks the beginning of an extended engagement with one of Haynes's principal concerns as a film-maker: combining his aesthetic and intellectual interest in formal experimentation with his desire to foster an emotional response to his works. Sheryl Farber's interview discusses the film's conception and production, as well as Haynes's newly formed production company, Apparatus.

His next film, *Poison* (1991), continues to articulate his attention to form, intercutting three distinctly separate stories in which each main character struggles with his place in his respective society. Released in the early days of what came to be called the New Queer Cinema, *Poison*'s section entitled "Homo" drew fire from conservative religious and political figures for its images of abjection and gay subject matter. This controversy earned the film a measure of publicity beyond the usual expectations for a Sundance Grand Jury prizewinner. In addition to discussing *Superstar*, Michael Laskawy asks Haynes about the higher profile and wider audience *Poison* attained because of the controversy. In his interview with Michael William Saunders, Haynes talks at length about *Poison* in the context of its debt to French author Jean Genet, representations of homosexuality in film, and the lineage of queer cinema. In Justin Wyatt's interview, Haynes discusses other contexts for the film, such as the AIDS crisis and the influences of theories of sexuality and feminism on the film.

Released in 1995, *Safe* is a contemplative film whose form poses challenges of a different kind and which brings back a female protagonist in a story about illness—recalling some aspects of *Superstar*. Unlike *Superstar*, however, the emotional points of entry for *Safe* are not as clear; the film questions and disrupts conventional modes of narrative and character development with its ambivalent portrayal of Carol's physical and psychological environment and the possible roles of both in causing her illness. Haynes's interviews with Collier Schorr, Alison MacLean, and Larry Gross allow him to talk about the origins of the film and his research process, as well as its cinematic influences and ideological implications. Blase DiStefano's interview covers all three of Haynes's films to date, and also includes discussions of his own coming out, his opinions on outing, and his preferred undergarments.

*Velvet Goldmine*, which Haynes calls his most affirmative film ever, returns to the theme that attracted so much attention to *Poison*: queer sexuality. However, the mythical glam-rock fan film, conjuring the brief liberatory moment of the seventies sexual revolution, is exuberant where *Poison* was comparatively dark. British writer Nick James asks

Haynes to comment on the differences and overlaps of the US / UK glam experience, while with *Hedwig and the Angry Inch* director John Cameron Mitchell, Haynes discusses their different youthful memories of glam rock in Scotland and California. With Amy Taubin, in two interviews, Haynes talks about the relevance of the seventies- and eighties-set film for its late nineties audiences and its emphasis on fan pleasure; editor Jim Lyons also explains his role in planning and working on the film. Keith Phipps asks Haynes about the movie's setting in 1984 and its implications about the conservative, heteronormative eighties that followed the path-breaking social revolutions of the sixties and seventies, as well as the film's place within the cycle of seventies-nostalgia films released around the same time. In my own interview with Haynes, we also discuss *Velvet Goldmine* at length, particularly the role of female characters in the film.

In 2002, Haynes revisits the woman's film for the third time, now without a disease plot, in the fifties pastiche *Far from Heaven*. Drawing on Douglas Sirk's domestic melodramas such as *All That Heaven Allows* and *Imitation of Life*, as well as Max Ophuls's *The Reckless Moment*, Haynes's first twenty-first-century film embraces the aesthetic and technical conventions and limitations of the 1950s. Haynes reached a still wider audience with this film, gaining numerous award nominations and wider theatrical releases than ever before. Dennis Lim explores Haynes's experiences writing and making the movie, his commitment to circumventing the possibility of ironic or condescending distance, and the challenges and delights of imposing restrictions on the creative process. In his interview with Anthony Kaufman, Haynes comments on his desire to produce a sincere emotional connection despite the film's obvious artifice, and the influence of 1950s melodrama on his stylistic choices. Close attention to cinematography and its expressive function characterizes Jon Silberg's probing interview with Haynes and his director of photography, Ed Lachman, revealing the exhaustive research process that laid the groundwork for shooting the film. In his analysis of *Far from Heaven*, Geoffrey O'Brien's insightful interpretations complement Haynes's observations drawn from an extensive conversation, covering topics such as social constraints, formalism, and parody.

*I'm Not There* (2007), a fragmented quasi-biopic of Bob Dylan represented as a chameleon-like figure with several names and played by several different actors, marks a return to the exploration of the power of popular music. Noel Murray draws out Haynes on the meanings of the film: specifically, its implications regarding the nature of the self. With

Stephanie Zacharek, Haynes encapsulates the movie's rhetorical goal: to express the ways in which Dylan's career and persona embody the ongoing reconfiguration of identity. Haynes talks in detail about each of the different "characters" who portray Dylan's various avatars in his conversation with Richard Porton, touching on the historical and cultural context of the 1960s and specifics about his research process in writing the film. Matt Prigge provocatively opens his interview by asking Haynes about the title of the *New York Times Magazine*'s cover story on *I'm Not There*, "This Is Not a Bob Dylan Movie," leading to a discussion about Dylan's star image and Haynes's approach to music biopics.

Scott MacDonald's extended interview ranges widely across Haynes's career, beginning with his student years. They discuss Haynes's early grounding in avant-garde and experimental film and the challenges of distributing and exhibiting *Superstar*, before moving on to the motif of spanking in his work, including *Dottie Gets Spanked*. Haynes explains that he learned about the 1950s of *Dottie* and *Far from Heaven* from watching the films of that decade, which have exerted a strong influence on his own aesthetic sensibilities. The interview returns to the subject of the avant-garde in the context of *Poison*—its origins in Genet's work, its intertextual links with other queer experimental films, and its publicity-generating controversies. MacDonald wraps the interview with questions about *I'm Not There* and its cinematic influences.

With *Mildred Pierce* (2011), Haynes achieves several firsts: it marks his first foray into the long-form television miniseries format, his first screenplay adaptation of a published novel, and his first Emmy nominations. Sam Adams talks to him about his commitment to James M. Cain's novel, its relevance to the contemporary audience in the midst of the financial crisis, and the naturalistic style of the series, inspired by the New American Cinema of the 1970s. In his interview with Amy Taubin, Haynes explains his interest in the serial form and the woman's film, as he revisits the genre from a more realist angle. Eric Kohn's interview covers, in two parts, the experience of working on *Mildred Pierce* for HBO and the reissue of *Poison* on the twentieth anniversary of its release. *Mildred* takes center stage in Michael Guillén's interview as well, touching on the power of the woman's film, *Mildred*'s economic and filial tragedies, and the dearth of opportunities for talented women performers in the film and television industries today.

I close the volume with my own interview with Todd Haynes, in which I ask him questions, some of which I had been saving up for years, about *Velvet Goldmine*, *Superstar*, *Safe*, *Far from Heaven*, and, of course,

*Mildred Pierce*. In the process, we discuss the woman's film and women's roles in his work, the constructedness of gendered and sexual identity, the centrality of melodrama and formal experimentation in his work, and the pitfalls of nostalgia when representing the past.

I must acknowledge my debt to Leila Salisbury for her vision and support throughout the process of putting together this volume: without her it would not exist. Sincerest thanks also to Michael William Saunders, Amy Taubin, and Justin Wyatt for going the extra mile in helping me obtain permissions to reprint their work. In the final stages, Nanako Ozeki's tireless assistance helped to ensure that the manuscript was formatted and ready to submit. But in the end, like everything, this book is for Christopher.

JL

# Chronology

1961   Todd Haynes is born January 2, 1961, in Los Angeles, California, to Allen E. Haynes and Sherry Lynne Haynes. Haynes attends Lanai Road School, Gaspar de Portola Junior High School, both in Encino, and the Oakwood School, North Hollywood.

1978   Haynes produces his first film, the short *The Suicide*, while still in high school.

1985   Haynes directs his first film, *Assassins: A Film Concerning Rimbaud*, and graduates from Brown University with a BA in art and semiotics. After graduation, he moves to New York where he co-founds Apparatus production company with Barry Ellsworth and Christine Vachon.

1987   Haynes co-writes, with Cynthia Schneider, *Superstar: The Karen Carpenter Story*. That summer he enrolls in Bard College MFA program and completes one term, during which he makes the sets and props for *Superstar* and shoots the film, which he edits in the fall in New York.

1988   Haynes is a founding member of Gran Fury, an artists' collective affiliated with the AIDS activist group ACT UP (AIDS Coalition to Unleash Power).

1989   Haynes receives cease-and-desist letters from attorneys representing Richard Carpenter and the estate of Karen Carpenter, as well as their record company A&M, ordering him to remove *Superstar: The Karen Carpenter Story* (1987) from public circulation. Bootleg videotapes of the film continue to circulate informally.

1990   Haynes receives funding to support post-production on *Poison* in the form of a $25,000 National Endowment for the Arts Grant, which draws attacks from fundamentalist Christian groups such as the American Family Association and the Christian Coalition. Right-wing "family values" activists characterize the experimental film as pornographic and protest the use of the government grant to support it, bringing Haynes and the film additional media attention and higher box office yields.

1991    *Poison* wins the Sundance Film Festival Grand Jury Prize and the Teddy at the Berlin International Film Festival. It is nominated for two Independent Spirit awards: Best Director and Best First Feature (with Christine Vachon).

1996    *Safe* is nominated for two Independent Spirit awards: Best Director and Best Screenplay.

1998    *Velvet Goldmine* is nominated for the Palme d'Or and wins Best Artistic Contribution at the Cannes Film Festival. It also wins the Channel 4 Director's Award at the Edinburgh International Film Festival and is nominated for the Best Director Independent Spirit award.

2000    After losing his apartment in Williamsburg, Brooklyn, Haynes moves to Portland, Oregon.

2002    *Far from Heaven* receives Academy Award nominations for Best Actress (Julianne Moore) and Best Original Screenplay. It is nominated for the Best Screenplay—Motion Picture Golden Globe award and the Best Director Independent Spirit award.

2008    *I'm Not There* wins the Robert Altman award at the Independent Spirit Awards and is nominated for the Best Director award.

2011    *Mildred Pierce* is nominated for three Emmy Awards: Outstanding Directing for a Miniseries, Movie or a Dramatic Special, Outstanding Miniseries or Made for Television Movie, and Outstanding Writing for Miniseries, Movie or a Dramatic Special.

# Filmography

ASSASSINS: A FILM CONCERNING RIMBAUD (1985)
Production Company: Brown University
Director: **Todd Haynes**
Screenplay: **Todd Haynes**

SUPERSTAR: THE KAREN CARPENTER STORY (1987)
Production Company: Iced Tea Productions
Producers: **Todd Haynes** and Cynthia Schneider
Director: **Todd Haynes**
Screenplay: **Todd Haynes** and Cynthia Schneider
Cinematography: Barry Ellsworth (uncredited)
Cast: Merrill Gruver (Karen), Michael Edwards (Richard), Melissa Brown
(Mother), Rob LaBelle (Dad/Mr. A&M), Nannie Doyle (Cherry Boone),
Cynthia Schneider (Dionne Warwick), Larry Kole (Announcer), Gwen
Kraus (narrator), Bruce Tuthill (narrator)
35mm, color, 43 minutes

POISON (1991)
Production Company: Bronze Eye Productions
Producer: Christine Vachon
Executive Producers: Brian Greenbaum and James Schamus
Associate Producer: Lauren Zalaznick
Director/Screenplay: **Todd Haynes**
Based on the Novels by: Jean Genet
Editing: **Todd Haynes** and James Lyons
Cinematography: Maryse Alberti (color); Barry Ellsworth (black and
white)
Music: James Bennett
Cast: "HERO" Edith Meeks (Felicia Beacon), Millie White (Millie Sklar),
Buck Smith (Gregory Lazar), Anne Giotta (Evelyn McAlpert), Lydia

Lafleur (Sylvia Manning), Ian Nemser (Sean White), Rob Labelle (Jay Wete), Evan Dunsky (Dr. MacArthur), Marina Lutz (Hazel Lamprecht), Barry Cassidy (Officer Rilt), Richard Anthony (Edward Comacho), Angela M. Schreiber (Florence Giddens), Justin Silverstein (Jake), Chris Singh (Chris), Edward Allen (Fred Beacon), Carlos Jiminez (Jose); "HORROR" Larry Maxwell (Dr. Graves), Susan Gayle Norman (Nancy Olsen), Al Quagliata (Deputy Hansen), Michelle Sullivan (Prostitute), Parlan McGraw (Newscaster), Frank O'Donnell (Old Doctor), Melissa Brown (Woman in alley), Joe Dietl (Man in alley), Richard Hansen (Narrator); "HOMO" Scott Renderer (John Broom), James Lyons (Jack Bolton), Tony Pemberton (Young Broom), Andrew Harpending (Young Bolton), John R. Lombardi (Rass), Tony Gigante (Inspector), Douglas F. Gibson (Van Roven), Damien Garcia (Chanchi), Les Simpson (Miss Tim), Joey Grant (Jamoke), Gary Ray (Basco), David Danford (Canon), Jason Bauer (Doran), Ken Schatz (Preacher), Maurice Clapisson (Guard 1), Matthew Ebert (Guard 2)
35mm, color and black and white, 85 minutes

DOTTIE GETS SPANKED (1993)
Production Company: Caboose Productions
Producers: Christine Vachon and Lauren Zalaznick
Coordinating Producer: James Schamus
Associate Producer: Craig Paull
Director/Screenplay: **Todd Haynes**
Editing: James Lyons
Cinematography: Maryse Alberti
Music: James Bennett
Cast: J. Even Bonifant (Steven Gale), Barbara Gale (Lorraine Gale), Julie Halston (Dottie Frank), Robert Pall (Steven's father), Harriet Sansom Harris (Sharon's mother), Irving Metzman (TV show guide), Ashley Chapman (Sharon), Rhea Silver-Smith (Darcy), Gina Gallagher (Kim), Adam Arkin (Dick Gordon), Richard DeDomenico (dream messenger), John Brian Rogers (TV director), Lenny Singer (photographer/assistant), Leo Ferstenberg (cameraman), Lindsay Rodio (Jennifer)
16mm, color, 27 minutes

SAFE (1995)
Production Company: American Playhouse Theatrical Films
Producers: Christine Vachon and Lauren Zalaznick
Executive Producers: John Hart, Ted Hope, Lindsay Law, James Schamus
Associate Producer: Ernest Kerns

Director/Screenplay: **Todd Haynes**
Editing: James Lyons
Cinematography: Alex Nepomniaschy
Cast: Julianne Moore (Carol White), Xander Berkeley (Greg White), Dean Norris (mover), Julie Burgess (aerobics instructor), Ronnie Farer (Barbara), Jodie Markell (Anita), Susan Norman (Linda), Martha Velez (Fulvia), Chauncey Leopardi (Rory), Saachiko (dry cleaners manager), Tim Gardner (department store dispatcher), Wendy Haynes (waitress), Allan Wasserman (client), Jean St. James (client's wife), Steven Gilborn (Dr. Hubbard)
35mm, color, 119 minutes

VELVET GOLDMINE (1998)
Production Company: Channel Four, Goldwyn, Killer, Miramax, New-market Capital, Single Cell, Zenith
Producer: Christine Vachon
Co-Producer: Olivia Stewart
Executive Producers: Scott Meek, Sandy Stern, Michael Stipe, Bob Weinstein, Harvey Weinstein
Co-Executive producers: Christopher Bail and William Tyrer
Director/Screenplay: **Todd Haynes**
Editing: James Lyons
Cinematography: Maryse Alberti
Music: Carter Burwell and Craig Wedren
Cast: Ewan McGregor (Curt Wild), Jonathan Rhys Meyers (Brian Slade), Christian Bale (Arthur Stuart), Toni Collette (Mandy Slade), Eddie Izzard (Jerry Devine), Emily Woof (Shannon), Michael Feast (Cecil), Janet McTeer (female narrator), Mairead McKinley (Wilde housemaid), Luke Morgan Oliver (Oscar Wilde, 8), Osheen Jones (Jack Fairy, 7), Micko Westmoreland (Jack Fairy), Damian Suchet (BBC reporter), Danny Nutt (kissing sailor), Wash Westmoreland (young man)
35mm, color, 124 minutes

FAR FROM HEAVEN (2002)
Production Company: Focus Features, Vulcan, Killer, John Wells, Section Eight
Producers: Jody Allen and Christine Vachon
Co-Producers: Declan Baldwin and Bradford Simpson
Executive Producers: George Clooney, Eric Robinson, John Sloss, Steven Soderbergh, John Wells
Director/Screenplay: **Todd Haynes**

Editing: James Lyons
Cinematography: Edward Lachman
Music: Elmer Bernstein
Cast: Julianne Moore (Cathy Whitaker), Dennis Quaid (Frank Whita-
ker), Dennis Haysbert (Raymond Deagan), Patricia Clarkson (Eleanor
Fine), Viola Davis (Sybil), James Rebhorn (Dr. Bowman), Bette Hen-
ritze (Mrs. Leacock), Michael Gaston (Stan Fine), Ryan Ward (David
Whitaker), Lindsay Andretta (Janice Whitaker), Jordan Puryear (Sarah
Deagan), Kyle Timothy Smith (Billy Hutchinson), Celia Weston (Mona
Lauder), Barbara Garrick (Doreen), Olivia Birkelund (Nancy)
35 mm, color, 107 minutes


I'M NOT THERE (2007)
Production Company: Killer, John Wells, John Goldwyn, Endgame
Entertainment, Dreamachine, Film & Entertainment VIP Medienfonds,
Grey Water Park, Rising Star, Wells
Producers: John Goldwyn, John Sloss, James D. Stern, Christine Vachon
Co-Producer: Charles Pugliese
Executive Producers: Philip Elway, Andreas Grosch, Douglas Hansen,
Wendy Japhet, Amy J. Kaufman, Hengameh Panahi, Steven Soderbergh,
John Wells
Associate Producers: Philippe Aigle and Charlotte Mickie
Director: **Todd Haynes**
Screenplay: **Todd Haynes** and Oren Moverman
Editing: Jay Rabinowitz
Cinematography: Edward Lachman
Cast: Cate Blanchett (Jude), Ben Whishaw (Arthur), Christian Bale
(Jack/Pastor John), Richard Gere (Billy), Marcus Carl Franklin (Woody/
Chaplin Boy), Heath Ledger (Robbie), Kris Kristofferson (narrator), Don
Francks (Hobo Joe), Roc LaFortune (Hobo Moe), Larry Day (government
agent), Paul Cagelet (carny/bell-hop), Brian R.C. Wilmes (circus man),
Pierre-Alexandre Fortin (Gorgeous George), Richie Havens (Old Man
Arvin), Tyrone Benskin (Mr. Arvin)
35mm, color and black and white, 135 minutes


MILDRED PIERCE (2011)
Production Company: HBO, MGM, Killer, John Wells
Executive Producers: Christine Vachon, **Todd Haynes**, Pamela Koffler,
John Wells

Co-Executive Producer: Ilene S. Landress
Associate Producers: Jessica Levin and Kendall McCarthy
Line Producer: Harvey Waldman
Director: **Todd Haynes**
Screenplay: **Todd Haynes**, Jon Raymond
Based on the Novel by: James M. Cain
Editing: Camilla Toniolo and Affonso Gonçalves
Cinematography: Edward Lachman
Music: Carter Burwell
Cast: Kate Winslet (Mildred Pierce), Brian F. O'Bryne (Bert Pierce), Melissa Leo (Lucy Gessler), James LeGros (Wally Burgan), Murphy Guyer (Mr. Pierce), Mare Winningham (Ida Corwin), Marin Ireland (Letty), Guy Pearce (Monty Beragon), Diane Kagan (Mrs. Pierce), Miriam Shor (Anna), Halley Feiffer (Arline), Hope Davis (Mrs. Forrester), Robb Webb (radio announcer), Christopher Koron (Archie), Margaret Hall (Mrs. Floyd), Morgan Turner (Veda Pierce), Erwin Falcon (Pancho), Elvy Yost (Sigrid), Laura Esterman (Mrs. Kramer)
16mm, color, 336 minutes (total run time)

### As Actor/Producer

CAUSE AND EFFECT (1988)
Production Company: Apparatus
Producers: Barry Ellsworth, **Todd Haynes**, Christine Vachon
Directors: Susan Delson and Evan Dunsky
Screenplay: Susan Delson
16mm, color, 11 minutes

HE WAS ONCE (1989)
Production Company: Apparatus
Producers: **Todd Haynes** and Christine Vachon
Co-Producer: Barry Ellsworth
Director/Screenplay: Mary Hestand
Editing: Barry Ellsworth
Cinematography: Stephen Kazmierski
Music: Alan Tubbs
Cast: Todd Adams (Davey), Salvador Barone (Dad), Susan Norman (Sally), Emma Strahs (Mom), Melissa Gardner (Shirley), **Todd Haynes** (Randy), Julia Haltigan (the bear)
16mm, color and black and white, 16 minutes

LA DIVINA (1989)
Production Company: Apparatus
Producers: Barry Ellsworth and Christine Vachon
Co-Producer: **Todd Haynes**
Director: M. Brooke Dammkoehler
Assistant Director: **Todd Haynes**
Cast: Michelle Sullivan (Greta Garbo), Christopher Renstrom (John Gilbert), Valda Z. Drabla (alter-ego)
16mm, black and white, 33 minutes

OFFICE KILLER (1997)
Production Company: Good Fear, Good Machine, Kardana-Swinsky Films
Producers: Pamela Koffler and Christine Vachon
Executive Producers: Tom Carouso, John Hart, Ted Hope, James Schamus
Director: Cindy Sherman
Screenplay: **Todd Haynes** (uncredited), Tom Kalin, Elise MacAdam, Cindy Sherman
Editing: Merril Stern
Cinematography: Russell Lee Fine
Music: Evan Lurie
Cast: Carol Kane (Dorine Douglas), Molly Ringwald (Kim Poole), Jeanne Tripplehorn (Norah Reed), Barbara Sukowa (Virginia Wingate), Michael Imperioli (Daniel Birch), David Thornton (Gary Michaels), Mike Hodge (Mr. Landau), Alice Drummond (Carlotta Douglas), Florina Rodov (receptionist), Jason Brill (delivery man), Eddie Malavarca (Brian), Doug Barron (Ted), Linda Powell (Naomi), Albert Macklin (Brad), Michelle Hurst (Kate)
35 mm, color, 82 minutes

QUINCEAÑERA (2006)
Production Company: Apparatus, Cinetic Media, Kitchen Sink Entertainment LLC
Producer: Anne Clements
Executive Producers: Nick Boyias, **Todd Haynes**, Mihail Koulakis, Avi Raccah
Associate Producer: J. Evan Shapiro
Line Producer: Shaun Young
Directors/Screenplay: Richard Glatzer and Wash Westmoreland

Editing: Robin Katz and Clay Zimmerman
Cinematography: Eric Steelberg
Music: Victor Bock, Michael B. Jeter, J. Peter Robinson, Micko
Westmoreland
Cast: Jesus Castanos (Ernesto), Araceli Guzman-Rico (Maria), Emily Rios
(Magdalena), J. R. Cruz (Herman), Listette Avila (Jessica), Alicia Sixtos
(Eileen May Garcia), Hector Quevedo (dancing boy), Germán Campos
(Chambelàn), Carlos Linares (videographer), Johnny Chavez (Uncle
Walter), Carmen Aguirre (Aunt Silvia), Margarita Lugo (Aunt Candy),
Jorge Ortiz (DJ), Veronica Sixtos (young girl), Jesse Garcia (Carlos)
35mm, color, 90 minutes
OLD JOY (2006)
Production Company: Film Science, Van Hoy/Knudsen Productions,
Washington Square Films
Producers: Lars Knudsen, Neil Knopp, Anish Savjani, Jay Van Hoy
Executive Producers: Joshua Blum, **Todd Haynes**, Mike S. Ryan, Rajen
Savjani
Director/Editing: Kelly Reichardt
Screenplay: Jonathan Raymond and Kelly Reichardt
Cinematography: Peter Sillen
Music: Yo La Tengo
Cast: Daniel London (Mark), Will Oldham (Kurt), Tanya Smith (Tanya),
Robin Rosenberg (waitress), Keri Moran (lawnmower)
35 mm, color, 76 minutes

WENDY AND LUCY (2008)
Production Company: Field Guide Films, Film Science, Glass Eye Pix
Producers: Larry Fessenden, Neil Knopp, Anish Savjani
Executive Producers: Joshua Blum, **Todd Haynes**, Phil Morrison, Rajen
Savjani
Director/Editing: Kelly Reichardt
Screenplay: Jonathan Raymond and Kelly Reichardt
Cinematography: Sam Levy
Cast: Michelle Williams (Wendy), Lucy (Lucy the dog), Michelle
Worthey (Sadie), Will Oldham (Icky), Wally Dalton (security guard),
Roger D. Faires (recycler in wheelchair), Boggs Johnson (recycling man),
Tanya Smith (grocery checker), Michael Brophy (grocery store stocker),
John Robinson (Andy), John Breen (Mr. Hunt)
35mm, color, 80 minutes

MEEK'S CUTOFF (2010)
Production Company: Evenstar Films, Film Science, Harmony
Productions
Producers: Elizabeth Cuthrell, Neil Knopp, Anish Savjani, David Urrutia
Co-Producer: Vincent Savino
Executive Producers: **Todd Haynes**, Phil Morrison, Andrew Pope,
Laura Rosenthal, Mike S. Ryan, Rajen Savjani, Steven Tuttleman
Director/Editing: Kelly Reichardt
Screenplay: Jonathan Raymond
Cinematography: Chris Blauvelt
Music: Jeff Grace
Cast: Michelle Williams (Emily Tetherow), Bruce Greenwood (Stephen
Meek), Will Patton (Soloman Tetherow), Zoe Kazan (Millie Gately), Paul
Dano (Thomas Gately), Shirley Henderson (Glory White), Neal Huff
(William White), Tommy Nelson (Jimmy White), Rod Rondeaux (the
Indian)
35mm, color, 104 minutes

### Other

"Disappearer" (music video for Sonic Youth) (1991)
Director: **Todd Haynes**

"Share the Good" (Heineken commercial) (2008)
Director: **Todd Haynes**
1:01 minutes

# Todd Haynes: Interviews

# Karen Carpenter: Getting to the Bare Bones of Todd Haynes's *Superstar: The Karen Carpenter Story*

Sheryl Farber / 1989

From *Film Threat* 1, no. 20 (1989). Reprinted by permission from *Film Threat* and Sheryl Farber.

On a New York oldies station tonight, the Carpenters are the featured recording artists. The DJ notes the *smooth as silk* voice of Karen Carpenter before he plays one of their hits, "Rainy Days and Mondays." The first few strains of the harmonica begin, heralding the melancholy voice of Karen singing—

*Talking to myself and feeling old.*
*Sometimes I'd like to quit.*
*Nothing ever seems to fit*

I can't stop listening. The DJ plays all of my Carpenter favorites and I am catapulted into memories of the seventies. "For All We Know" comes on and I am in a music class full of pubescent pimply-faced junior high school kids, reluctantly waving plastic batons, learning how to conduct to Karen's soothing voice and her brother Richard's elaborate arrangements. Actually this is the late seventies and I am wondering why my teacher has chosen a song that I remember from my early childhood—a song that is now only played on the annoying muzak station my mother listens to in the car on the way to the supermarket and piped into the speakers above the aisle of lemon fresh Joy and Bounty. Nonetheless, I am, unlike most of my baton-slinging peers, captivated by the voice of the songstress of the seventies.

The hits just keep coming out of my radio. "We've Only Just Begun," written by that diminutive troubadour John Williams. "Close to You," written by Burt Bacharach, who called Karen, at the time of her tragic death at thirty-two, "A magical person with a magical voice." I fall asleep with "Superstar" ringing in my ears.

My reawakened interest in the Carpenters' music began after I sat through a slew of bad films at the New York Film Festival Downtown. The evening seemed like it was going to be representative of the bleak state of underground filmmaking in New York. The last movie to be shown, however, was Todd Haynes's *Superstar: The Karen Carpenter Story*, a 16mm, forty-three-minute film made in 1987 that has been receiving critical acclaim for over a year now. Along with strong recommendations to see the film from friends I was usually given a brief description—"It's made with Barbie dolls." Like most American women (and even some men) I was no stranger to the Barbie netherworld, and like most women (but unlike many men), I had been forced to reconcile myself with the fact that I would never be built like a Barbie. I was interested to see what director Haynes would do with the issue of anorexia, the disease that eventually led to Karen Carpenter's demise and wondered if the use of Barbie dolls would be purely comic.

The film opens with Karen's mother's point of view in February 1983. She discovers the collapsed, silk-shrouded body of Karen in their Downey, California, home. Then we are shown the outside of a middle-class suburban house (which incidentally was the actual Carpenter digs in Downey) and the question "What happened?" is posed by the narrator. "Let's go back," he says as we are about to enter a journey, first through the streets of sunny Southern California, providing a backdrop for fancy seventies stylized credits, and then through the simulated doll life of Karen Carpenter. With a straightforward narrative we are hooked into the story of Karen Carpenter's life, her rise to stardom and her problem with anorexia that accompanied it. Haynes has also managed to capture the period brilliantly with detailed sets, music that includes the Captain & Tennille and Gilbert O'Sullivan, clips from television such as *The Brady Bunch* and *The Partridge Family*. There are clips of Richard Nixon, bombs over Cambodia. This seems to counter the clean-cut, close-knit youthful wholesomeness that the media tried to bolster with such teen stars as the Brady Bunch, the Osmonds, and the Carpenters.

I spoke with Todd Haynes at a restaurant that serves healthy, non-fattening foods.

**Sheryl Farber:** Which came first: the idea to make a movie about Karen Carpenter, or the idea to make a TV docudrama-type of film with dolls?

**Todd Haynes:** Well, the idea to do a film with dolls actually came before anything. I saw this promotional black and white little trailer on television—a vintage piece of TV from the fifties, that introduced the Barbie to the American public. And it had a little miniature interior scene with the doll sitting around the living room, and then Barbie came in and showed Midge her new dress and it also intercut with live action—a little girl opened up a mailbox, shot from inside the mailbox, getting her Barbie fan club mail. And I was really intrigued with the idea of doing a fairly straightforward narrative drawing on pre-existing popular forms, but simply replacing real actors with inanimate objects, with dolls. And being very careful with it and detailed in such a way that it would provoke the same kind of identification and investment in the narrative as any real movie would. But in watching it, this emotional involvement in dolls or something completely artificial, that would possibly make us think. Maybe that's what happens when we see movies, it's more the forms and the structures that they take that provoke the emotional responses; more than the fact that there was, at one point, a real actress or actor in front of the camera. We were watching shadows on a wall carefully fitting into pre-existing forms that we know very well, that we still cry and laugh as if it were a real person.

**SF:** So you are using the star story docudrama form to grip the viewer but at the same time you're being critical of that very form?

**TH:** Yes, I think so. The form I used definitely comes from probably the most tabloid form of narrative filmmaking, which is always telling the rise and fall of the fated star and revealing all the inside dirt in careful pre-determined ways. I juxtapose it with other kinds of styles sort of faux documentary style.

**SF:** The anorexia films we saw in high school—

**TH:** Exactly. Instructional kinds of films. And also montages which begin like the typical image montage that accompanies a song number in a movie, but beginning to get a little more abstract and more experimental as the film progresses. The film is basically held together by the narrative. And that's what makes people move from being cynical, critically engaged or laughing, to being implicated and emotionally attached to the character. And in a sense, I like it better when the narrative works than when it fails because since it's with dolls it hooks you in, and you have to admit to your implication by realizing you've been lured into a trap.

**SF:** This movie seems to appeal primarily to people between the ages of twenty and thirty, particularly I think because of your images of popular culture from the seventies.

**TH:** The film supposes a kind of turning point in popular culture from the sixties and the seventies that caught all of us in a certain generation at a vulnerable point because we were just starting to think of ourselves autonomously in the early seventies because of our being eight, nine, ten, eleven. And when the music came out, it was such a strong kind of suggestion that everything was fine. The turmoil of the late sixties was over in a second and Nixon was in the White House and things were going to be just great. The family gained new value, of a new pertinence that had been questioned for the previous decade.

**SF:** It was also the taming of the youth culture.

**TH:** Yes, completely. Although at the same time the Viet Nam War was raging, Kent State, there was a continued explosion of social protests and causes but at the same time, because of our age, I responded much more to the images of safety and tranquility that were on television and the radio—the Carpenters represent that to such a complete extent. What seemed to happen then is that everything started to fall through like Watergate pulled the rug out from under the Nixon administration. The Carpenters dropped in popularity and disco happened and we just began this really self-absorbed generation of hedonistic pleasures. I think we got cynical and the eighties celebrate that cynicism in a way that we never really anticipated. So when I look back at that period and when I heard the music, after not really hearing it for a long time, it was almost for me like the last time I believed in popular culture and that it worked for me. It manipulated my view of the world and it also united me with my family and their values. Like, this friend of mine said to me, "It was pre-irony." It was the last moment for our generation that was one of the last earnest sentimental times. The music gained all its resonance that probably, at the time, you would never have thought it carried.

**SF:** How long did the movie take to make?

**TH:** The whole film took about a year and a half from writing to completion while carrying on other jobs. I shot it in upstate New York at Bard College. I began an MFA program there, a three-summer long program and I basically utilized the first summer—I haven't gone back since—to build all the sets and make all the props and by the end of the summer we shot it. I worked on it with three close friends. Cynthia Schneider co-wrote it with me and co-produced it as well. Barry Ellsworth, who is part of Apparatus, helped me shoot it and write it and is really responsible for how beautiful the film looks. Bob Maneti worked on it laboriously as well. So it was a very small core group of maniacs working insane hours. I mean the film was fun but it was really hard. I underestimated how long everything would take.

**SF:** The film has a strong feminist viewpoint and I know you had a female co-writer; I was wondering how you became sensitive to such issues?
**TH:** Well, I think the film couldn't have been conceived without Cynthia's participation. Neither of us have experienced anorexia personally but through the process of researching it and involving ourselves I think we both found connections to it that I may never have considered otherwise. I think the pressures and the kinds of neurotic motivations that would result in eating disorders are the same pressures and neurotic feelings that I've experienced but taken out in other ways. But definitely the roots and the causes that I began to see of anorexia were all things I knew really well. I found the whole thing intriguing, the whole story, but I don't think I found it personally comprehensible in the way that I did after researching it. But the response basically has been extremely supportive from the feminist community. There had been a couple of incidents of what I would call a more narrow and dogmatic side of feminism which recoils from the idea of humor being engaged in any way in a film or a work about anorexia—that humor does not have a place in it. And the film does not at any point make fun of anorexia but I do think humor is a tool. It can even be a weapon and it's been a part of cultural production, a really interesting part of it for a really long time. And it can be an incredible political tool and to simply say, "That's not allowed!" I find to be the worst side of feminism or any other kind of political critique of our culture—when it takes on the same dogma that the culture imposes. That's wrong to me.

**SF:** Did you use those high school-type health films that you imitated to help research anorexia?
**TH:** No, but we found general material that's available to the public that has the whole tone. And which is just as limited in the whole view of the problem.

**SF:** You really managed to physically transform Karen's doll to show the effects of her anorexia. How did you get that emaciated effect on her face?

**TH:** We carved down the plastic cheeks of the doll head. I found dolls at flea markets. I don't think they were actually Barbie dolls. These were dolls that were extremely thin already but the faces were kind of round so I wanted to carve down the cheeks and then cover it over with pancake makeup and have very creepy effects.

**SF:** I saw a picture of Karen Carpenter from that time and the doll really looks like her. Are the dolls actual Barbie dolls from Mattel?

**TH:** No, in fact none of them are literally Barbie dolls. The doll that portrays Karen is the Tracy doll, a Mattel product who's the dark-haired current Barbie friend on the market. A Ken doll does portray Richard but he has various wigs and hairpieces throughout the film and by the end of the film we changed his face a lot so it's no longer a Ken doll.

**SF:** More like some strange mutant.

**TH:** Exactly. I love the part in *Superstar* where Karen turns around and she says, "I am sick, Richard," and he says, "What do you mean sick, mentally?" And he looks so much sicker than she does.

**SF:** Did you know about Richard's Quaalude addiction and choose not to explore it?

**TH:** I didn't know about it, although my film's reference to his private life could be interpreted as referring to his drug habit.

**SF:** Or his homosexuality.

**TH:** Yes. But I don't have any solid evidence to what his private life entails so I guess I could leave it open.

**SF:** So what did you think about the TV movie?

**TH:** I enjoyed every second of it but I also found it disturbing. I thought it was interesting how it both very carefully revealed and concealed information about them.

**SF:** Yes, especially the way they treated her eating disorder. I charted scene by scene their showing of her voracious appetite like when the Carpenter family goes bowling, Karen yells eagerly, "Pizza, yeah!" Then "Hot dogs, sure!" They always had her stealing from the cookie jar.

**TH:** And then "all of a sudden" sort of reversed tack. There were things I didn't know. That they lived together during that period. That was really interesting to learn. I didn't know that Karen's first recording contract was a solo contract. That was really extraordinary. They're really hot. I hear the solo album and it's really an exciting collection of songs that don't sound like Richard Carpenter productions.

**SF:** They weren't his arrangements?
**TH:** No. It was during the time that he was detoxing apparently, that's what the movie tells us and she went to New York. They bring it up in the TV movie. She tells him and he immediately gets mad at her but then it switches to the anorexia as the issue. She went to New York during that time and cut an album with Phil Ramone, who's a producer of Billy Joel, and some classics and some disco classics. And it was '79, '80, so it was very disco influenced. It's really interesting because it's her voice up against stronger percussion and none of that saturated vocal background bullshit, which I hate, which is the Richard Carpenter trademark. This is really cool because it's so sad. I don't think people think of Karen Carpenter as diversely as she could have been considered as an artist. She never really got a chance to be anything but Richard Carpenter's product. She never got to experiment with sounds and playing with her voice in different ways. I think maybe if she had, and thought of herself more autonomously, she might have been able to live longer and give herself incentive to not think of herself solely in context of the family and Richard's world. What's really sad is the solo album may never get released because of Richard Carpenter even today. Karen Carpenter's image is still being controlled and manipulated by Richard and the family. That's so sad.

**SF:** I know that this is getting into the private family stuff that you may not know about. But do you know what Richard's relationship to his parents is? I know he had control over this TV movie and the content is real derogatory to his parents.
**TH:** His mother gave it her approval. And most people find the mother's depiction extremely critical and harsh. But it only makes you think if the mother okayed this version, you could only imagine what it was like in real life.

**SF:** Parts of the TV movie seemed to overlap yours, for example the use of the song "Masquerade" when Karen meets her husband Tom Burris. What was your reaction?

**TH:** I knew that there would be parallels. Partly because I was drawing on the TV movie form to begin with, and obviously when you're doing a TV movie genre about an anorexic pop singer there's going to be similar dialogue. I'm also from California so that the whole colloquialism of that world is familiar to me. People tell me, "They must have seen your movie and stolen from it," but I really think it was accidental.

**SF:** What is Apparatus involved in now and where are you taking it?
**TH:** We're still producing work by emerging filmmakers who submit scripts to us. We provide funding and production facilities and guidance. But the director maintains the creative control throughout these projects. We recently signed a contract for a really wonderful partnership with Zeitgeist. They want to fairly aggressively distribute packages of short films each year that we produce or that we're affiliated with in some way called "Apparatus Presents" and try to get them shown theatrically and non-theatrically across the country. They are also very eager in that we travel with the films and discuss the philosophies behind this push toward short filmmaking and experimental narrative filmmaking.

**SF:** Are the other people involved in Apparatus friends from school?
**TH:** Yes, we all met at Brown and have worked on each other's films since then. We've all basically continued to work on our own projects on the side, as filmmakers. It's been great. The two films that are coming out this year are even more radical and experimental in a lot of ways than the ones we did last year. One of them is called *La Divina*. It's a heightened, stylized account of a thirties star in the sort of style Garbo shot. It's a very self-critical, perhaps self-conscious look at that whole world. And the other one is called *He Was Once*, sort of based on the *Davey and Goliath* show almost as a reverse to *Superstar*. This takes actors and dresses them up as Claymation puppets and enacts them from that way.

**SF:** I ask a general state of underground filmmaking question—New York, around the country, etc. . . . where do you see it going?
**TH:** I think in a small way we've helped. Both Apparatus and the amazing response to *Superstar* have helped the national scene to take more account of marginal filmmaking, short filmmaking, and filmmaking that experiments with narrative forms and styles in ways that I think the general film audiences have been able to take seriously for a long time. At least there's been sort of precedent of fifties and sixties avant-garde, which no one seems to improve upon or we're always comparing

ourselves to, that very high moment in experimental filmmaking in this country. Totally disavowing or ignoring the fact that we've had a lot of important strains in filmmaking since then. That there's been the punk movement in the late seventies. There's been a neo-narrative movement in the early eighties. There's been a conceptual movement in the early seventies and no one seems to talk about that stuff as much as this "high moment" of avant-garde film which still gets screened primarily at places like the Anthology Archives and the Millennium and, until recently, the Collective for Living Cinema. I think we're all eager at Apparatus to push forward and begin to diversify the ways in which we look at narrative again. What's really funny is that I think Hollywood and the studios and the people with money and the cable world are hungry, starved, even, for innovative work so they're not missing a single punch when it comes to small films that get shown at festivals or circulated.

**SF:** Have they shown your films on cable yet?

**TH:** No, they haven't. Unresolved music rights really prohibits that. I can't, and they can't, take that risk. The festival showings of *Superstar* have generated a lot of response—not just for that film but for films of its kind. So I think that's really hopeful, I don't think we're seeing the revolution yet but . . . it really surprises me that the big professionals of the industry have also found it inspiring. To me that means that everyone is eager for something different.

**SF:** What is the fascination with pop culture?

**TH:** I think it's inevitable given that we're in such an information-ridden society and we appropriate the past so quickly that you can barely call it the past. Things get taken up so quickly and become retro at this sort of hyper-accelerated speed, so that I sometimes think that the context gets lost and this massive attempt to re-examine the past kind of equates and collapses meaning or I guess purpose. It also comes out of Hollywood. I think in *Blue Velvet, Hairspray, River's Edge,* and even Coppola's *Tucker,* there's a real official fascination with popular culture. I think those films are actually a better example of a lot of commercial films that are also obsessed with the past. But I think it's cool. We're learning how to refer to and play with other genres; I just think sometimes the style precedes the purpose and the content. We need to know why we're looking at the past and what we're trying to learn from it and ultimately how it's informing the present. It gets really fun to do sometimes. It may be more fun than valuable and I think there's a danger there in just collapsing the reasons behind it.

I think the one thing that is evident with *Superstar* is that it's all contrasted examples of artifice. It's all fake. It's a doll world that's made to look like a real world. Or it's sort of a pseudo-documentary, collages that are also scripted and completely constructed. So it's different examples of so-called truth that you, as a viewer, have to weigh against each other. I also think I was lucky in subject matter because the Carpenters provided a perfect dialectic, almost a before and after. The before being this one image of purity and wholesomeness and good-naturedness, and the after being this despair and anorexia. So you could very easily read one against the other and that was helpful both at looking at the early seventies, just culturally in this country and whatever memories we associate with them as viewers, but also in the music itself. At first those songs seem banal and manipulative and overly sentimental. They gain a new kind of depth as we've learned how Karen Carpenter has suffered. There's a real sadness and the voice gets all the more beautiful as you find out. You listen to it and you can't stop.

# Todd Haynes: The Intellectual from Encino

Jeffrey Lantos / 1991

From *Movieline*, January 3, 1991. Reprinted by permission from Jeffrey Lantos.

I've just caught up with a remarkable film. It's called *Superstar: The Karen Carpenter Story*, and it was made three years ago by Todd Haynes, a Brown University-educated writer-director who is now thirty. Regrettably, you won't find this film in the video stores or catch it on cable. That's because Haynes received a cease-and-desist order from some big-shot lawyers who also wanted him to destroy every print of the film. Even if Haynes had agreed to that (he didn't), it wouldn't have mattered, because boot-legged video copies of *Superstar* are available, although if you're lucky enough to get hold of one, it'll probably be a grainy, ninth-generation copy.

The person who hired the big-shot lawyer, the person who has done all he can to prevent you from seeing a fresh print of *Superstar*, is Richard Carpenter, the older, living half of the brother-sister singing duo, the Carpenters. Remember Karen and Richard of Downey, California? She of the honeyed voice? He of the syrupy arrangements? Both with the bangs and the showbiz teeth? Emblematic of seventies youth, they were invited by Richard Nixon to perform at the White House. We see that scene in the film. Well, sort of. The Carpenters are not exactly in the White House. And, to be honest, they're not exactly singing either, because the actors who play Karen and Richard are not really singers. In fact they're not actors, either. They're dolls. That's right, folks, this is a movie starring dolls from the Ken and Barbie collection. Have you ever seen one doll goading another, anorexic doll into eating a piece of choc-olate cake? You will here. What about a chiseled-down, sunken-cheeked doll collapsing on stage during a concert? Hey, welcome to the wacky world of Todd Haynes. It's a world you enter laughing and exit disturbed.

*Superstar* isn't the kitsch oddity it sounds like. It's done in a kind of faux documentary style, the dolls notwithstanding, and it sets out to answer the question, what happened to Karen Carpenter? Haynes depicts Karen as gifted but vulnerable, easily exploited by her career-minded brother and ultimately destroyed by a controlling family and a demanding public. At twenty, she hasn't the inner strength to stand up for herself. Her ego is as undernourished as her body.

*Superstar* is a film of contrasts. We see the sunny, suburban neighborhood where, behind closed doors, mothers devour their young. We watch the All-American siblings who, offstage, are drowning in drugs and acrimony. We hear Karen's mellifluous renditions of "Close to You" and "We've Only Just Begun," over footage of Nixon lying to the nation and bombs dropping on Vietnam. At the height of her fame, Karen dumps package after package of Ex-Lax into the same orifice that produced those magnificent sounds. Her life, literally, goes down the toilet. When the film was over, I said, "Wow. They don't make 'em like this in Hollywood."

And director Todd Haynes didn't make *Superstar* in Hollywood. He shot the film over the course of a couple of weekends at Bard College, where he had gone for an MFA degree.

Haynes grew up in Encino, California, home of Michael Jackson and lots of other entertainment people, though Haynes's father is a sales rep for various fragrances, not a producer, and his mother is a decorator, not an ex-starlet. He attended the Oakwood School, in the San Fernando Valley, before heading off to Brown in 1980. There he majored in art and semiotics, which is, in case you're a rocket scientist not an English major, the general philosophical theory of signs and symbols that's been the rage among academic intellectuals since it was imported to Yale from France in the early seventies. There was no film department at Brown in 1980. If you wanted to make films, you majored in semiotics.

"Before you could make a film," says Haynes, as we sit at his parents' home in Encino, the suburb from which he defected thoroughly but returns to comfortably, "you had to study cultural theory, literary theory, and film theory. Then if you found a niche, say, Marxism, feminism, or psychoanalysis, and figured out what you wanted to squawk about, you made a film. It was very different from going to the USC/UCLA/NYU film school. There were not a lot of facilities, not a lot of emphasis on technique, so people had to find creative solutions. We ended up having to think a little harder about what we were doing and why. Many of the films coming out of film schools are thoughtless. They're just playing out modes of filmmaking they've seen before without much consideration about what they're saying. They mimic mainstream cinema without adding anything or commenting upon it."

And they never make movies with dolls. "The idea to do a film with dolls," says Haynes, "came before anything. I was intrigued with the idea of doing a straightforward narrative but replacing real actors with inanimate objects—and being careful with it and detailed in such a way so that it would provoke the same kind of identification as a real movie would."

Why the Carpenters? For Haynes they represented safety and tranquility after the turmoil of the sixties. "That was the last time I believed in the popular culture. Images of the family were everywhere. There were the Osmonds, the Jackson 5, the Partridge Family, the Brady Bunch, the Carpenters. And you're not fully aware what those images do to you until you find yourself under their spell. The images manipulated my view of the world and united me with my family and their values." Haynes calls those years the last sentimental moment of his generation. Then Karen Carpenter died of anorexia nervosa at the age of thirty-two, and just around the bend was eighties cynicism and corruption. In retrospect, the Carpenters, says Haynes, "provided a perfect dialectic, almost a before and after."

I wonder, what will studio executives make of this kid who looks like a surfer and talks like Noam Chomsky? I find him a tad didactic and theoretical—but hell, it's refreshing to meet a Valley boy who speaks in paragraphs and is currently reading *The Brothers Karamazov* because he never got to it in college. The Hollywood powers, though, are they going to see their meal ticket in this guy?

Well, they did pick up on *Superstar* when it showed at the U.S. Film Festival (known today as the Sundance Festival). "It was exciting and strange to receive attention like that after a film I thought I was making for myself and a few friends," says Haynes. "I would have been happy to have gotten a few downtown club screenings in New York City. I was also surprised the Hollywood community was so thorough in its search for new talent. They found me."

So, after all the accolades and feelers, Haynes hopped the next plane to Hollywood, right? Wrong. He went back to New York and Apparatus Productions, a film cooperative he founded with some Brown cronies. Apparatus is a nonprofit organization that provides resources and money for emerging filmmakers. They've also put together a book for publication called *The Guide to No-Budget Filmmaking.*

Haynes says, "I knew I wanted to make my next film on my own terms. I needed to feel like I could handle a feature. I wasn't ready to do anyone else's script, and I wasn't ready to direct a $10 million film. I feel bad for filmmakers just out of graduate school who are handed big-budget studio projects and watched like hawks. It's tremendous pressure for people who are just learning their craft. I want to protect myself from that and make my own films for a while."

Haynes's new film is called *Poison*. Shot in 16mm, it is feature-length and stars New York stage actors. According to Haynes, it is inspired by the writings of Jean Genet. The budget on *Poison* was $250,000. Seventy-five thousand came in the form of grants from several sources, including the New York State Council on the Arts and the NEA. The rest of the money came from private investors, "people who've known me for a while."

It's one thing to make a defiantly non-commercial film when you're in school. It's another to make one with other people's money. I ask Haynes about this. "Everyone who invested in *Poison* knew it was not the sort of film from which to expect full return and profits. But most of the investors are looking less at the individual film and more at the career of the filmmaker. In that way I feel justified in the support I've received. People like to help a director who might go somewhere."

So what's the story here? Is this guy delusional or is he going somewhere? It's still too early to say, although *Poison* should yield some clues. It's a film made up of three different stories with different casts and different visual styles, though the three stories interconnect throughout. The overriding theme is how society deals with behavior that deviates from the norm. Or, to put it another way, it is about the need of a society to turn against an individual or group who threatens the conventions of that society. (Sounds like *Edward Scissorhands*? It isn't. You won't hear the machinery creaking in the third act.) Part of *Poison* is a send-up of the B-movie, horror genre. But Haynes is not Mel Brooks. He doesn't merely parody, or plead for laughs. He's going deeper than that. He says he wants us to be aware of subliminal themes rooted in films like *Invasion of the Body Snatchers* and *I Was a Teenage Werewolf*. In these films, and others like them, there was, he says, a "symbolic message about the bad element—be it communism or teenage delinquency—that was being worked out in the film. Ultimately, the 'monster' is put in his place and society is relieved and made safe again." Another segment is about a seven-year-old boy who disappears after apparently killing his abusive father. Haynes explains that in this segment he questions the definitions of normality that inform the Long Island community where the story is set. The third segment is based loosely on Genet's novel *Miracle of the Rose*, and deals with a prisoner's romantic obsession with a fellow inmate.

Haynes likes stories of deviant behavior. Stories that exist in a kind of parallel world that isn't ours but looks like it. On the other hand, Haynes says he wants to make films that a lot of people will see. But unless *Poison* generates the same kind of heat that, say, *sex, lies, and videotape* did, Haynes will stay a directorial curiosity with a cult following.

Are there any directors working in Hollywood who interest Haynes?

"I like Tim Burton, although I found *Batman* disappointing. That's an example of [a director] thrust into a scale of filmmaking he might not have been ready for. Yet. And when you work with Jack Nicholson and a $40 million budget, how do you have a voice?" And then there's Spielberg. "If you're doing a movie about the suburbs you have to deal with the question, how do I dramatize the dark twisted side? How do I depict the peculiar? Spielberg [in *E.T.*] does it by having a weird thing happen in the narrative. Which is great. But then he pulls back and reaffirms the good mother and the sweet kid and the reigning community values. That pulling back destroys the peculiar part of what Spielberg does. And it's that peculiar part that makes him a success. I liked *Heathers* [directed by Michael Lehmann]. It was smart and twisted and funny, but the ending smelled of studio interference. I try to see the work of the newer directors, but I always end up going back to the older ones for inspiration."

Like who? Well, how about Bertolt Brecht?

"Brecht," says Haynes, "wanted people to think during a work of art. He wanted the audience to maintain their objectivity, to analyze what was transpiring. Fassbinder took it a step further. He wanted to engage the viewer emotionally while at the same time revealing the structure for what it was. That's an exciting premise. Of course, Hitchcock did it better than anybody. In *Vertigo*, for instance, when Jimmy Stewart wants the girl to look exactly like that image of Kim Novak—with her hair in a bun—you look at it objectively and realize how cruel it is; you realize, further, what men do to women, and yet when she walks in and her hair is hanging down you desperately want her to put it back in a bun."

In effect, Hitchcock shows you his hand, then makes you fret about whether he'll pull out the right card at the end. It's a variation on this strategy that Haynes put to work in *Superstar*. The use of the dolls is, of course, the ultimate artifice. It turns the characters into grotesques, and you giggle for the first five minutes. But then you stop, and you start to get into it, because the situation (dinner table chit chat) is so commonplace. "Conversations between kids and parents are familiar," says Haynes. "That's why people stop laughing at the dolls."

Haynes also succeeds in taking several hackneyed themes—the self-destructive star, the suburban nightmare, the over-protective mother—and turns them into a potent brew. One that lingers and provokes discussion.

Haynes says, "I wanted to redeem Karen Carpenter." Talk about audacious. If someone said that to me before I saw the film, I would have said, "Why?" It's one thing to try to redeem a supposed villain, because in that case, the audience brings passion to the theater. The director's job is to re-channel that passion and make you think about your allegiance, as Barbet Schroeder did with Claus von Bulow in *Reversal of Fortune*. But Karen Carpenter? How do you redeem someone who has no claim on our imagination, someone whom few took seriously to begin with? Amazingly, Haynes succeeds. You come away from the film missing Karen and humming Carpenters tunes. And suddenly the lyrics lodged in long-term memory—"Talking to myself and feeling old. Sometimes I'd like to quit. Nothing ever seems to fit . . ."—take on a new level of meaning.

Haynes says that after he heard from Richard Carpenter's lawyers he made them a counteroffer. He said he'd only show the film in clinics and schools, and he'd give all the money to the Karen Carpenter Foundation for Anorexia Research. Richard refused. "He's still controlling her," says Haynes.

"What would you say if you met Richard Carpenter at a party?"

"Fuck him. He's a jerk."

It'll be interesting to see if Hollywood has the same reaction to Todd Haynes or whether, after *Poison*, they embrace him and turn him into the Lynch/Burton/Waters of the nineties.

# *Poison* at the Box Office

Michael Laskawy / 1991

From *Cineaste* 18, no. 3 (1991). Reprinted by permission from *Cineaste Magazine*.

Todd Haynes first came to critical attention in 1988 with *Superstar: The Karen Carpenter Story*, a highly praised short mock-documentary whose featured performers were all Barbie dolls. Due to subsequent legal action taken by A&M Records, the film has presently been withdrawn from circulation; *Poison*, the first feature by the thirty-year-old director, made for under $250,000, has already generated similar attention. Earlier this year, it won the Grand Jury Prize at the Sundance Film Festival and provoked protests from the religious New Right over its depictions of homosexual eroticism and its reception of an NEA grant. Inspired by the works of French criminal-cum-author and playwright Jean Genet, *Poison* consists of three stories, each in a different genre, but all rooted ultimately in their concerns with the outsider in society.

**Cineaste:** Where did you get the inspiration for *Poison*, and specifically the way you chose to structure the film?
**Haynes:** It's an extension of concerns that were evidenced in *Superstar*, taking what was a single story and looking at it from different perspectives, both as a pseudo-documentary and subjective montages which are almost experimental. What I found was that the typical viewer could adjust, could switch formats and narrative styles very easily. They had no trouble with that, partly because it was one story and also, I think, because people are very sophisticated viewers these days. People can read narrative styles and strategies very quickly. I wanted to take that further with *Poison*, to have different stories, and different styles of telling stories, without a common plot binding them. I wanted to push a little further and impose on the viewer the obligation to interpret the film as it goes along and find a reason why these three stories are sharing one film.

**C:** Why did you choose the three genres that you chose—the documentary, the horror, and what is essentially an experimental section?

**H:** I definitely knew that in one story I wanted to work more explicitly in Genet's world, though I was thinking of a genre in that element as well—the pulp heroic novel, almost a romance in some ways. The characters are introduced in heroic voiceovers and Bolton is introduced, somewhat self-consciously, in a slow pan up his body with a description of his height and weight. But, in contrast to that story, I wanted things that were American, stories that I associated with a perspective that was societal. I wanted at least two of the stories to be coming from without, from the dominant perspective of the outcast in society, one in a documentary style, and one in a horror style. These are styles which I think often come out of a need to deal with threats to the social norm, a need to explain them in ways that I think are misleading, but ways that we know really well. So the prison story is definitely in contrast, coming from the perspective of the person who has been shut out, as opposed to reflecting society's opinions about what deviance or what transgression is. That's basically what informed my choices. I didn't really waffle a lot on different kind of stories. I settled on those styles pretty quickly.

**C:** When the *New York Times* reported that the film won the Grand Jury Prize at the Sundance Festival, the paper headlined its article, "Gay film wins award." I'm curious how you felt about it being labeled a gay film, or your being labeled a gay filmmaker, as opposed to a filmmaker who is gay?

**H:** It's a good and complex question that I do not have a simple answer for because so many different people read that same headline in the *New York Times* and feel so many different ways about it. Even if the journalist who wrote it meant it in some ways dismissively, there are so many gay and straight readers who would sympathize with that and say, "Great, a film that comes from a different perspective." So it's both reductive, and, at the same time, can be really important to identify; I don't consider myself a gay filmmaker, and I don't consider *Poison* an exclusively gay film. For me, the problem is always in content: we want to define the perspective of a film solely through its content, and not through its form. The films that are so incredibly conventional in form that are about gay characters, like *Longtime Companion* or *Making Love* or *Cruising*, are so straight. It's because, formally and structurally, they're unchallenged. They follow the rules completely without any attempt to look from a different perspective, so I can't look at the work itself as being different either. And there are films that aren't by gay filmmakers that play with narrative form; some of the best films of Hitchcock or Billy Wilder are films that might be looked at as more gay.

**C:** When you say gay in that respect, what do you mean? A breaking of conventional societal boundaries?

**H:** I'm talking about it more as a structural idea than a content idea. Heterosexuality is part of the structure of a society that has its rules in place about what's normal and not normal. Narrative structure comes out of that society and is adhered to in dominant film practice over and over again. These rules can be broken and looked at from different perspectives; you might call that a gay approach to filmmaking. I think you can look at it as a transgressive approach. Just like I think the way certain Hollywood films that were made by Cukor or Sirk or Hitchcock are, for feminists, strongly feminist works, although they weren't created by women. That can happen in a lot of different ways and I think it depends what kind of minority term you're applying to that transgression. I don't think it has to be about gay characters to challenge the straight world.

**C:** Let's talk about Genet. In his work there is a continual denial that you can escape from the way society is structured. Richie Beacon, the subject of the documentary, does, in a way, manage to escape. Do you think escape is possible?

**H:** Possibly; I think the message that runs throughout Genet's work is that the structures we all suffer under are inescapable, and that minorities inflict them on one another. At the same time, Genet did enact a sort of escape. I see him as someone who attempted to reject his success, the intense need to assimilate him at every stage. When his success as a writer became the dominant thing in his life, it inspired him to stop writing and run away from that world and spend his time in a political revolt that was more closely aligned with the way he felt about things. He couldn't do any more in his writing. I also look at him as someone who rejected the world far more completely than I will ever be able to. In a sense, he challenges my own participation and involvement all the time. At the same time, he wasn't some purist who never participated: he was completely involved in it. In some ways, his sainthood was a literary construct. His work sanctified him. That's what Richie is as well—he's a device, very much like Genet, the combined pervert child and the superhuman saint who can fly away.

**C:** Much of your film focuses on childhood—Richie's story and the experiences of Broom and Bolton at Batten being obvious examples. Is there a particular reason why you emphasized childhood and childhood influences?

**H:** Well, I imagine because the root of all of our psychosexual knots are in childhood. We play them out our whole lives. So, in a film that is literally a knot of three stories which by the end coalesce into what can almost be read as a single psychology, childhood influences are essential. Desire and the idea of sexuality in childhood is a really fascinating theme to me. All the things we don't want to associate with childhood are things that *Poison* continues to assert throughout, that children are often in control of situations that they seem to be victims in, that they are full of desire—sexual desire, that children are the objects of rituals of severe humiliation. It's an opening up of things that people want to close down about childhood but that I just don't think you can.

**C:** What about the opposite of this desire? What about the self-loathing that a lot of your characters exhibit?

**H:** Well, I don't really see it as self-loathing. I see it as this process of transforming, to refer to James Baldwin, from a victim to a threat. He says a victim who can articulate his experiences as a victim is no longer a victim; he or she has become a threat. I think that's what happens to all the characters in *Poison*. They undergo tremendous suffering in various ways but they gain from it. Through it, they see the world more clearly than anyone around them, and, in some ways, they transcend their situations as a result. Richie is ultimately revealed as the complete master over his own situation. Graves becomes a human full of pathos and empathy through what he undergoes. Up until then he's a grouch, a pretty miserable guy. Broom is an enlightened observer. He's involved with Bolton, but in his ability to articulate his desire in a way that Bolton can't, he survives. Though the feelings that they do have for each other come out in pretty violent ways, I think it's pretty clear that it's the conditions that they're living in that make that violence a necessity.

**C:** Do you see the film operating in that same way? Turning a victim into a threat?

**H:** The film as a whole? Well, it seems like it has without me ever setting out to make it like that. I don't see it necessarily as a threat. I think the film asks you to watch these victims in the process of articulating themselves. The threat part is left with you, the viewer, to do something with, to think about, to apply to the world we all live in now, but I don't think the film does that for you.

***C:*** But don't you think that a film with fairly explicit depictions of homosexual sex or such a graphic, unsettling spitting sequence would be seen by some viewers as a threat?

***H:*** I mean threat less in terms of shock value but something more profound than that, something that could possibly change things. I don't think the film takes you there. I don't think that any film can, but maybe it gives you some tools or some questions that you can ask about the world. Films that set out to shock don't really interest me, and that wasn't my intent with *Poison*. Again, it's what you do with the film that makes it a threat, or makes you the threat rather than the film on its own acting as some self-powered machine that will accuse society of its ills. It takes the viewer to do that. The film can suggest and provoke and ask questions. The tradition of cinema is to answer all the questions that it asks, and I think that's where film dies, when it closes itself up with answers. It's bullshit. We don't have these answers. I think films that open up questions, that provoke you and get you involved, but don't provide answers are much more powerful and may be much more politically potent than films that neatly tie themselves up and let you passively leave the theater.

***C:*** Has the success of *Poison* surprised you?

***H:*** The Sundance Film Festival was a surprise. These extenuating circumstances have thrust *Poison* into a much more mainstream world than I ever would have thought possible. What surprised me was that the mainstream press could get into it and sometimes really love it. And when they didn't love it, to think about it complexly. That surprised me. I just thought this was a film for a very few people. I didn't think so many people could get into it. And I'm glad. It's good people can.

***C:*** Do you worry about cooption then? Do you worry about the film becoming too mainstream?

***H:*** No, not really. There are all these points of irony, seeing *Poison* among all the other movies in the box office chart, next to *Teenage Mutant Ninja Turtles*. In a way all you can do is adore that. But it still kind of rubs me the wrong way.

***C:*** I guess that's what I'm getting at is, do you worry that, when it appears on the same newspaper page as *Teenage Mutant Ninja Turtles* and *Pretty Woman*, that it's a way of removing the questions from the film, of turning it into entertainment?

**H:** I'm not sure. Hell, let all those people stumble unknowingly into *Poison*. A percentage of them are going to be deeply struck but in a way they wouldn't ever have been prepared for. And other people will dismiss it and not know what to do with it, and that's OK. The fact that some people are encountering something completely otherworldly, that's good. In many ways, this whole idea of mainstream vs. art-house is a myth. As soon as you show your work, even in some dive club in downtown New York, you are involved in exchange. You're showing it to people. They are looking at it. They can talk about it. They can think about it. They can reject it. It begins there, and it can end there too, but there's no way of controlling what will happen as a result of that. It enters into this exchange world, which is the world around us, and I don't think it's so different from what happens on a much larger scale. I think people still see the big movies and some people see the small movies and they all go into our heads. I don't see one as so different from another.

**C:** Have you gotten offers from Hollywood?

**H:** Yes, enough to make me feel guarded. Though I'm encouraged about finding funding for my next film, I'm guarded about the necessity of my control over my further work which, unfortunately, I haven't had time to write and get into, so I'm not really talking about it yet. I think it will be quite different from *Poison*.

**C:** You open and close the film with quotes from Genet—"The whole world is dying of panicky fright" and "A man must dream a long time in order to act with grandeur, and dreaming is nursed in darkness." Why did you choose these selections?

**H:** Originally the script to *Poison* ended with the long quote from *Our Lady of the Flowers* that begins, "The whole world is dying of panicky fright." We first conceived of using it as an epilogue, allowing you to reflect back on what you had just seen. But, after moving things around, it made sense to set the stage with the state of severe despair that *Poison* takes off from. I think it completely clues us in to where we are in the world right now. That's what I wanted it to do, to be very much about what's going on in the world in the shadow of the AIDS epidemic and a far right administration and climate in this country that we've had for a while. That was the thinking on the first one. The quote that completes the film seemed to speak more for what was common about the three characters and their plights. It seemed to be a more satisfying way to end the film.

**C:** And what do you hope an audience comes out of *Poison* with?

**H:** I think *Poison* might force you to mourn a little bit, to feel sad a little bit. In really bad times I think people have this survival mechanism that disables us from feeling every blow, every death, every horrible thing that happens, and we just go on with our lives. There's something really tragic about that. If a film can make you stop for a second and feel sad, or feel some sense of loss, or think that something's wrong, then I hope *Poison* can do that at least.

# Cinematic/Sexual:
# An Interview with Todd Haynes

Justin Wyatt / 1992

From *Film Quarterly* 46, no. 3 (1993). Reprinted by permission from the University of California Press and Justin Wyatt.

**Justin Wyatt:** Has your academic background had a bearing on your filmmaking practice?

**Todd Haynes:** In high school I had a teacher named Chris Adams. Chris had studied with Beverle Houston at USC and that was really important to her way of thinking about film. Chris showed a lot of experimental films in her classes, which was great. We saw James Benning, Stan Brakhage, Ken Jacobs, *Oh Dem Watermelons*, even the trash classics of early American avant-garde cinema.

I remember that it was a big breakthrough for me when Chris Adams said, based on Beverle Houston's writings, that film is not reality. Reality can't be a criterion for judging the success or failure of a film, or its effect on you. It was a simple, but eye-opening, way of approaching film. You would go to these new Hollywood films and you would say, "It wasn't very realistic, that wasn't a very 'real' scene." This sense of real all the time was pervasive, very easy, and a completely accepted form of critiquing and analyzing what worked and what didn't work. But it wasn't a way of critiquing at all: it was really a way we represent ourselves. So that approach was planted in my brain as a way of looking at film as completely constructed, and then trying to create different criteria for how to look at film.

I actually made my first film in high school—with a crew and a big production. It was called *The Suicide*. We emulated the Hollywood practice of oppression: script girls and all the obligatory hierarchies and stuff. I was the co-producer. I wrote the story for a thesis exam in high school, and it's a film that actually is very similar to *Poison* in structure: it has all these different voices and intercuts all these different realities. We started to shoot it in tenth grade, and we worked on it for two years. The entire second year was devoted to the sound track. We started in Super-8, but by the end of the year we had blown up all the tracks to 35mm. We were able to use the Samuel Goldwyn studios to do our final mix through film brat kids' connections. We went in and did it right after *Barnaby Jones* and right before *The Last Waltz*. At the end, for our final party, we rented a theater in Westwood and somebody hired a limo to pick us up and take us to the theater. I was so disgusted with the whole thing that I vowed to make weird, experimental, personal films, with no sound, for a while. This idea continued to develop and become clearer throughout college.

At that time I was also very seriously into painting. A lot of people who know me from Brown probably think of me more as a painter than as a filmmaker. While studying film theory and getting pretty excited about it, I found that there was something very different about what could be expressed in film. To me the difference was societal and political. It was a matter of using images and representation.

In a way, I felt that I had acquired a skill about representing things as a child. I would practice and practice—I would draw all the time. It was replication of what representation is. By the time I was in college and painting abstractly, I felt that these acquired representations were a weird burden that I carried. Just ignoring them would be a denial that I thought was important to address. In a way, I wanted to use these emblems, these images of the world that I had perfected: images of men, images of women, who look this way and that way, that you can take apart to put on the canvas, and then take apart and discuss. But I kind of hated them. I hated representation, I hated narrative, and yet I felt that I had to deal with it, I had to. I thought that film was the most appropriate medium for an exploration of that idea.

**JW:** You've said that one of the reasons you made *Superstar* was to experiment with questions of identification and to see whether audiences could become emotionally connected to these Barbie dolls. What did you learn from this experiment?

**TH:** I learned that people will identify at the drop of a hat [laughs] at almost anything. I think that it's an essential need when we go to a film, and a really exciting need to know about and not simply fulfill. There's this aspect of creating narratives in a commercial sense that I hate, and you see it in so many ways in movies over and over and over again: this need to create a likable central character with quirks and interesting things to say. It's a horrible mirroring of the need to affirm who we are through stories and make ourselves big and huge on the screen. I hate it and yet, at a very basic level of narrative, I think that it happens. So I'm always caught in the dilemma of feeling that it's still absolutely necessary to work with stories, because they are a weird mechanical and emotional hybrid that we all react to. There is an incredible potential since people go in with expectations that you can never meet part way, and then alter—because you have them, they're emotionally engaged.

**JW:** Your experiments with genre, narrative, and character identification destabilize a lot of the traditional ways through which pleasure is derived from film. What do you think the relationship is between cinematic pleasure and style in your films?

**TH:** I think that there is real stylistic play in both *Superstar* and *Poison*. In a way, it's the most on-the-surface example of the films' element of fun and play. I think in *Superstar*, more than in *Poison*, the way style is played with is what makes you laugh. It's this absurd miniaturization of the bourgeois success story, and you laugh at how all the obligatory elements of the 1970s family are miniaturized and present in the film and how it follows the genre of the star film with Barbie dolls. I think what is actually pleasurable about the film is the identification which you finally achieve with Karen through all the distancing. In a way, the play of style can be an alienation. You laugh, but you're not really interested in the story or the ideas or the emotions. It's not helping you identify with the film; in fact, it's keeping you outside of it in ways that provoke as much thought as the weird feeling of having identified with a plastic doll.

  I think *Poison* works in different ways. Again, I think the style is the intercutting of disparate stories and that's the fun and it is funny at points. I don't know what's pleasurable about *Poison*, except something very sad, that is only pleasurable because it's hopefully truthful to people's experiences.

**JW:** How interested are you in deconstructing generic frameworks? *Poison* relies strongly on the documentary and horror genres, while *Superstar* could be read as an affliction movie or a star story.

**TH:** I don't know if the films are interested in deconstructing those genres as much as in referring to them, using common knowledge about them to talk about other things. The affliction movie gives the central character her identity through her disease and all of a sudden that's supposed to be a complete identity when the disease is determined. In the star story, the star is the dual identity of success and fame, and then an evil element brings about the decline or fall.

Similarly, in *Poison*, it's how all three of these genres or styles have a history of dealing with the notion of transgression and taking care of that threat in various ways. For a genre fan, maybe the film is really fun and fulfills all of those deconstructive and, at the same time, recuperative instincts. I just thought that the film needed to be in three different styles and that I wanted all the styles to relate to the central theme.

**JW:** But are you looking for an emotional response?
**TH:** Yes, definitely. I think what makes *Poison* really work for some people is that it gets under your skin and makes you feel something . . . usually something very sad or disturbed. For other people, though, that doesn't happen. For some people, it's an intellectual game: it's just, "Oh, the documentary and the horror one are funny, and the other one is serious all the way through." In some sense, it's a very conventional, very mainstream, very Hollywood wish on my part that the film saddened you, and becomes more than what you're seeing—maybe by the end or by the last third. If it doesn't touch you in some way, if it ultimately doesn't overcome its structure, its intelligence, its cleverness, I would be unhappy.

**JW:** What are your views on the argument of essentialism versus social constructionism in homosexuality? How does this influence your filmmaking?
**TH:** Oh, a really easy question [laughs]. I tend to have a continued gut-level criticism that kicks in whenever essentialism is brought up. In a way it wasn't until gay theory was ushered in by people like Diana Fuss, identifying the essentialist versus social-constructivist perspectives, that I realized how significant and important feminism is. Gay theory as well, of course, but there's been so much more written about feminism. There's more of a multiplicity of perspectives around it. It was the first time that you had to acknowledge essential differences, not simply say that the whole idea of femininity and womanliness was solely a societal construct, that the traditions of femininity were imposed and constructed by men. To counter that with something else, a perspective that has to do with a not necessarily biologically different way of existing in the world, but a biological difference that creates social reaction

and institutions—really interesting and complex ways of fighting these societally imposed notions of essential difference . . .

With homosexuality and my films . . . I don't know that in *Poison* there is evidence for arguments of essential difference in homosexuality. Instead there is an attempt to link homosexuality to other forms that society is threatened by—deviance that threatens the status quo or our sense of what normalcy is. I don't believe that there is an essential gay sensibility either. What is so interesting about minorities identifying themselves historically and rewriting their own history is that, in a sense, it is an attempt to create an essential difference that isn't really true. But it's one that they are writing, as opposed to the status quo. So it's a way of disarming the conventions of difference that have been imposed on us and rewriting our own differences.

**JW:** David Ehrenstein used as the headline for his review of *Poison* in the *Advocate*: "*Poison* is the most important gay American film since *Mala Noche*." How do you feel about the film being appropriated in that way by gay culture?

**TH:** I think it's fine. The film is absolutely the result of AIDS and also a result of Genet. Obviously both of these facets are essential to gay history, to gay texts, and I think there are all kinds of ways that the film can be important to reexamining, at this particular point in history, being gay. To begin with I was just frustrated with this defensive, fearful acceptance of the terms that AIDS imposed on what being gay meant: provoking gay people to clean up their act and become inoffensive to society. All of a sudden there was this metaphor for homosexuality lurking, this awful, horrible metaphor of AIDS that had to be continually distinguished, and I think it should be distinguished, from homosexuality.

At the same time, what is so fascinating about Genet is that he was deeply interested in what was particularly transgressive, and only what was transgressive, about homosexuality—and what was erotic about it as well. That went along with the underground, disturbing, dark, and at times intense betrayal of lovers and trusted people that is hard for a lot of people, including myself, to deal with. I think Genet wrote about a strangely united political and erotic charge that he experienced with regard to homosexuality that was violent, that was based on upsetting the norm and not at all on finding a nice, safe place that society will give you.

**JW:** Does that relate to your personal feelings about homosexuality?

**TH:** Yes, definitely. I felt that it was so sad to be weak and apologetic about who we were as a result of AIDS when the fucking society was letting us die. So it was like, look around, people don't give a shit about you. If the only power we have is the power to upset the norm, then let's use it and not try to iron it out. AIDS is inert, it doesn't have a brain, it doesn't choose, it's just the accident of a virus. Someone's sick joke has single-handedly affected all the disenfranchised, all the oppressed; it's the cruelest twist of fate. It gives so many people the ammunition to maintain things the way they are. That definitely inspired the film, and I feel that it is really important for gay people to look at it.

**JW:** The concept of labeling seems really important to *Poison*: the first scene with Broom being admitted to prison—centering on his acceptance of the label "homosexual," the ways in which the neighbors are bothered by Richie because they can't label him. Can you talk about how labeling structures the film?

**TH:** It was something that I was definitely thinking about—from Genet, who so eloquently writes about how language provoked his violence more than anything. It was as though being called gay, thief, provoked the need to react, and in a sense reclaim those terms, make them uglier, more disturbing and abject than society could ever imagine. Maybe just being in possession of the labels was enough. It was the world that Genet could create to survive those years in prison and enjoy them as fully as he did.

I was really interested in the initial aspects of that—the whole idea of naming and branding people, and what traumas it provokes. Basically, I wanted to investigate the James Baldwin quote about the victim who can articulate his experience no longer being a victim. He has become a threat. So it's about articulation. That's the thing that gets these people: Richie is probably the most in control of anyone in the film, Broom learns how to speak, he is always able to articulate his desires, even if it is just to us. That's how they survive and also how they learn from their suffering. In a sense it's also why they seek out their experiences—there's something masochistic about that strain in Genet, and in *Poison* . . . absolutely. It's about accepting terms only in so far as you can use them and turn them back around.

**JW:** What responsibilities, if any, do you feel you have being a filmmaker who is gay?

**TH:** I think that I should be creating positive images of homosexuality to spread around the world, on television, through the mass media to show people that gays are positive, they're just like them. That's my role. That's my job [laughs]. I am being sincere.

**JW:** So you want to make a film like *Making Love*, for example?

**TH:** . . . and *Lost Companion*. Is it *Lost Horizon* or *Lost Companion*? I get those fantasy things mixed up. "Let's imagine all the AIDS people return-ing at the end." Obviously, I have problems with the protocol of that. In fact, I have a lot of frustration with the insistence on content when people are talking about homosexuality. People define gay cinema solely by content: if there are gay characters in it, it's a gay film. It fits into the gay sensibility, we got it, it's gay. It's such a failure of the imagination, let alone the ability to look beyond content. I think that's really simplistic. Heterosexuality to me is a structure as much as it is a content. It is an im-posed structure that goes along with the patriarchal, dominant structure that constrains and defines society. If homosexuality is the opposite or the counter-sexual activity to that, then what kind of a structure would it be? I think that it has been documented in film theory that conven-tional narrative form adheres to and supports basic ideological positions and structures in society and enforces heterosexual closure and romance in films. For me, it's the way the narrative is structured, the way that films are machines that either reiterate and reciprocate society—or not.

**JW:** What are your feelings about those mainstream films concerning homosexuality?

**TH:** I think that they're straight because of the structure. Most films don't experiment at all with narrative form, basically fitting a very con-ventional boy-meets-girl, boy-loses-girl structure. If you simply replace boy meets girl with boy meets boy, it's not really doing anything differ-ent at all. Of course, seeing two men kiss in a movie is important, but I think it needs more than that. That just replaces the content and pre-tends that the structure is natural. It's not as if the content has been de-termined by the form in the way it's being told to you. It's more exciting to think of revising, rethinking the ways that films are put together—the way you are positioned as a viewer, the way you are told to identify with characters or not, the way that the film is alive because of the work that you do as a viewer. It's a really just a reflection on the wall otherwise.

# Appendix: An Interview with Todd Haynes

Michael William Saunders / 1995

Following is a transcript of a phone interview I conducted with Todd Haynes on January 16, 1995. In the text, "T" refers to Mr. Haynes, and "M" refers to Michael Saunders. In redacting this interview, I have attempted to keep the transcript as close to being a word-for-word account as my typing abilities will allow. Inevitably, this attempt will convey to the reader both my own verbal sloppiness and the extraordinary elegance and acute focus of Mr. Haynes's conversation. I apologize to the readers for asking them to endure the former, and I am pleased to be able to present evidence of the latter.

**M:** To begin with, what I'm doing with this work is I'm looking at images of homosexual characters as monsters in film. So my departure point is first backing up and asking some questions and getting some things in the foreground of my awareness as I think about all this and trying to see how I want to define homosexuality in terms of monstrosity from the beginning and play with that idea. And it seems that, when I try to put all of what I know about homosexuality and monstrosity and images together, my departure point is this: namely, that traditional culture tends to view homosexuality as monstrous in two senses: first as a deformation of the natural order as defined by sexuality, as defined by expressions of relationships—human relationships—in the first sense, as a kind of deformation; and in the second sense, as a kind of omen: homosexuality tends to be viewed in conservative culture which, now frighteningly seems to be reasserting itself, but it tends to get viewed as a form of

33

expression or living that is doomed. The homosexual gets viewed very often as being a person who is doomed to undo himself, and as such serves as an omen: look what will happen to you if you deviate from the natural order. So those are the two basic senses in which I'm beginning to try to play with the whole idea of how I think homosexuality works in terms of talking about monstrosity. What I get to after that is, given the strength with which this sense of the homosexual as monster and the variety of senses with which that sense expresses itself in the culture, it seems interesting to look at images, particularly images—not just defined as visual images but images in any sense, images in writing, for instance—but where images of the homosexual as monster tend to come up. So here I'm crash landing into my first question for you: How do you see those images coming up in film? Does it seem to you that such images are a significant part of film imagery?

**T:** Yes, definitely, especially in the way that you just defined monstrousness. Do you want to name a couple of films or a range of films that you might be talking about or have already talked about in your dissertation?

**M:** Basically I'm dividing film into—I'm trying to gather a cluster of what probably most people talking now would consider new queer cinema on the one hand, and setting that as the focal point of my analyses—what I'm actually doing readings of in the dissertation—setting that on one side and looking at what I'm vaguely and probably sloppily calling traditional cinema on the other hand.

**T:** I'm just thinking really off the top of my head of films like—and you should tell me if these are films you've thought about or not—*The Living End* or *Swoon*, even *My Own Private Idaho*, which still had one step in mainstream production probably more than the others.

**M:** *Querelle*?
**T:** Fassbinder's *Querelle* and what else?

**M:** The granddaddy for me is Genet's *A Song of Love*, and Kenneth Anger—*Fireworks* and *Scorpio Rising* and all those other things. So Genet is the granddaddy and then you—with a quiet underground in the form of people like Kenneth Anger, you move forward into the sixties and seventies, then comes Fassbinder with a bang in movies like *Fox and His Friends* and *The Bitter Tears of Petra Von Kant*, and finally *Querelle* and all the other films of his that deal with homosexuality or that feature homosexual characters. I'm also including films like Jarman's *Edward* *the Second*, Almodovar's *The Law of Desire*, a film by Agustin Villaronga called *In a Glass Cage*; Rosa Von Praunheim, his films, Jennie Livingston's film *Paris Is Burning*, Monika Treut's film *Female Misbehavior*, some of her other documentaries. So there's the pack that I want to look at, with you in that pack, on the one hand.

**T:** Yeah. I would definitely see elements of—when you first described those two aspects of monstrousness and applied them to the way gay characters are portrayed, I thought of how that certainly is true of more mainstream depictions of homosexuals in film, where they are often not the agents of the narrative in the way that they might be in some of the queer productions—films by gay filmmakers that come from the margins more than from the mainstream. And yet I think that you could probably find that both of the two aspects that you brought up—the sort of deformation or redrawing of traditional relationships, and then the kind of doomed element—would probably come up in various ways in both categories. I just think there is a level at which the gay filmmaker is purposely manipulating tropes that are both already constructed by the culture and circulating within the culture and activating them in various ways, but maybe without some of the corrective or cautionary elements that you will usually find in more mainstream productions, where it's necessary that the gay character dies or it's necessary that they're drawn as somewhat—that whatever those images are contrasted to within those films, that they're slotted in a more derogatory or more threatening category. But all the films that you're talking about from queer cinema seem to me to be the ones which, under the banner of Genet himself, are films that aren't striving to, quote unquote, "reform" and create positive images of homosexuals and happy narratives in which everyone walks off in the sunset at the end, but instead where these tensions and these threats—the monstrousness of homosexuality per se is maintained and utilized. And that's certainly a tradition that I've come from or studied or find myself associated with.

**M:** And in so many ways that's a very dangerous thing for a filmmaker like you to be doing. I mean, you get things like the flak that you caught over *Poison*, the response to the "gobbing" scene at Sundance that's sort of become part of the myth of the film. Working with that kind of image puts you in a very dangerous position, it seems to me, from all sides.

**T:** Yeah. I agree, and yet what's funny when I think back to that whole period—it was strange that very few people from the right, or places where the film was getting its strongest criticism, said, See, the film simply proves that homosexuals are monsters and that there is this self-hatred of homosexuals—it's all there, this is a total indictment of the homosexual life from a homosexual case in point. Instead, the film seemed to generate the same anxieties about homosexuality itself that the film was absolutely trying to talk about and in fact preserve. In other words, whatever anxieties homosexuality continues to unleash to main-stream society, I felt like my film was absolutely serving to do that for these people, and so you watched it being played out in their own range of anxieties, fears, denials, and obsessions and all of that more than you saw it being taken out on me, the homosexual. And in some weird way— I don't quite know why that happened—it happened exactly as I would have hoped.

**M:** From the other side of that, then, though, do you feel in your experi-ence of the film after the fact, you may have gotten into a tight spot with gay people who said, Now wait a minute, what are you doing here, Mr. Haynes, do we need this?
**T:** Yeah, that did happen, it did come up, and I imagine that those feel-ings and mistrust of my film were felt even more strongly than was com-municated to me directly. It did come up now and then, and I guess I was supported by a critical rethinking of the questions about positive imagery and identity politics that were circulating then and now, and in many ways there was always full critical support of the kinds of issues I was raising in the film. I think people often shouted down the poor ques-tioners in an audience who would say, Why is it so negative? There were certainly screenings that I attended where that came up.

**M:** In choosing to go back to Genet, in choosing to mine him for things to do, for things to say about all these issues . . . Genet seems to focus so intensely on the notion of abjection, this extremely spiritual sense of the meaning of abjection, and of course that does show up in *Poison*, the process and the whole experience of abjection, in a number of really dif-ferent ways. Do you see yourself, among other things, as reading Genet's four-novel discussion of abjection; do you see yourself as reading that or responding to it? Are you recreating your sense of what Genet does with the idea of abjection in the film, either with respect to gay people or with respect to people in general?
**T:** I'm not sure if this exactly answers your question, but I definitely feel a dual reaction to those issues in Genet's work and in his general philoso-phies and that is, on the one hand, feeling this innate understanding

of what he's talking about and identification with it and maybe even more a sense that it's describing a kind of isolation or antisocialism that I've always felt at some basic level. But, at the same time, it completely challenges me in what then feels like my complete assimilation in the world and in the evil society that he so much more fully distanced himself from than I do mine. And so I am both encouraged and completely fascinated by it, but at the same time I feel chastised by it as well, and almost, what he said once about André Gide's work and life, that he was of questionable immorality. I feel the same question placed on myself. And it challenges me, but I don't feel that I've failed and that I'm wrong, but that I'm encouraged to look at our culture with the same kinds of absolute suspicions that he did his; that it's a source of strength to turn to and that *Poison* has a strange kind of fixation on abjection, almost from the scatological—it's almost a science experiment of various body fluids. I mean, I've looked at the film and it's almost obsessed in a juvenile way with blood and guts and spit and shit, all of these literal versions of abjection. But those are the markers that differentiate the characters from the world in which they live, so naturally the film would focus on those pieces of evidence.

**M:** Then I'm led to another question, and it's this: does that abjection into which these characters are thrown or into which they're born or whatever, does that describe a position of power or does it describe a condition of being defeated from the very beginning?

**T:** No, I don't think it describes a position of being defeated from the very beginning in the slightest, in fact. But it's not solely a position of power. It's certainly not just a position of power that they discover in this acknowledgment or even in this celebration of that abjection. I think it's much more a position of—it's a dual position of masochistic power. Because abjection is part of every body—every internal body is full of the same fluids and juices and excrements that the characters in *Poison* either emit onto one another or are the subject of the abuse of language and fluids and abjection from other characters or from the society around them. But I guess to me it's something that singles them out as these marked bodies [who] are different from the world in which they live, but who are in the process of articulating that relationship to their respective societies and, in the act of that articulation, do become powerful and threatening to the society, but without that articulation are mere victims of the society. And so I think it's in the process of the realization and the understanding and the acknowledgment of those differences and the ways in which they're played out or literalized in these acts of horror—bodily instances of horror—that we all share, but that have a particular importance and meaning to these people and their lives that makes them into something more, and that is probably more on the line of powerful than not by the end. Or at least you see it being enacted differently—the distinction between the character Broom and the character Bolton: Bolton, who is ultimately acted upon by the people around him, is in a different relationship with respect to his society than Broom, in that he can't speak about his homosexuality, he can't articulate this desire. It's in him but he's not able to express it, and so he becomes this symbolic subject of masochistic pleasure, basically, that doesn't, maybe, transcend the world. Broom watching Bolton being spat upon is the way in which that image becomes something more than it is, through his watching of it; it's not simply the act itself, it's somebody transcribing it in their minds and transforming it as Genet did in *Miracle of the Rose* into something of an ecstatic nature. Without that, it would just be an act of abuse.

**M:** Just to be sure I haven't overread—are you comfortable with my talking about the characters in *Poison* as monsters? I tend to look at Richie as being a kind of monster in that he's a prodigy—he's referred to as a gift from God. Of course, Dr. Graves, I suppose there's not too much of a problem with seeing him as a monster. When you get to Jack and John, essentially you're talking about monstrosity as sociopathy, monstrosity as gay men, and linking up with sociopathy and all that.
**T:** I guess one thought is . . . initially that there's a tradition in which monsters have been depicted in film and sometimes that tradition links up with the way traditional film deals with homosexuality. I think you're bringing up all these different uses of the monster, not necessarily derogatory or negative ways of discussing monstrousness or abjection. And *Poison* has all of it, almost every variant, every application is found within the various stories. I intended the "Horror" story to be more about the way traditional film—[presents] morality in traditional depictions of the monster—and applying that to depictions of people with AIDS or people with disease that I became very sensitive to around the time I was writing the film, where I saw the same kinds of moral divisions between the monstrous AIDS patient and the safe subjects watching these stories as I saw in traditional horror films. It's just that we have this great historical distance from the moral positions of the classic horror films, and so we can laugh about it, we can see the distinctions between the monster

and the safe public as more absurd or ironic or funny or over the top or whatever. But, in the midst of your own history, you often don't see that. So I was trying to apply that to a more contemporary situation. So it's not about the Genet appropriation of monstrous terminology and his attempts to turn it around against the society and not having the society have the final word in those representations—which was, I think, more in the "Homo" section.

**M:** As I think about and look at all this, one of the things that finally seems to come out about monsters is how completely ambivalent our reaction to them tends to be. On the surface, they're disgusting things, but, of course, there's obviously something wonderfully exciting and fascinating about them. We keep bringing them back to life after we kill them, you know? The sequel business will never end.

**T:** That's so true. I think what's fascinating is the pleasure of being scared that's so evident in our history, in our culture. Mainstream film and mainstream novels are so fully aware of that market, that desire, the pleasure we feel in being terrified. I think it's a great analogy for homophobia. At times you are just shocked at how obsessive heterosexual society is about homosexuality, how incredibly sidetracked it can become with something that [it] shouldn't ultimately. If it's really so marginal, if it's really such a small percentage of the mainstream and so negligible, then why would they care? But there's this deep fascination with it that, obviously, has to do with what's inside every person, that is a great analogy for the intense fascination and pleasure that we feel being scared or upset.

**M:** It's exciting. Someone quoted recently to me, and I don't know if I'm mangling the quote, but: People have imagined all kinds of really interesting hells, but no one has yet to come up with a heaven that anyone with any great sensibilities would want to live in. Horrific images have a great deal of charm. Finally, not to take too terribly much more of your time, I have a few questions about how you assembled *Poison*. Were you very much aware of *A Song of Love* when you were thinking about the film, or did it provide you with any kind of model for the film?

**T:** Actually not. I had seen it before making *Poison*, but it had been several years before, and there was a point where I wanted the director of photography, Maryse Alberti, to see it—she hadn't seen it before. We couldn't get a print, no one had a tape, and I thought well, maybe it's just as well that we embark on it without too much attention to its detail.

It would invariably have a huge effect on me and would probably make me feel awful about anything that I would come up with. So, let it go, you know? Let it be the vague memory. But, in terms of its structure, it didn't have any direct effect on *Poison*. There are just scenes in it that you'll never get out of your head, and I remembered them when writing the film—the scene where Broom is kissing his hand in prison reminds me of some of those images of the wall and the smoke and stuff like that, but beyond that there isn't a real close analogy that I'm aware of.

**M:** How did the whole strategy of intercutting stories evolve, or can you say how it evolved? Was it sort of an organic decision?
**T:** I knew that it was something I wanted to expand upon from previous films I've made and from the structure in Genet, the structure of *Our Lady of the Flowers* or *Funeral Rites* that, *Funeral Rites* particularly, have these very distinctive stories that are linked. *Our Lady of the Flowers* is more fluid, but still, the way he's constantly paralleling different stories, I wanted to incorporate that in the film. But it was also something I had done a little bit in *Superstar*, the film I made about Karen Carpenter that at least used different stylistic narrative forms, although also in the same story: they would go into this constructed documentary section or this more subjective montage style, and then it would be the doll, the fictional-star story-doll parts. But I was pleased to see how audiences could easily jump from one narrative trope to another, and I wanted to see what would happen if that was taken even further. And, if the different styles told different stories as well, sort of force the viewer to interpret the film as it went along. I always like to try to force them to do something while they're sitting there in the theater. The original script was intercut, because I wanted people who read the finished script to get a sense of what it would be like, the finished film; but I knew that it would change, it would have to change, the suggested points of intersection that the script reflected. Although a couple remained or they were embedded in the way we actually shot the scenes, and they made a narrative sense that persisted throughout the editing of the film. But really the film, which is so much about editing itself, needed to be open to that process to the greatest extent that it could be and so, when I cut the film with Jim Lyons, we really rewrote it and reconceived it in the process in many ways. So I think it really happened in the editing room. And it was a long editing process, which it needed to be, and I don't regret a day of it; it was really necessary to continually rethink it and reshape it and make it streamlined in the process of intercutting. It took a while to keep

simply the dramatic tensions from one story alive while cutting into the next; at certain points you want to cut them off, but more often than not, I wanted to think of ways that that energy would just continue into the next story and inform what was happening to that story or add to the tensions that we left with the next story when we last saw it. So, it was hard, but it was certainly worth it.

**M:** My last question: Do you see yourself as either being shaped by or somehow in line with or proximate to other people that are identified now with new queer cinema, both in terms of the appropriation of the notion of queerness and all that that implies? Is that very much a part of what you're doing in your work or did you park it once you got finished with *Poison* or was it never any part of your work, really?

**T:** Well, as opposed to feeling part of a current cinematic movement among gay filmmakers, I would think that my films are more uniformly affected right now by AIDS than they are by what's happening among other gay filmmakers at this moment, and it's arguable that their films and perhaps even mainstream Hollywood films are equally affected by AIDS; maybe that's actually the thing that we are all, in various ways, working out. The film I've just completed, called *Safe*, which is my second feature after *Poison*—it took quite a while to get it made—doesn't have gay themes in it at all. The film is completely about illness and immunity, basically. And so, if there's any universal theme in all my films, it seems to be disease, so far. And, I hope that changes, but I have a feeling it may not until things change in the world; but I am really happy to see, almost without it being a conscious construction—I don't think it is that much more so, by other gay filmmakers—that the work that is coming out shares a criticism of mainstream culture that goes beyond content and that does affect forms and the ways in which characters are constructed and the ways in which our sympathies and our identification are complicated in the way we view the films. So, in that sense I'm incredibly proud to be part of this current moment in gay filmmaking.

**M:** Thank you, very much.

# Diary of a Sad Housewife: Collier Schorr Talks with Todd Haynes

Collier Schorr / 1995

*Safe* is what *American Gigolo* has become; *Safe* is where *American Gigolo* has gone. The hustler glamour of Paul Schrader's erotogenic Los Angeles is affected and then dismembered in Haynes's title sequence which bathes in appropriated gloss. Post- and pre-outbreak respectively, *Safe* drags the images and conceits of Schrader's *Gigolo* into the current crisis, advancing its discussion of AIDS in metaphorical terms. Oddly and involuntarily, the two films bracket the AIDS crisis by implanting danger or susceptibility within the heterosexual orbit, without posing the "virus" as antagonist. Playing Haynes's straight act off Schrader's homosensual and phobic voyeurism might seem fanciful but consider their parallel exploration of banishment and loss of identity. In polar L.A.'s, both housewife and whore (Richard Gere) are edged out of worlds they occupied only as surrogates. The sexless sex and sleek suits, the spiritual and physical toxicity of excess, and the subsequent exodus into mainstream monogamy, lead us fifteen years later to the insular world of *Safe*, where illness rather than intrigue unravels complacency.

In *Poison*, Haynes serenaded the archetypal gay male dystopian utopia: the Genet prison. Now he inverts this strategy, casting the heterosexual utopian locale—the suburban home—as a wife-killing entity.

I talked with Haynes this May on the heels of *Safe*'s quiet triumph at the Sundance Film Festival as we looked toward the film's early summer release.

**Collier Schorr:** Why open *Safe* with such a shamelessly gorgeous and seductive sequence?

**Todd Haynes:** I wanted the opening to be a glossy, slow entry into this world. The way it's described in the script is that the viewer is driving up a hill and watching houses go from small to large to larger, all more and more simulated in their architecture. I was thinking of Encino, where my parents just happen to live and where the architecture is at once stunning, frightening, and fascinating—fake Tudor, fake country manor, at night bathed in the iridescent blue-green glow of street lamps and landscape lighting, with that buzz of electricity in the air. Everything in the film is about what can be seen in those houses from outside at night. The music adds to it, as well as the credits, which appear to pulsate and then evaporate into fumes.

**CS:** Did you look at any particular L.A. films before filming *Safe*?
**TH:** I looked at *2001*. I looked at films that took the notion of L.A. as a futuristic spaceland where every trace of nature has been completely superseded by man really far. L.A. is like an airport: you never breathe real air; you're never in any real place; you're in a transitional, carpeted hum zone—which is what I wanted to convey in *Safe*.

**CS:** The prison scenes in *Poison* were so full of visual pleasure. What was it like filming in the home of Carol White?
**TH:** The two films represent absolutely opposite approaches. I align *Superstar* with *Safe*. *Poison* is closer to *Dottie Gets Spanked* and an earlier film I made about Rimbaud called *Assassins*. The latter three are gay themed, and they are messier films because I was taking something I felt really passionate about and trying to describe artists, their lives, and their acts of transgression—all the while knowing and mistrusting the tendency to think that film can portray transgression and give it to an audience intact. It can't. You have to interrogate transgression or present it in pieces. With those projects I had to guard against my love of the material and how my own fantasies revolved around it. *Safe* is not my world, it's the construction of another world. *Superstar* and *Safe* were very conceptual projects about people in whom I didn't have an initial investment, but while I was constructing the films I found myself in them. I completely identified with Karen's anorexia, although I've never been anorexic, and I completely understand Carol's relationship to an identity she inherited and her need to be affirmed by a society that intellectually she knows sucks.

**CS:** Carol's world seems less a construction and more a reconstruction of the heterosexual environment you grew up in. It says a lot about mythologized inheritances that you feel closer to the prison locale of *Poison*.

**TH:** The textures, colors, and smells of that world did not feel like mine. I always saw it from the point of view of somebody who didn't really feel like a part of it.

**CS:** So is Carol you?

**TH:** Yeah, I think she is. In *Safe*, I'm putting this unborn version of myself deeply into that territory and then slowly scratching my way out.

**CS:** I thought about Natalie Wood in *Splendor in the Grass* when I watched Carol's ladylike collapse. Both are models of restraint—with the exception of Natalie's breakdown in the bathtub and Carol's seizure at the dry cleaners. In *Safe*, does chemical illness replace hysteria, which seems ever stuck on the feminine?

**TH:** Yes, of course. One thing about *Splendor in the Grass* is that Wood's character's sexual hunger is continually being tamed—by society and its rules of what a woman is supposed to be. Unfortunately Carol White doesn't have that hunger. The history of illness associated with women has been a continual interest in my films, from *Superstar* to *Safe*. I loved what seemed particularly inexplicable about environmental illness when I first read about it—how it was affecting housewives. It wasn't until men in the workplace started to come down with similar kinds of sensitivities that environmental illness became something the medical establishment would even begin to investigate. The ability to dismiss illness as feminine and the way illness completely undermines identity are what *Safe* explores.

**CS:** Why has female illness been of continual interest to you?

**TH:** I think it's illness first and foremost, but there's a tradition of illness being projected onto the "female" that I identify with. I clue into that history. I feel that AIDS as it's associated with homosexuality has a historical connection to illnesses attributed to women.

**CS:** If Carol White didn't suffer from chemical illness, would she have been all right?

**TH:** No. I think the illness is the only thing that's telling her the truth in the movie. Illness is the thing that makes her look at her life in a completely different way and forces her out of these patterns. Unfortunately the illness takes her to a place, Wrenwood, that is supposed to provide answers or explanations for physical conditions, but ultimately what Wrenwood provides is as destructive and confining as the L.A. home and life she fled. We leave Carol White almost where we found her in the beginning of the film—suffering in a repressive system that is supposed to have been the answer to everything.

**CS:** *Superstar*, *Poison*, and *Safe* all explore illness through a low-impact version of the horror movie. Can you talk about that genre's capability to represent the other as protagonist?

**TH:** Carol is kept at bay from the viewer. In *Safe*, the distance usually felt toward the "monster" in horror movies, the feeling of removal, is furthered by the fact that there are very few close-ups of Carol. It's quietly horrific. People who have chemical illnesses get really intense physical reactions from chemicals. Some of the stuff I saw doing research was so extreme—cysts draining black discharge, for example—I couldn't put it in the movie because the audience would think it was just outrageous. I think the audience does feel this weird distance from Carol, though it may not be immediately associated with the "monster" lurking within her. Carol White doesn't know who she is, she's at a distance from herself. The film reflects this distance, mirroring the way her illness literally distances us from her. Carol's process of figuring out who she is gives us a sense of how to care about her.

**CS:** It seems as though being sick has become a metaphor for having AIDS. How is it helpful to make an AIDS movie that's not specifically (vis-a-vis story line) about AIDS?

**TH:** I'd like to make a film about AIDS, but I do find that the specificity of AIDS right now in our day-to-day lives gives everybody the ability to set it aside from their lives out of a survival instinct. There are always ways of separating ourselves from a completely overwhelming experience when we don't have the means to deal with it. When I set out to do *Safe*, especially after I did *Poison* (because *Poison* was completely informed by AIDS, and neither film could have existed without the epidemic), I did have this instinct to take the metaphor of AIDS as far as possible away from the war zone—*Poison*'s realm, where you're in the trenches and everything's pushed to an extreme, operatic level—and instead to try to discover illness in the most unlikely place on the planet: in the safest, most protected, most comfortable, most sealed-off kind of life.

**CS:** Illness doesn't look as dangerous or life-threatening in a place like that.

**TH:** Initially. All of this is an elitist version of illness. One of the internal concepts of *Safe* is that while you're watching it the film provides all these reasons why you should doubt Carol's illness and find it unacceptable.

**CS:** For Carol, "unhappy" is a ridiculous concept. Who in her world would believe she could ever be unsatisfied? So she blearily says she's under a lot of stress.

**TH:** Stress becomes a code word. I created a difficult situation for myself by providing the audience with all these ways not to care about Carol. But the ammunition the audience has just reiterates all the mean messages Carol is told: You are making yourself sick; it's all in your head; go see a shrink; you don't love yourself enough; you lead this empty life; you're not really stressed out. I wanted to touch that little bit in everyone where you just aren't convinced that who you think you are is really who you are—that moment when you feel like you're a forgery.

**CS:** Getting away or fleeing—often from the oppression of normalcy—has been a constant in your work, from Karen Carpenter's eating to disappear to a child's flying away to leave home. Carol leaves her husband and stepson for a desert retreat; it's a pretty powerful image of separation. Can you talk about stripping a family away from a female character, and whether or not one could read this exploration as a kind of reflexive heterophobia?

**TH:** Well, there's no question, the film is completely—valiantly—heterophobic. But perhaps it's more masculine-phobic, or patriarch-phobic. I feel there's an unconditional sympathy for Carol, who is heterosexual. One goal in the movie was to create the least sentimental image of a kid—a kid Carol has no real relationship to. Rory [Chauncy Leopardi] is a child from her husband's first marriage, but neither Carol nor Rory have their hearts in this sort of placating—of being mother and son, assuming roles. At the very beginning, before the illness, you see Carol not getting fulfillment from a sexual life with her husband or from a maternal life with this child. I didn't want to create a perfect home that was undermined by illness. A problem already existed, and the illness was a circumstance that alerted her to it.

**CS:** After *Poison*, many viewers might expect something a little sexier than *Safe*.

**TH:** A lot of people are in for a slow, quiet shock. *Safe* is a film that resists telling you what to think. It does have a very clear point of view, but some may not know how to look for it. These days, movies have gotten didactic and instructive, heavy-handed in every way.

**CS:** While all conventional wisdom would suggest Carol engage in extra-marital sex with the recognizably Hollywood-ish Chris (James LeGros), she remains unsatisfied. Is it satisfying, even thrilling, for you to with-hold from gratifying the audience's desire for desire?
**TH:** The film withholds the kinds of rewards that are usually assured. From the beginning, Carol is not fully accessible to us. We don't really understand why all this is happening to her. What always is wanted in a film like this, especially in all the TV disease movies, is a transcendent ending when the protagonist either survives the illness or doesn't. In terms of selling the film, it definitely would have been easier to include some romance. The focus of concern while trying to raise money for *Safe* was the film's resistant ending, which has continued to be a ques-tion for critics. I was never tempted to make a romantic spark between the characters. I really wanted to frustrate narrative expectations to the point where you want Carol to become independent, and at the same time you learn enough about Wrenwood to know that Wrenwood's an-swer for Carol is horribly cruel—she is blamed for her illness and basi-cally locked in a sealed-up vault. That's not the narrative resolution we look for in movies.

**CS:** The un-spa-like, unheimlich retreat that Carol moves to brings up issues of quarantine and segregation. While quarantines have generally been set up to protect those outside, one gets a sense of the comfort of being separate. Can you talk about the film's elusive title and what quar-antine means to you?
**TH:** The film investigates the safety of immunity—various kinds of im-munity, like emotional immunity to the world (how we find Carol in the beginning). Carol's illness forces her out of such numbness, but Wren-wood's kinds of spiritual diagnosis of illness have a great deal to do with controlling the world and information—keeping newspaper ink, televi-sion, and transportation at bay—and re-creating a sense of quarantine, what immunity becomes in holistic language.

**CS:** Your depiction of a spiritual retreat, complete with a mansion-own-ing guru, is somewhat detached, which I think may make some viewers uncomfortable. You resist making the retreat an easy target of ridicule.
**TH:** I found the least interesting thing I could do with New Age stuff was

to completely dismiss it. The cut we had at Sundance didn't have the shot showing the mansion. That single shot has allowed people to have a slightly more solid reading of the film, which I have to say is disappointing on some level for me because I feel like the film is so full of strong indicators of what my critique is.

**CS:** Why cast Peter [Peter Friedman], the retreat guru, as someone with AIDS?
**TH:** A lot of it has to do with Louise Hay's book *The AIDS Book: Creating a Positive Approach*. In the mid-eighties Hay developed a following among gay men with AIDS. What is it that makes people with AIDS read a book that says, If you loved yourself more you wouldn't have gotten sick, and now that you are sick if you learn how to love yourself you will be cured? This puts the subjects in an impossible situation where they will never overcome their illness because they'll never love themselves enough. I think I made Peter someone with AIDS not only because it's another immune-system illness, like environmental illness—they're often linked—but also because there was this history of New Age thinking and AIDS that I wanted to bring into the film.

**CS:** *Safe* breaks from television and Hollywood by withholding any resolution. Safe in her safe house, Carol whispers "I love you" to her reflection in the camera lens, following a counselor's advice. Ordinarily this might function as some kind of happy-ever-after beginning, but in Carol's case it is just another example of her malleability.
**TH:** I did want some kind of tension. Carol adopts the words of the new world she's entered, and she is repeating the lingo that she didn't know how to repeat earlier on, but that must be weighed against all the evidence that's piled up against Wrenwood. Without all those critiques of Wrenwood, you could leave the theater feeling fully resolved and hopeful, but in *Safe* there's no escape.

# Todd Haynes

Alison MacLean / 1995

This interview, "Todd Haynes" by Alison MacLean, was commissioned by and first
published in BOMB Magazine, from BOMB 52/Summer 1995, pp. 48–51. © Bomb
Magazine, New Art Publications, and its Contributors. All rights reserved. The BOMB
Digital Archive can be viewed at www.bombsite.com.

I've been a huge fan of Todd Haynes ever since my first trip to New York
in 1989 when I saw his film, *Superstar*, featuring Karen Carpenter as a
Barbie Doll. *Superstar* was subsequently and tragically banished to pirate
video limbo by the Carpenter estate. I'd never seen anything like it—the
sheer audaciousness of it took my breath away.

As did his next film, *Poison*, which intercut three very different stories: a fifties B-horror spoof about self-inflicted disease; a Genet-inspired
love story set in a prison; and a mock TV "documentary" about a deviant
boy who literally flies out a window.

Then there was *Dottie Gets Spanked* about a young boy's obsession
with a Lucille Ball character on TV, which explores, among other things,
the erotic fascination of spanking.

Todd's films always open new doors for me, show me rooms I never
knew existed before. They're beautiful, puzzling, and very passionate,
and always informed by a radical, unshowy intelligence.

*Safe*, his new film, is no exception. It's a horror film unlike any other
horror film—cool, mysterious, and emotionally devastating. Like his
other films, it creates its own unique, coherent world—a very rare thing
these days. Which is to say, in seeing it, I felt I'd dreamed it. Stated simply, *Safe* is a film about a woman who develops an allergy to the twentieth century. It's terrifying, yet at the same time, unusually—wonderfully—restrained, building a sense of dread from the smallest details: a
black couch in a suburban living room; a man spraying deodorant under
his arms. There is never a false moment. Todd is one of the most exciting
directors I know. As a filmmaker myself, he gives me courage.

**Alison MacLean:** When you wrote the script for *Safe* did you see it as a horror film?

**Todd Haynes:** Definitely. But a completely latent horror film where everyday life is the most frightening of all.

**AM:** What's so unusual about *Safe* is the way in which it refuses to tell you what to think, whereas most films we watch take us by the scruff of the neck and tell us what to think and how to feel. *Safe* is ambivalent, almost as if you're undecided yourself. It's similar to the experience it's investigating, of being hurt and going to one of those New Age retreats with equal feelings of hope—that there is some answer in their cure—and also skepticism and fear that their philosophy is completely hollow.

**TH:** I wanted to interrogate my own knee-jerk reactions against these kinds of places. I researched New Age philosophy with an open mind to see what it was doing that I didn't like. And to see what it was doing that people were so in need of right now. Why is it taking on such a huge predominance in people's lives? Why are they choosing it as a way to comprehend their illness, unhappiness, or their emotional uncertainty? The book that really got me revved up was Louise Hay's book on AIDS.

**AM:** I don't know her.

**TH:** She's a California-based, middle-aged woman whose life changed from her illness and her subsequent recovery. With the best intentions, she wrote a series of books with little daily meditations. This was in the mid-eighties, when AIDS was taking off, and she developed a strong following among gay men. Her book literally states that if we loved ourselves more we wouldn't get sick with this illness. And that once you get it, if you learn how to love yourself in a proper way, you can overcome it. That's scary. I kept thinking of the people who have no answers to their situation and who turn to this. And my motivation wasn't to demonize the instigators or to victimize and reveal the blind ignorance of the followers, but just to understand this phenomenon for myself. *Safe* is a guarded interrogation of the whole thing with a careful sympathy for its central character, Carol White. I didn't want to overpower her with my own opinions or allow the film to overpower her with its narrative instructions. This character has her own uncertainty about who she is, and the vastly changing face of her world becomes our guide to her.

**AM:** She's a very unusual character. I was intrigued by your comment about deliberately choosing an ordinary woman, someone you'd meet at a party and not necessarily remember the next day.

**TH:** There are many more people like her in the world than the ones with strong personalities we're used to seeing on film. People aren't taught to project themselves in dynamic, articulate ways. And most people aren't gorgeous or absolutely sure of who they are. I know that I make films, I'm an artist. But there are times when I don't really know who I am. The unconscious assumption of who we are and what we're here for, those questions are fragile in most people's minds. There are times when that unconscious sense of ourselves slips through our fingers.

**AM:** Carol's character seems so lost at the beginning and perhaps even more so at the end. There's that moment halfway through the film when she starts to question everything and comprehend the emptiness in her life, but it's a terrible knowledge. It's a powerful scene: Carol's sitting on her bed and her husband comes to the door and she says, "Where am I?" And she looks at the photograph of the two of them beside the bed and it no longer reassures her.

**TH:** When she writes a letter to an environmental illness group, to say, "My name is Carol White and this is my history," at that moment her husband and normal life rushes through the door and she completely forgets everything. It's all taken away. But I agree, she's lost at the beginning and at the end of the film. The film is a very sad circle that returns her to a perfectly sealed-off version of where she started. There's some hope in the middle of the film, when she goes to this group and begins to take steps out of her protected, isolated world. Her body tells her that something's terribly wrong with her life and her world. Whether it's a material problem or a larger symbolic problem, it's something that everything in her life has been encouraging her not to look at. The chaos of that middle section is the most hopeful moment in the film, because suddenly she is forced to re-examine her life and see it as troubled and needing a change.

**AM:** You don't make it easy for us, it can be seen equally as a physical or a psychological manifestation. And of course that's such a false distinction we make. It's such a horrifying scene, Carol's at a baby shower, sitting in her party dress with that little girl on her knee and—what's interesting is the way the girl reacts first, as if she senses Carol's distress before we do; then Carol completely falls apart. It looks like an anxiety attack.

**TH:** A journalist said the other day, "I still didn't know whether her illness was psychosomatic or not." I discovered for myself at least, that whether the problem is the chemicals in our society or the conditions in which this woman is living, in both cases the problem is cultural. And most of the time it's a combination of both: emotional and physiologi-cal, concrete. Carol goes to Wrenwood, a New Age health center, to try and find all the answers and is told to find them within herself. Wren-wood's project is to internalize everything as psychological: an issue of self-love or self-hate. My tendency is to look at the world we live in, and the conditions we all share—ultimately, society is what determines ei-ther the material or the psychological manifestation of the illness.

**AM:** It's a very complex way of looking at illness. There's a point where Carol embraces it.
**TH:** It gives her a new identity.

**AM:** Yes, you can see that—I've seen it myself in certain people I know. The film is a metaphor for something else. But the metaphor keeps changing. Sometimes it seems to be about a spiritual vacuum or emo-tional alienation. . . .
**TH:** Void.

**AM:** And then of course AIDS. What's so uncanny is that the people are so real. Did you do a lot of research?
**TH:** I talked to a lot of people who are chemically sensitive or environ-mentally ill, however you choose to define it. I also wanted to get ele-ments of the vernacular and the vocal qualities of contemporary subur-ban America, particularly Los Angeles, in the film.

**AM:** How did you do that?
**TH:** I hung out in the San Fernando Valley and haunted those clubs and malls and department stores. My parents live in a world not unlike that, so I'm familiar with it. Some of the visual information and the locations are places that I know myself. There is a manifestation of Valley dialect in *Safe*, a tinny, depthless vocal quality that you're hearing more and more among younger generations, particularly women. It's a vocal laxity you don't hear often in films, certainly not Hollywood films, or when you do it's accidental, it's a bit part. You hear it on *90210*. I didn't want to make a big camp parody of it or criticize it, but I did want it to be part of the film.

**AM:** It seems to me, perhaps because I'm a foreigner, but there's some-thing quite girlish about it.
**TH:** I know. (laughter) And then there's a whole other vernacular for the

way the New Age people speak. I'd visit those places and feel like the evil spy with my notepad.

**AM:** Did you make some real contacts?
**TH:** My closest personal contacts were with people who are sufferers of environmental illness, and they really aren't the target of any specific critique in the film. They range in class, and place and sex. There's no definable voice or singular quality about them. Their sole concern is that people are alerted to this illness, that it's real, that it exists. Lynne Montandon of the Response Team for the Chemically Injured, which is a group in Atascadero, California, was wonderful, really supportive and helpful. As was Susan Pitman of the Chemical Connection in Wimberly, Texas, another little community of people with environmental difficulties. But I did visit some New Age places and steal from them, and didn't develop any personal contacts there.

**AM:** Did you visit a place like Wrenwood?
**TH:** Yeah. I stole some aspects of Wrenwood from a place called Kripalu, a yoga center.

**AM:** Oh.
**TH:** Do you know Kripalu? In Lenox, Massachusetts.

**AM:** Yes, I've been there for a yoga class.
**TH:** You went there! (laughter)

**AM:** For a yoga class.
**TH:** Did you stay over?

**AM:** No, I didn't stay over. I've thought about it, though.
**TH:** There's something completely restful and recuperative about it. But it also has an element to it—you can't call it a cult particularly, but there's certainly a following.

**AM:** There's something that makes my flesh crawl.
**TH:** It's that institutionalization of the spiritual.

**AM:** Exactly. It's very political in a way. You touch on that in one scene at Wrenwood: a group therapy session and where that older woman is grieving and very angry and the therapist tells her to let it go, and she refuses. She's the odd one out.

**TH:** She's resistant. And there's no room for that in New Age language.

**AM:** He just cuts her off.

**TH:** That was from Kripalu. I have to admit, the rules at Wrenwood, the asexuality, the silent meals for breakfast and lunch, men on one side of the room, women on the other, no sexual interaction or affection displayed. . . .

**AM:** Not wearing provocative clothes, or anything that might draw attention to itself.

**TH:** Exactly. The assumption of men on one side of the room and women on the other is a perfect example of how New Age thought often reiterates power structures that exist in the world without examining them. It's reiterating this heterosexual idea of safety. By separating men and women there'll be no sexual distractions from the higher goal.

**AM:** Carol's a wealthy suburban woman.

**TH:** Suburban ideal.

**AM:** And then she goes to what you would think to be the opposite end of the spectrum—in terms of an alternative lifestyle—and yet they seem to be equally life-denying. It's fascinating.

**TH:** When I first heard about environmental illness it was in some tabloid TV piece about women. They called it a twentieth-century illness. The very name was so fascinating my mind started to go. But what cinched it for me was that the solution to this problem was not some return to nature. Instead, women went to these trailer homes where everything was covered in plastic, and their lives became hyper-insulated and hyper-sealed off. That's really what convinced me that this was something I wanted to pursue. It was not taking you toward an essentialist position, but into this excessive control over your life and every substance and every piece of information that could disrupt your system. That's scary.

**AM:** It's very sad. Were they all actors in the film? It was so realistic, those people at Wrenwood, I wondered whether some of them were non-actors.

**TH:** All the speaking parts were actors, unlike *Poison* where I used a

ALISON MACLEAN / 1995   55

combination of actors and non-actors. I think I'm spoiled for life by the quality of the actors I worked with—they brought that sense of reality to everything they did. Even the extras, who my brother Shawn cast, were excellent. Because extras have to act too. Directors forget. There's always that species of extra in movies who are so wooden. . . .

**AM:** They can ruin a scene. I've had that experience where I cast an extra to be a nurse and they can't be believable doing a simple task.
**TH:** Did you have a bad nurse experience? I had a really bad extra nurse experience too. (laughter)

**AM:** I had to fire her on the spot and cast a real nurse.
**TH:** I didn't have that much gumption. I wish I did. My nurse couldn't spray the spray can.

**AM:** So what did you do?
**TH:** I just kept shooting her over and over again.

**AM:** Right, right. Everyone's waiting. You get more and more distressed. What I find so exciting about your films is the way they all seem to expand the experience of what it is to view a film. In *Poison*, you did that audacious thing of intercutting three distinct genres throughout the film. When I saw it at Sundance it made me think about how film—unlike music or the visual arts or fiction—has this unwritten rule that it must be completely homogeneous in style, not including flashbacks or fantasy sequences, of course. And then, in *Superstar*, casting Karen Carpenter as a Barbie doll. What's interesting about that film is how emotionally involved you become, how you start to forget they're dolls.
**TH:** Thank you. I mean it was an experiment, like most of my films. Each one takes various risks, but their experiments seem to locate around identification—that's the place where we all participate in making real or making alive this two-dimensional, technological gimmick projected on the wall. When we fill it in with our emotions as spectators it becomes powerful and alive, that's the place where I feel the most curiosity as a director.

**AM:** Many films don't allow much room for the viewer to enter into them.
**TH:** They don't want that narrative process interrupted. It's a perfect system, let's not mess with it. But it's exactly at that place where we

unfortunately find ourselves identifying in stories and messages that reaffirm the world exactly as it is, in its worst aspects. And that's where I find narrative film to be the most frightening, because it's so powerful. It's hard to find an equivalent in other art mediums, for me at least, that has such a symbolic impact on the way we think about the world and about ourselves. Films reflect and instruct us at the same time, and that's strong stuff. So I do delight in the idea that by playing around, tinkering or upsetting that process of identification a little bit, people have to think more about what they're seeing, who's telling them what and why. A viewer has to ask the question: where's this idea coming from? Without losing all the pleasure that's part of that process.

**AM:** There's pleasure in your films, but there's a different kind of engagement. *Safe* has a detachment, a restraint that oddly enough draws you into the film all the more strongly. It takes some getting used to. It's a different rhythm, a different pace, but once you adjust—because it's more open-ended—you fill it up with your own thoughts and experiences. Like those shots you have where Carol's walking through the house and garden, and it's quite wide and we only see her back. What is it about backs? They're often so much more mysterious and eloquent to me than faces. You're dying to see her face and that desire makes you fill in her face for yourself.

**TH:** *Safe* won't have that effect on everyone, but I did feel my own frustration with the volume and aggressivity of current Hollywood film practice, where each film has to out-shriek, out-pace the next. And the amount of histrionics and technological gimmickry and assault that each film displays, one-upping the next, again and again. I walk out of those films absolutely numb, feeling nothing, because they assume everything. Whereas a Chantal Akerman film is a real inspiration because it's so restrained and resistant. What you see in it in real time is what every other movie would cut out. But it creates a suspense and curiosity, and a huge role for the viewer in the telling.

**AM:** I worry that that kind of filmmaking and experimentation ended with the seventies. People are much less patient because of this MTV sensibility. All the experimentation goes into creating the spectacle, but is not focused on the level of storytelling or the way a film engages with an audience.

**TH:** The formula for successful filmmaking has been so reduced to a single set of prototypical characters, enormous events, and perfect resolutions that it's almost inconceivable for films that are produced by the studios and larger independents to escape that formula. The seventies were the last time that there were a range of possibilities, even in mainstream films.

**AM:** It seems like you draw from television, or from the television you saw when you were growing up. As a filmmaker, has television been important to you?

**TH:** Yeah. It is, but tell me more. I'm curious. I mean, sometimes I'm scared by how much television I watch. I don't know if I want it to be as much of an influence as maybe it is.

**AM:** You reinvent it. It seems to be part of the genre vocabulary that you draw on. *Safe* is nothing like television, but on one level there's all that banality of suburban life—it deals with the ordinary. It's kind of an anti-TV Movie-of-the-Week.

**TH:** *Poison* was influenced by the TV disease movie genre, totally, but to a very different end. Disease movies have this guise of teaching the viewer, informing them about breast cancer, about AIDS. . . .

**AM:** Towards the cathartic death or towards hope.

**TH:** In all of these TV films there is a burden on the part of the central character to have a transcendent realization as a result of their illness. In *Safe*, Wrenwood becomes the institutionalization of that transcendence. Basically, *Safe* is on the side of the disease and not the cure. It's the disease that completely opens Carol's eyes and makes her rethink her life, and the cure that returns her to this sealed-off existence. The values in *Safe* completely reinvent the disease movie, but the structure is very much the same.

**AM:** Do you think about what would be required of you to reach a wider audience, to have a bigger budget in relation to the kind of films you want to make?

**TH:** I'm always surprised when films of mine which I think are intellectual experiments are received by a wider audience. Whether it happened by fluke or because of the NEA scandal surrounding *Poison*.

**AM:** But it won the Sundance award too.

**TH:** Yeah, that as well. But *Poison* was getting a lot of mainstream coverage because of the NEA censorship stuff. It was seen by far more people than I ever thought it would be, even after Sundance, because many films win at Sundance and don't really take off. And I thought, is this film up to that? Is this really what I want for this film, to be scrutinized by mainstream audiences? And not because of the homosexuality but because of the structure. And I found that people in little towns across the country where I accompanied the film and talked about it, were really eager for something more than what they were being given by Hollywood and were excited by the challenge of it. And were also very sophisticated narratively, could read and identify genres. I felt very pleased that the assumptions we all make about American filmgoers versus European filmgoers are not always the case. I do admire filmmakers like Hitchcock who could, through the formulas he created in narrative, reach such an enormous audience and be absolutely mainstream and popular, but at the same time be so completely subversive. It's always something to marvel at. And he wanted to be popular—I love that. But that's not my main goal. Is it yours?

**AM:** No, but it's a factor if you want to make films that cost more than a certain amount of money. It seems that you have to be enormously clever in the way that Hitchcock was or somehow . . . I guess I'd like to achieve that.

**TH:** You're right there. There's the practicality of budgets, and trying to get your film made the way you think it needs to be made, and sometimes that requires considering name stars and structures that might differ from your first choice. But I've learned from making what I make that I am an experimental filmmaker. I don't need to be a feature filmmaker as a personal reward. The limitations in that world alone are so profound in terms of what you can get made—it's always an internal debate in my head. I don't know.

**AM:** The films that get me really excited, that give me huge pleasure, rarely achieve that popular success.

**TH:** I know. I feel that way too. I certainly felt that way after this year's Oscar ceremony. Way out of touch. Is there this pulse, zeitgeist, this basic trend that we're all supposed to find and make our own? What becomes more and more apparent, particularly in America, is this multiplicity of ideas and points of view that have strange, unexpected crossovers from topic to topic but take place in heterogeneous worlds. Maybe that's the way it should be.

**AM:** But you don't really see much of that diversity in films. You have the black film or the gay film, I hate to use those categories, but it's not really reflective of . . .

**TH:** Money doesn't recognize them. But by the same logic, the attempt to pre-plan ahead by Hollywood standards, to use everything they know from previous hits, to prefabricate it using audience tests at every stage, to fashion films identically after other films, always fails. There's something accidental that occurs even in successful blockbusters. Film is a cultural habit. There's a ritual to going to films. What do you do on a date? You go see a movie. It's not necessarily because it's touching people or really moving them or rocking their world, it's just what's there. It's out of a lack of anything else to do that we keep the film industry going, maybe.

**AM:** This might be my skewed perspective, but it does seem that going to films is such a significant part of people's lives. It scares me how much it dominates our lives.

**TH:** And more and more so in the era of fiber optics. You don't need to go out anymore, but people do. At least they do. There's something about the big screen that's still an allure.

**AM:** I was going to ask if you had a good Los Angeles earthquake story.

**TH:** The earthquake coincided with a break in our schedule, so it didn't brutally affect the shoot, but we continued through numerous aftershocks, which as I'm sure you've heard, are sometimes really sizable and frightening.

**AM:** Just that anxiety. . . .

**TH:** Exactly. So we were shooting the final scene in the film where Carol gives her awkward speech to the group, saying, "You have to be so much more aware, reading labels, going into buildings . . ." all of a sudden it started to shake and the windows started to vibrate. It was a reaction shot and the actors kept their fake grins on, but the pain in their faces was really kind of brilliant.

**AM:** Could you see it in the image?

**TH:** Yeah, we used that take. What you see on the film is the actors actually reacting to the aftershock. (laughter)

# Antibodies: Larry Gross Talks with *Safe*'s Todd Haynes

Larry Gross / 1995

From *Filmmaker Magazine*, Summer 1995. Reprinted by permission from *Filmmaker Magazine*.

Todd Haynes, director of Sundance Grand Prize Winner *Poison* and the underground classic *Superstar*, was inspired to make his latest feature, *Safe*, by his visceral response to New Age recovery therapists who tell the physically ill that they have made themselves sick, that they are responsible for their own suffering.

Carol White, played superbly by Julianne Moore, is an archetypally banal homemaker in the San Fernando Valley who one day gets sick and never gets well. Her doom is first her own unique physical condition. But her "action" is to be exposed to two kinds of discourse about illness. One is a conventional discourse that tells her that since what's wrong with her can't be diagnosed, it must not really exist. The other, found at a New Age–styled retreat called Wrenwood, is an unconventional remedy that acknowledges her condition with a certain sentimental empathy but which further alienates her from the social reality around her, rendering her even more incapable of taking significant action in her own defense.

*Safe* is a political film that almost never directly mentions political issues, a horror film without any monsters, special effects, or killings, and a relationship film without any regular psychological inflection. It is on the surface an utterly traditional narrative film, but one which is also secretly a work of difficult abstractness. Working with a bigger budget and trying to reach a larger audience, Haynes has wound up making his most demanding and elaborate film yet.

**Larry Gross:** It was three or four years between *Poison* and *Safe*. What were you doing in that period and when did the idea for *Safe* come along?

**Todd Haynes:** I wrote *Safe* pretty quickly after *Poison* and anticipated that the ability to get [the film] together at that time would be easier than it ended up being.

**LG:** And the difficulties were what?
**TH:** To raise $1 million for the film. We didn't think we could do it for less, and just that minor commitment was more than people felt they could make based on the script.

**LG:** What was a typical rejection like?
**TH:** "Oh, it's really interesting. We don't know." Getting people to say no is what's hard, and excluding them from your list and moving on. People weren't sure. They wanted somebody else to take the first step and American Playhouse basically did. But that was in the midst of their restructuring their finances and getting much less money from PBS. This is before the recent move away from public funding. They're now Playhouse International Pictures, associated with Goldwyn, and I think they may have no public funding involved anymore, but at this point that wasn't the case. They were fully dependent on money that they expected more of. They made a commitment to *Safe* and then immediately said, "Oh we don't have the money we thought we had. We're going to have to wait." They eventually came back on for a portion of the budget and we went to Cannes to secure the rest. It was my first experience there and we were like, "Okay, we're going to get the rest of the money together in three days" and we did. And a month later, everybody changed their mind again. So two-and-a-half years went by before we felt we could really begin.

**LG:** Who came in with money that was real and stayed?
**TH:** American Playhouse, Channel 4 in England. And then the Kardana Company, these two guys, John Hart and Tom Caruso, who produced *Tommy* and *Guys and Dolls* on Broadway, came in at the very end to kind of get us through the last notch. They had never been involved with independent filmmaking up to this point and they loved *Dottie Gets Spanked*, the short film I made during that time, and really liked the script to *Safe*. So they completed the financing.

**LG:** So you began producing when?
**TH:** First of the year, '94.

**LG:** And you shot for six weeks?

**TH:** Shot for six weeks in L.A.

**LG:** Discuss working with [producer] Christine Vachon.

**TH:** The film wouldn't exist if she hadn't fought the fight that I just described. It was really due to Christine's persistence. I would've given up.

**LG:** And the DP?

**TH:** I wanted to work with [New York DP] Maryse Alberti who had shot *Poison* and *Dottie Gets Spanked*, and who I love working with. She's brilliant—she just shot *Crumb*, by the way—but she was pregnant at the time. So I started talking to people in L.A. The differences between [New York and L.A.], particularly in low-budget filmmaking, became clearer to me.

**LG:** What are the differences?

**TH:** Oh, they are staggering. The L.A. mentality is dominated by the industry in every possible way. It's all by the money. So, we [ended up hiring] the people who work for $850 a week—basically, the L.A. sexploitation crews. The DP, Alex Nepomniaschy, had shot *Poltergeist 3* and I was immediately blown away by his lighting in that film. I thought it was very natural, but it had the appropriate industrial-chemical feel to it. I wanted a very natural feeling that would create a strong mood but not be like, green light to your face, the very obvious sort of flashy approach you see more and more of these days.

**LG:** How did you describe the movie to the cinematographer?

**TH:** He read the script and immediately said, "Have you seen *Red Desert* by Antonioni?" And I hadn't. I had seen the others, *Zabriskie Point*, *Blow Up*, *The Passenger*, but I hadn't seen *Red Desert*, which is an amazing movie. So from the descriptions in the script, he already had a very specific and appropriate vision of the film; we really connected right away. But the basic, almost funny restrictions that we placed on ourselves was this restrained coverage and distance from the character. The joke was, okay, let's move in for a close-up but we never got very close. All of our proportions were appropriately adjusted from the starting point, which was wide. Minimal camera movement.

**LG:** Relative to *Poison* and *Superstar*, *Safe* would be classified as less of an experimental film. Did you want this to be a more traditional film?

**TH:** No, not at all. And I think it's the hardest, the most difficult film I've made for audiences.

**LG:** I agree with that, but I believe that its extraordinary quality . . . as a [kind of] facsimile of a conventional film . . . is part of the difficulty of it.
**TH:** I think you're right. The film creates expectations for a more linear, accessible type of film that it doesn't fulfill.

**LG:** And indeed, it employs some of the procedures of more conventional films at the same time that it turns them over in a variety of ways.
**TH:** As *Poison* and *Superstar* did as well.

**LG:** But they're more aggressive in their critical procedures. The fact that they're engaged in critical procedures is more of an empathic part of the experience of those two films.
**TH:** The structure and style tells you so.

**LG:** The thing is, in asking for $1 million and hiring Julianne Moore and doing various things like that you were moving in slightly more "conventional" territory. Did you say, "This is going to be my version of a conventional film, this is going to be my critique of the conventions of a conventional film?"
**TH:** Actually, I was looking at movies like *Jeanne Dielman* by Chantal Akerman and eventually *2001* for some stylistic pointers, so I was looking at things that were extreme.

**LG:** The margins.
**TH:** Yeah, strained, kind of cool presentations of stories. For me [*Safe*] had to do with restraint and playing with narrative expectations in very subtle, controlled ways. I was much more attentive to the structure of conventional storytelling in *Safe* than in *Poison* and *Superstar*.

**LG:** Let's talk a little bit about the narrative genres that are being invoked, that are being "read" by the film in a sense. I saw two strands of regular filmmaking being referred to in the movie and then a third that was more like television. On the one hand the film is linked to a certain tradition of horror film that I see in people like Hitchcock, Cronenberg, and Polanski—what I call a narrative of deterioration. Then there's something else that Cronenberg in particular compared his film *The Brood* to that I'm going to call for lack of a better word, a critique of the "family values" movie: the *Ordinary People* movie, the *Kramer vs. Kramer* movie that begins with some criticism of inauthentic bourgeois life which the film then narrates the triumphant overcoming of. Now of course there's this third genre that combines this and illness, fusing elements of the horror movie, and that's the "disease-of-the-week" TV movie. How did you think of them when you were constructing the film?

**TH:** Most overtly, I was thinking of the TV-disease film, but the film language of horror films was also inspirational. I love that moment in Hitchcock when you know something is about to happen and suspense is created by prolonging the ordinary mundane events that precede this event.

**LG:** One could argue that in *Safe* you're involved in torturing Carol White in the same way that Hitchcock is involved in torturing Janet Leigh. She's the object of the narrative's inexorable machinery and he has a very grim view of what that machinery is doing to those people.

**TH:** He takes a lot more pleasure in that torture than I do in *Safe*, whatever that means. He got off on it.

**LG:** Yes, absolutely.

**TH:** He makes us get off on it. It's the most interesting thing that he did. He made the viewer get off on it and parallel that to what is innately pleasurable in watching movies.

**LG:** Talking about the "disease-of-the-week" genre. Do you see those films? Do watch them with some degree of artistic respect?

**TH:** Absolutely. *The Boy in the Plastic Bubble* was an obvious starting point.

**LG:** We should go back to this question of how you remain and how we remain compassionate towards Carol and interested in her fate, regardless of how the film teases her or is ironic towards her.

**TH:** Or to the genre. Getting back to what I think you're asking about—how close I am or how uncritical I can be with regard to those kinds of TV movies. Yes, certainly there are scenes throughout that I feel absolutely sincere in wanting to develop a certain kind of affection for Carol, a sense of compassion for her that you would find in a TV movie at that particular point in its narrative. That's partly done so that you care about her but also for you to be taken in by those expectations.

**LG:** The film induces the hope or the expectation that something can turn out well which in fact can't turn out well in the world of this particular film. It's very interesting. I'm thinking about Cronenberg's movies. My problems with *The Fly* and *Dead Ringers*, two very interesting films in a lot of ways, is that they're not suspenseful enough about their negative outcomes. Cronenberg obsesses a little bit too completely on the sheer horribleness of it. You are so restrained in these terms. There's this program of continually elongating the hope of a way out for Carol when there's no way out.

**TH:** That's interesting, what you said about Cronenberg, because it's also where his films I think become kind of fun but often where the tension is lost.

**LG:** Let's talk about the wide shot style. The film's visual style seems exceptionally aggressive and powerful and yet it's strongly functional. I don't think there's anything in your technique that's beauty for beauty's sake. The wide shots that dominate the film have many functions. They isolate the heroine. They undermine the rigidity of her pattern of life. They universalize the character in a way. They remind you to read the character as a kind of symbolic entity. And yet, at the same time, they're all beautiful shots. I'm interested in beauty versus function in the conception of this stuff.

**TH:** I'm definitely drawn to minimalism aesthetically. I think it's beautiful and so the film is beautiful to me although . . . what's beautiful about *Safe* is also hard and rigid and cold and controlled and so it's scary. I definitely felt the need to depict Carol constantly in relation to her environment and as part of its architecture.

**LG:** And that makes a political statement right away. It says this is about a character and her environment is a meaningful component of her life.

**TH:** Right. We were trying to define her and feel her and find her as a character but we always [did] it in relation to her space. You don't really have full access to the character, to her psychology, history—things that we're usually pretty quickly given access to in a movie.

**LG:** From an opposite standpoint, what if I want to argue that this look dehumanizes Carol? What do you say in response to a person who says the stylization performs a destructive operation on the heroine?

**TH:** I don't think it performs a destructive operation. I think it reflects and mirrors what the destructive operation is in her world. I mean, it's really about a person who doesn't know who she is, whose illness forces her to look at her life and her self and her world in different ways. We could get back to the disease movie. The thing that is interesting in the disease movie is that in the guise of telling you a story about illness, these movies are really [telling] the story of people's personal victories over the odds. The disease teaches you an "invaluable lesson" about becoming who you are through your illness. I don't ever want to portray a sense of natural being—comfortable, unconscious, secure being. That's what I want to exclude from the film so that the whole time you're trying to think, "How could I possibly get back to that 'not thinking about myself' mode," that supposedly natural mode that we know is not natural at all. And then you get to Wrenwood and it's this parody of the natural world, of this discourse telling you how to be natural.

**LG:** The *New York Times* mistakenly described the film as set in the future.
**TH:** I know, I love that.

**LG:** You made it specifically in 1987. The futuristic side of the film does very much resemble *2001: A Space Odyssey*, which also relies on a lot of wide shots. What led you to *2001* in this film?
**TH:** I stumbled upon it accidentally. Of course I had seen it when it came out but I hadn't thought I should look at *2001* for *Safe*. I had considered *Safe* like *Jeanne Dielman*, but taking place in an airport. I just kept thinking that certain homes in Los Angeles have the quality of airports. All traces of human life, or natural life, have been excluded and taken over. Air is controlled and space is controlled. There's no trace of humankind, of the mess of human beings.

**LG:** You, the filmmaker, are the producer of that. But you kid Carol White for being the producer of that. In other words, Carol White freaks when things aren't color coordinated. I could imagine Todd Haynes walking through the set and seeing the set not being the right color and freaking in a somewhat similar way. Do you identify with Carol?
**TH:** Julianne Moore and I probably share this "nice" problem where we don't freak out on the set. We have this very nice demeanor and we repress it and so I think both of us bonded in this unconscious way on the movie because we were both traumatized while making it. She just stopped menstruating for six months. But you think my identification with Carol White is something that I don't let myself feel very much because it's too scary. I know what it's like to sometimes not feel confident

or know who you are or why you do what you do. I felt like I wanted Carol to represent the most vulnerable part of identity, the most uncertain and fragile part of myself.

**LG:** This brings me back to Kubrick in a way. When *2001* came out, people pointed out this tough subtext of life in this denaturalized future world. The film is hard on these people. They're very dull. Life in the future is dull. They're not very personalized; they are people totally used up in a role that leaves their inner lives pretty much gone.
**TH:** Very much so.

**LG:** But Kubrick utterly admires that world at the same time. What's involved in constructing that reality absorbs him to such an incredible degree. That's finally what seems to me to be true of your relationship to the world that Carol White lives in. There are some feelings of love for this cold world. Coming back to Hitchcock again, I don't think you love punishing Carol the way that he loves punishing Tippi Hedren, but there's a way in which this "unreal, denaturalized" world was your aesthetic esteem. Is that right?
**TH:** Well, it's a world I know really well. It's my family's world, basically. It's quite a bit more extreme and grotesque but it's a world that I know and I've tried to not hate. I've tried to find something very common and sympathetic about it. But what I think some people may miss in the film is a camp appreciation of that world. I think some people go expecting the same camp treatment of the nouveau riche L.A. of the eighties that you may find in *Poison* and it's not there. I think the film is a very sincere attempt to find something common and something human about these people. It's not a happy film but I think that its sadness is an extension of its compassion. It's not part of its critique.

**LG:** I came across something today in a 1949 book of Maurice Blanchot where he's trying to tease at the relationship between Surrealist literature and its ambition to be political: "And we can also see that the most uncommitted literature is also the most committed because it knows that to claim to be free in a society that is not free is to accept responsibility for the constraints of that society and especially to accept the mystification of the word 'freedom' by which society bides its intentions." He's talking about the fact that Surrealism attempts to be revolutionary even while moving completely away from direct, explicit engagement with social and political questions. It tries to produce the image of freedom and at the same time reveal the mechanisms by which freedom is constrained. That sounds to me to be similar to the political discourse in *Safe*. And what's interesting about it is there's no explicit political discourse in the film. Do you worry that people won't understand that there's a political meaning to the film?

**TH:** It's something I've been thinking about since Sundance, absolutely. It's disappointing to me because what *Poison* taught me was that a lot of people out there are eager to see different kinds of films. They wanted to be challenged. Not necessarily art-film goers—people a couple of steps outside that world still want to be engaged and challenged by film and aren't given the chance most of the time. It's pretty clear to me what's going on in *Safe* at the end. It's a pretty unambiguous condemnation of a New Age answer to life's problems.

**LG:** I think it's more than that. I think this is the one movie that describes the complete collapse of left-wing oppositional culture in this country.

**TH:** That's so interesting.

**LG:** Because it's made clearly sympathetically to the criticism of conventional institutions that left-wing causes are supposed to undertake.

**TH:** And it targets left-wing audiences and left-wing expectations in a fairly nasty way. [In the Wrenwood section of the film,] the first time you see the black character, Susan, you think, "Oh, this has got to be a cool place," and then you see Peter, who is described as having AIDS and you think, "Oh, he's got to be cool, it goes without saying, Todd Haynes is a gay filmmaker." So it's like all these things mislead your expectations. People of color, minorities, people from backgrounds different from Carol's in the film keep prodding you toward thinking that there's going to be some political rhetoric or some revolution that will tell you what's right and what's wrong and it continues to trip you up till the end.

**LG:** You could've addressed it more directly. You chose not to.

**TH:** I realized before we started shooting how much of a critique of leftism this film is. What did initiate it was a series of personal questions about recovery treatments and therapies in relation to AIDS. Why so many gay men seemed to be drawn to people like Louise Hay in the eighties, people who were literally telling them that they made themselves sick, that they could make themselves well if they simply learned how to love themselves. I didn't really care about the Louise Hays of the world, the Marianne Williamsons. But, ultimately, what was it in people who were ill that made them feel better being told that they were culpable for their own illness than facing the inevitable chaos of a terminal illness?

**LG:** It's an attempt to sort of escape the catastrophe of a complete absence of genuine political power. It's about making yourself comfortable with powerlessness.

**TH:** I guess that's it, but why is there such a complete and total replacement of what was once an outward-looking critique of society by this notion of a transcendent self that can solve all our problems?

**LG:** I think it's a persistent strain in the progressive side of American culture that leaps off the tracks and becomes a weird individualistic-type mysticism. It's very Thoreau and Emerson in a different way. People who at one stage in their career are critical of a lot of American capitalist society and then move in some strange pre-Nietzschean way off the tracks into some elevation of the private individual person as the only incorruptible unit left. Let's talk about Wrenwood a little more because it's obviously a source of tremendous controversy in the film. I'm going out on a limb and say your characterization of the San Fernando Valley applies to Wrenwood. I don't see you completely demolishing Wrenwood as an ideological delusion. There's tremendous human sympathy for the people of Wrenwood. Peter, with all of his authoritarian-totalitarian aspects, has another side. He's also a human being who is trying to do the right thing.

**TH:** I think part of that is a ploy to paint him very carefully and more sensitively at the beginning so that you think this might be the answer for Carol. The other part of that is due to Peter Friedman's performance because you really believe that the character is real and not a narrative device. It was just a really subtle and intelligent performance. During the writing, I felt that the least interesting thing you can do with New Age stuff is totally accept it or totally dismiss it. So I really tried to look at it. But ultimately, there are certain phrases and markers that I don't have any ambivalence toward whatsoever. Like saying, "I've stopped reading the newspaper, I've stopped watching the news on TV." I can't get past it. There's another place in the film where I wanted to start tightening the screws. When Peter goes around the circle and, one by one, beats these poor people down into this self-confession of their pure culpability for their illness, and thanks them afterwards as they break into tears. It's an assembly line, packing these people down into their little holes.

That to me is not a very subtle depiction of New Age thinking, as far as I'm concerned, and yet I still think people want something more, you know, Jean-Claude van Damme breaking through the screen and shooting them all down with a machine gun. Then you *know* it's bad.

**LG:** You've been the object of criticism because certain people think you agree with this character.
**TH:** That's true. But now we've added a shot of Peter's house on the hill that was not in at Sundance. [After the Sundance Screening, Haynes re-inserted a shot of Peter's opulent home to clue the audience into the character's hypocrisy.]

**LG:** And you think that helps locate Peter?
**TH:** I do think it helps clarify him.

**LG:** What does Carol's relationship to Chris [a fellow resident of Wrenwood played by James LeGros] mean to you in the movie? Is it one of those things dangled in front of the audience as a kind of way out that can't be a way out?
**TH:** I guess I wanted it to be another red herring, where you'd think, okay there will be a romantic resolution and Wrenwood has all the potential for perfect closure and happiness. Instead, one by one, these hopes fall away and you're left with Carol and Chris in this sort of platonic day-camp friendship. I didn't write him as a gay character. Did you think he was?

**LG:** I didn't know. It crossed my mind.
**TH:** That's great. Julianne told me later that [actor James LeGros] had decided that he was Peter's boyfriend. Julianne also felt very strongly that there should be no sexual magnetism between Chris and the Carol character.

**LG:** Wrenwood to me is a kind of mirror image of the Valley. Were you conscious of trying to construct it visually so it referred back to the Valley?
**TH:** Did you see that? I didn't go overboard in doing it and sometimes I think, "Oh I should've made that a little more clear." That really is what I wanted to convey.

**LG:** Leaving the world of the film for just a second, do you ever feel ambivalent about making a film that's this pessimistic? Is somebody watching the film going to say, "I should give up, there's no hope" or do the opposite and develop a new political awareness at the end?

**TH:** If the film is constructed with any kind of target, it targets that unbelievably persistent "warm feeling" in Hollywood filmmaking that every clumsy narrative is moving towards achieving in the last five minutes, where the central character is really the director, is really the writer, is really you and we're all the guys and we're all in it together and we get the girl and feel so good about life. It's so upsetting to me, I can't tell you. It's such a fucking lie and that's what I wanted to dispel in most of the films I've made. So, to feel really sad for one fragile woman for two hours. . . . If anything, what *Safe* does is refute the sense we make of identity, the sense we make of cures, the sense we make of notions of wellness and health. I think its most hopeful place is in the middle of the film. [Carol] gets angry in the hospital and says, "It's the chemicals that did it to me." There's something about saying, "It's the chemicals," which up to that point, until you know that it *may* be the chemicals, all you can think of is, "It's her. She's a mess. It's in her head. She's a nut. She's a fruitcake."

**LG:** Julianne Moore was such a key element in the film working. How was working with her and how much did she understand about the film, and how much did she think of it as her job as an actress?

**TH:** I think she understood it completely in an innate way. Her approach is not to overly theorize what she's doing or to do tons of method preparation.

**LG:** She does not condescend to the character. She finds a way to respect this character without letting you know that she's smarter than the character.

**TH:** Her courage as an actor was in knowing how little to do to communicate Carol's paralysis. This is something many actors don't understand. Some people can't open their mouths very big, can't move their eyes very far, can't move their necks very far. There are reasons why each of these things is blocked or limited and that's something [for an actor] to use. But instead of demonstrating all the blockages and all the limitations she was so incredibly secure about how to approach it. It was amazing to me.

**LG:** What's your next film going to be?

**TH:** It's funny, when you were asking me if I was ever nervous about

creating such a pessimistic, dark film, or such a hopeless political statement . . . it's almost the reverse. I'm doing a film about the glitter-rock era
of the early seventies. Things have changed a lot culturally and politically
since then and that's why I want to do this film now. It was that bisexual
moment in the early seventies. You had to pretend to be gay or bisexual
to make it at the time. [It was] just very different, and, in my opinion, far
more progressive than the identity politics at work today. So now I find
myself feeling nervous to be making a film about something I really *like*.

# Briefs, Barbies, and Beyond

Blase DiStefano / 1995

From *OutSmart*, August 1995. Reprinted by permission from Blase DiStefano.

Thirty-four years ago on January 2, 1961, the film industry gave birth to a gifted writer/director. Of course, at that time, neither the industry nor the director himself had any knowledge of the event. The writer/director, Todd Haynes, would become somewhat conscious of his talent when he was playing with dolls with his sister; the film industry would become aware of his talent BECAUSE he played with dolls with his sister.

"We used to go into my sister's room," Haynes tells me, "and put a blanket over her bedroom table and create stories for each other. We would sort of take turns making shows for each other under the table, using all of her international dolls and her little plastic horses.

"All the stories that I did for her were about these little girls who would fall in love with their horse, then the horse would run away or get shot, and my sister would cry. I would spend a lot of time with the lighting—I think that's where the whole *Superstar* idea came from ultimately."

*Superstar: The Karen Carpenter Story* is a short film in which dolls (some of which are Barbies) were used to portray the characters. You may not have heard of it, because shortly after its release in 1987, Karen's brother Richard Carpenter put a stop to it. Haynes used the Carpenters' songs without authorization from A&M Records, and "that's where the problem lies," says Haynes. "Richard Carpenter is basically given full authority over the Carpenters' cuts."

This "Barbie-doll" story of Karen Carpenter is told in a very nontraditional way, and if you haven't seen *Superstar*, it may seem inconceivable that it could be a positive portrayal. However, says Haynes, "it's actually a very, very sympathetic film about her. It takes some issue with the family and ultimately paints Richard Carpenter more critically. If he did see the film, he could have objections along those lines. Whether he's seen it or not, there are a lot of reasons why he would react this way."

73

And how did Mattel react to Haynes's use of Barbie dolls? Mattel was the first company that created some problems, according to Haynes, "but there's no real way of knowing for certain how many Barbies are in the film. And, in fact," Haynes continues, "a lot of the dolls are dolls I got from thrift stores." Mattel was offered a credit or disclaimer according to their needs, but they didn't respond, Haynes says, "probably because they realized they didn't have a very firm case."

Probably because he played with dolls, I assumed he is gay. So I ask Haynes if his parents were accepting of his homosexuality when he was a child, at which point I immediately apologized for the assumption.

"It's been previously published that I'm gay," Haynes graciously offers, and without missing a beat, he continues to answer the original question: "They were eventually very supportive, yes."

Eventually?

"I really didn't know I was gay when I was growing up," Haynes tells me. "I knew when I was in high school, but I didn't know when I was a child, or I didn't call it that. It was tough on my parents—their difficulty was more the difficulty that very progressive, liberal-thinking parents encounter when their own child brings information home that they've always been saying is completely fine. People you expect to have the harder time with it, like your father, often surprise you and are much more solid and supportive from the beginning. Mom had the hysterical period, but it was short. My grandparents were incredibly supportive. I'm very lucky. I can't complain."

Haynes also couldn't complain when his first feature film, *Poison*, won the Grand Jury Prize at Robert Redford's Sundance Film Festival in 1990. In fact, he "was very surprised and shocked."

Others were shocked, but not for the same reason. It seems that Haynes received partial funding for the film from the National Endowment for the Arts (NEA), which prompted Donald Wildman of the American Family Association to write a letter that targeted *Poison*, even though he had never seen the film.

"It was based completely on hearsay," says Haynes. "Wildman called the film *Homo*, which is actually one of the subtitles of the four sections of the story. He described it as a feature film about men having sex in prison." I ask Haynes if he thought Wildman was more upset about the funding or the homosexuality.

"It was absolutely the homosexuality," he replies, "the homosexuality of his imagination, actually."

Wildman wasn't the only politician freaking out over *Poison*. Senator

Dick Armey (who hadn't yet called Barney Frank "Barney Fag") appeared with Haynes on *Larry King Live*. Similarly, Ralph Reed (spokesperson for the Christian Coalition) shared the spotlight with Haynes on *The Today Show*.

I wonder if these people just HAPPENED to be guests on these shows at the same time as Haynes.

"They would have me on with somebody from the far right who basically opposed the idea of NEA funding," Haynes says. "Most of them hadn't seen *Poison*, and they were objecting to the film abstractly. Armey, for instance, took the libertarian perspective and was like, 'No, no. I think a film like *Poison* SHOULD exist—it just shouldn't be funded by the NEA. The NEA shouldn't exist, because it's invariably a biased association.'

"So it was this weird, false conversation we would have," Haynes asserts. "I'm not from the NEA, and I can't speak for the NEA—I'm just an artist who received a grant. He's someone who didn't see the film. So we spoke very abstractly."

While on the subject of politicians, I ask Haynes how he feels about politicians being outed. He is all for outing for those politicians who promote anti-gay legislation, but "I've never really condoned outing as a project," he says, "particularly how it's been so focused on the entertainment world, where I think the emphasis is a little bit misplaced. There's so many people in politics and in positions of power who misuse their homosexuality—or their denied homosexuality—in all of these ways. If we're going to target public figures, it seems to be a more appropriate direction to do so. But I think the problem is larger than whether gay people are in or out of the closet, and we have to work on things that go beyond outing to really make a difference."

Haynes has made a difference with his latest film *Safe*, which is about as safe as toxic fumes are to one's health. There are no car chases, though the fumes from cars' exhaust systems do play a major role. There are no bombs going off, though the fumes from those roach bombs we occasionally set off would enter into *Safe*'s realm. And there is no violence per se, though some of the film's characters do have violent reactions to the sixty thousand chemicals that have become part of our environment.

*Safe*, then, is about environmental illness.

Haynes didn't know anyone with environmental illness before he became intrigued with it. He researched it, started thinking about the story, and then he began talking to people with the illness.

"The more I learned about environmental illness," he tells me, "the more I was struck by its many parallels to AIDS. The difference is that environmental illness has a known origin—chemicals. It is a disease that is embedded in the very fabric of our material existence."

Does he think that these same chemicals might contribute to the AIDS virus, or at least the breakdown of our immune systems?

"Certainly," he says. "I think the chemicals that make people ill—that we all encounter, but that certain people develop extreme sensitivities to—must affect the immune systems of people who have debilitations. It seems inevitable to me."

Also inevitable is Todd Haynes's success as a writer and director. Though he came out of a more experimental background as a filmmaker, his films have actually crossed over and found larger audiences than one usually associates with experimental films.

"So, in a way," says Haynes, "I've been forced into a more commercial venue or perception than I may have otherwise, and so I feel like I have a foot in each world—I have a foot in feature filmmaking with stars like Julianne Moore [*Safe*'s star], in telling dramatic stories, and then I have a foot in a more experimental tradition that tries to keep stretching the envelope of how we tell stories in films.

"I'm proud that *Safe* got made," concludes Haynes, "because it was a very difficult film to get made, to interest people in financially, and ultimately I think it's a demanding work of filmmaking more than it is a message or a story or a piece of entertainment. And to have gotten it made and gotten this far is a miracle."

Though it might be more appropriate to conclude this interview with that miracle, a somewhat more personal ending seems fitting. Hey, I figure if Bill Clinton and Newt Gingrich can be asked if they wear boxers or briefs (Clinton answered, "boxers"; Gingrich replied with something like, "I'm not going to answer that! What a stupid question!"), maybe Haynes wouldn't mind.

So I ask him if he wears boxers, briefs, or nothing. His reply: "During the day or when I'm asleep?"

Curiosity begged for answers to both.

"During the day, briefs," he continues, "and when I'm asleep, briefs or nothing."

Sweet dreams. And play safe.

# All That Glitters: Todd Haynes Mines the Glam Rock Epoch

Amy Taubin / 1997

From the *Village Voice*, November 11, 1997. Reprinted by permission from Amy Taubin.

For the audience that still worships at the intersection of art and pop culture, no film, probably not even Quentin Tarantino's *Jackie Brown*, is more longed for than Todd Haynes's *Velvet Goldmine*, currently in post-production and due for release in the fall of 1998.

A musical set in England during the glam rock era, *Velvet Goldmine* stars Jonathan Rhys Meyers as a Bowie-like pop star, Ewan McGregor (even more on display than in *The Pillow Book*) as a kind of Iggy Pop/Gary Glitter amalgam, and Christian Bale as an ardent fan who, years later, becomes a journalist and is assigned to cover a mystery surrounding one of these music idols. The nineties film thus looks back on early seventies glam from an early eighties perspective. But there's an even larger framing story involved. "It examines the English relationship to homosexuality and pop culture," says Haynes. "Oscar Wilde looms over the film."

Filmed in London with a cast of British actors, and financed largely with money from Britain's Channel Four and CIBY Sales, *Velvet Goldmine* is more an English than American production. (Miramax's involvement is limited to distribution in North America.) And although producer Christine Vachon, editor Jim Lyons, cinematographer Maryse Alberti, and music supervisor Randy Poster are American, other key creative people—production designer Christopher Hobbs, costume designer Sandy Powell, hair and makeup artist Peter King—are British.

But *Velvet Goldmine* is also profoundly English in its content. It delves into the history of dandyism—in other words, camp, drag, or faggotry—from Beau Brummell to its pop-culture climax in glam. In looking back at the seventies, Haynes is doing what camp has always done—mining the past for evidence that gender is a masquerade—a mutable cultural construction rather than a natural absolute. Think of Jack Smith's obsession with Maria Montez or Andy Warhol finding himself in Shirley Temple.

This is not, of course, the first time Haynes has revisited the seventies. In 1986, fresh out of Brown University's semiotics department, he made a forty-three-minute biopic of Karen Carpenter, the pop star who died of anorexia, using miniature sets and a cast of Barbie Dolls. Although A&M records (the Carpenters' label) won an injunction to keep the film from being publicly screened, *Superstar: The Karen Carpenter Story* put Haynes on the Downtown cultural map. Bootleg VHS copies are still feverishly circulated in art schools across America.

Like *Safe* (1995)—Haynes's first foray into 35mm, which starred Julianne Moore as an upper-middle-class housewife afflicted with environmental illness—*Superstar* was set in the SoCal valley suburbs, where the filmmaker grew up. He remembers that the Carpenters were the last pop group he and his parents agreed on. "I was sitting in the bathtub and my father walked in and said, 'Oh Todd, I've just heard this groovy new song on the radio,' and he started singing 'We've Only Just Begun.'" About fifteen years later, Haynes heard a Karen Carpenter song on some FM-lite station and knew immediately he had to do the Karen Carpenter story. "At that time, there was not a glimmer of a seventies reexamination. You weren't hearing that music or seeing those images as you do now everywhere. It felt truly like something I hadn't thought about in a long time."

Glam was scarier to the preadolescent Haynes. "I was a little too young for glam when it first hit." (He was eleven when *Ziggy Stardust* broke in the U.S. in 1972.) "But oddly enough, there were these girls my age who were right in the center of it—these tough cigarette-smoking glam girls who were really into Iggy and Elton. I remember being on the school bus and hearing one of them say, 'Bowie's bi.' And that was scary. Not confusing, it was clear what it meant. But it thrilled and repelled me at the same time. I also remember going to a friend's house and listening to *Diamond Dogs* and *Million Dollar Legs*. But I wasn't really into it until high school."

The idea of doing a glam rock movie originated with Jim Lyons, one of the stars of Haynes's first feature, *Poison*, and the editor of *Poison*, *Safe*, and *Velvet Goldmine*. "In 1990, while we were working on *Poison*, Jim had this idea of doing a three-part glam movie," says Haynes. "Glam is the period most suited to film because it's the most visual period in rock. As the script developed, it took on more of my obsessions than Jim's. Jim was more involved with the Dolls and Iggy and the trash-culture, New York aspect. I was more involved with the English part—Roxy Music and Bowie."

"A lot of people are inspired by seventies movies like *The Last Picture Show* and *Five Easy Pieces*," Lyons says. "But when Todd and I and Christine Vachon, producer of *Poison* and *Safe*, as well as *Velvet Goldmine*, started to watch movies in the seventies, we wanted them to take us to a different world. Movies like *Performance* or *Cabaret* or *The Damned* or Kubrick's movies or cheapie head films—they were all about blowing your mind. And all of Todd's films do that. So we wanted *Velvet Goldmine* to take off on those kinds of midnight movies—movies that use the spectacle of cinema. And I locate that same impulse in glam, in *Aladdin Sane* or in Eno. You'd make this artifact and distribute it to the world, and it would whisper secrets into the ears of a kid like me stuck in Long Island suburbia."

Anyone who's expecting *Velvet Goldmine* to be the next *Trainspotting* most likely will be disappointed. Haynes, who's the only American indie filmmaker able to give Wong Kar-Wai competition for the Godard crown, has always been a formalist at heart. He often describes *Superstar* as an experiment to determine whether viewers would identify with Barbie dolls.

"The challenge in doing *Velvet Goldmine*," says Haynes, "was to go against naturalism. That's what glam did. It was about artifice, camp theatricality, performance. When it worked best—as in early Roxy Music—all those campy things were there, but it also worked emotionally. It moved you. You don't see that kind of artifice anymore in Hollywood movies, except occasionally in comedy. Glam could only have existed in British culture. Roxy Music at its most radical failed in the U.S. So the film comes out of my intense curiosity about that aspect of British culture."

"The film," says Lyons, "is about the strength of desire, about a moment when desires were high and people were willing to act on them. You could surprise yourself with your dream. What if I were Rita Hayworth? It was a moment when it was cool even for straight people to appear bisexual. Eno vamping in a platinum pageboy and blue eye shadow on the cover of *Here Come the Warm Jets*. *Velvet Goldmine* was conceived in 1990, when sex had become straitjacketed, so there's a clear nostalgia for that period when we believed that we were going to have a better and better society, and that feminism would win, and homosexuality would be completely accepted."

If the seventies revival seems to spring back to life every time someone proclaims it exhausted, it's both because it takes so long to get a film
financed (like *Boogie Nights*, *Velvet Goldmine* involved a lag time of about
seven years between conception and production) and because there are
so many versions of the seventies. Nothing could be more opposed to
the puritanism of *The Ice Storm* than *Velvet Goldmine*.

"Part of the reason the seventies are so fascinating to us now is also
that the seventies is when this whole thing of looking back first started,"
says Haynes. "So here we are in the nineties looking back at the seventies, which looked back at fifties glamour to give a kick in the pants to the
sixties. And what's sad about all this seventies revisionism is losing the
sense of what was shocking at the moment. If the sixties were about authenticity, then the seventies were about artifice. The whole rediscovery
of glamour and nail polish must have been a shock. In America, lots of
the seventies revival has been just silly and kitsch and fashion-oriented.
But the seventies was one of the last progressive moments—aesthetically
and politically. *Velvet Goldmine* is about that time—about something
that couldn't have happened in any other time or place—and it's also a
historical movie about how things have changed so horribly since then.
And at the same time," he adds, laughing, "it's all fake."

"The main thing," says Lyons, "is that we want it to be the most fun
rock movie it could possibly be—and everything else, we just sneak in."

# Todd Haynes (Interview)

Nick James / 1998

From *Sight and Sound*, September 1998, published by the British Film Institute. Reprinted by permission.

**Nick James:** Glam rock was primarily a British phenomenon. How did you become aware of it?

**Todd Haynes:** I was ten in 1971 and I remember traces of it—the first inklings of something new defying the previous generation's sensibility. But in the States the sixties sensibility was still fully in place because it encompassed things Americans love, like authenticity, naturalism, and a direct emotional experience between audience and performer—the tenets of sixties music which remained the dominant mode into the seventies through the singer-songwriter. I got to know Roxy Music and Bowie stuff much better later, in college, along with Velvet Underground and Iggy Pop. It wasn't until then that I saw how mutually influential these artists were.

**NJ:** *Velvet Goldmine* is very good at reproducing the spirit of that time. Who did you talk to?

**TH:** It wasn't meeting people or tracking people down as much as following a trail of written material. I went to the sources that inspired those artists. I was reading Richard Ellmann's Oscar Wilde biography, and there were so many fascinating intersections. I was interested in glam rock's flag-waving of artificiality—and there's no more articulate spokesperson for artifice than Oscar Wilde. It's that incongruous relationship you also find in Roxy Music's work between a strong anti-naturalist statement—a pose, a stance, and ironic wit—and an ability to be poetic and beautiful and moving. My goal as a filmmaker was to incorporate this duality into a narrative context.

**NJ:** *Velvet Goldmine* illustrates powerful social forces that are specific to Britain, especially through journalist Arthur.

**TH:** Initially I didn't have an angle on glam rock and class. But as I was comparing it with sixties rock—and the Stones' middle-class interest in American R&B and their need to slum it in this more authentic culture for inspiration—I kept realizing how working-class many of the architects of glam were, mainly the art-school set, and how it was a fantasy of an aristocratic persona, with Bryan Ferry maybe the most extreme. It's the period when Ferry was becoming Noel Coward that's the most resonant in his work. But these class angles wouldn't be apparent to an American voyeur of his period.

**NJ:** One of the great things claimed for glam rock was a liberation of attitudes towards homosexuality and bisexuality. Isn't this close to New Queer Cinema?

**TH:** New Queer Cinema came out of the AIDS era, a time when bisexuality wasn't the issue. But I wonder to what degree that glam attitude was from the heart. Things have changed now: there's a boredom setting in with the conformity of gay life, and it's healthy to question that conformity instead of just replicating the structures we've been trying to free ourselves from. The courage of the glam rock era still blows me away—it was so much about blurring boundaries between gay and straight, between men and women.

**NJ:** What was your structural approach to the film?

**TH:** The only way to approach a film about rock stars is from a great distance, with barriers between the viewer and the stars. It could never have been a behind-closed-doors, what-Iggy-said-to-Bowie kind of movie. So *Citizen Kane*'s classic structure of the search for the missing truth to find out what defines a character seemed the best thing to quote from.

It had to be about a lost time from the start, about something repressed—and great fears had risen up around whatever this was, which had changed it completely and buried it. That's why for Arthur it's an ambivalent search back. When you listen again to Roxy, the music is already mournful of a lost moment—it's full of melancholy.

**NJ:** The narrative interweaves three or four strands, which may make it difficult for some audiences to follow.

**TH:** Having a dreamlike, trippy feel from the start does that. And that's also what defines *Performance* for me. The equivalent in America was

Warhol: the emergence into the mainstream of a combination of under-ground strands—from experimental film and art to crime—that were so close to each other at that time. That combination creates unusual, one-of-a-kind works. It made possible the kind of filmmaking that moved me the most when I was young. You go to *2001* and you come out at the other end with a whole new discovery. I wanted that feeling. But it's probably the most affirmative film I've ever made, and I have trouble with that. I don't believe in films that give you the answer.

**NJ:** Did you intend the film to be longer than it is now?
**TH:** The script was such a jigsaw puzzle it wasn't possible to deviate much. I was trying to get it as tight as it could be and it was hard—any way you look at it, it's a full meal. There were also economic factors: how we ended up having to do the film for a great deal less than the lowest budget we could conceive of. This made the shooting difficult, to say the least.

**NJ:** Who did you want to reach with this film?
**TH:** I hoped it would be like those trippy movies you'd go to and then analyze with your friends; buy the record and play it over and over again and ponder its meaning. That's how Arthur gets to be opened up by this period in the film, and through him you see it all from the fan's point of view. It's rare that pop culture can do that.

**NJ:** When you were shooting the music, how conscious were you of try-ing to make it not look like MTV?
**TH:** This is sad. The way so many people refer to the stylized mini-scene in the film as "the video scene" marks such a change in perception about experimental film. I don't watch MTV, I get bored by it, but it steals from such a rich, diverse history of experimental film and Hollywood musi-cals that people now call almost anything that deals with style, artifice, and fakeness "MTV." It's a reduction of an entire tradition, a rich and buried history of film in which images lead and dominate and tell stories without words.

**NJ:** Did you look at D. A. Pennebaker's *Ziggy Stardust and the Spiders from Mars* from 1982?
**TH:** Meticulously. And *The Last Waltz* by Scorsese from 1978 and classic sixties documentaries. I tried to mirror the simplicity of them. We wanted some camera moves, but they shouldn't dominate or over-determine

where your eyes go. The best thing about live performance is that it has to be spontaneous—so if Ewan fell down over there, we had to follow him. But the camera was static for a lot of it. What I was looking at mostly for the "Ballad of Maxwell Demon" number against the white sets with the lizard character were promo films from that period. I'm sure our editing is more flamboyant at times, but for the most part I was trying to keep it crude, amateurish, and hokey.

**NJ:** The visual style is so different from *Safe* which was very tightly controlled.
**TH:** I forced my camera department to zoom, rack, and swish constantly rather than to track. It was early seventies-style filmmaking: Altman, Scorsese, Coppola, and *Performance*. It was about framing, exploring the surface of the grain, and not entering the space physically so much as zooming in and finding your subject matter. Those amazing searching zooms in Altman's *McCabe and Mrs. Miller*, for instance. And we spent a lot of time trying to restore grain in the stock, the lenses and in the final lab process. Today's stocks are all founded on minimum grain, and grain can be so beautiful.

**NJ:** When seventies revival began in UK clubs in the late eighties, people going to thrift stores to buy clothes discovered that seventies bodies were much less nourished.
**TH:** My first film was about anorexia and I seem to turn my actors into anorexics. It's horrible. Julianne Moore had to lose so much weight for *Safe* and Toni Collette had a complete transformation for *Velvet Goldmine*. Ewan wasn't even allowed to drink beer!

**NJ:** The orgy scene is particularly effective.
**TH:** It had to have a decadence and an ugliness to it—it couldn't be glamorous. Unfortunately actors and extras who are willing to appear nude often have a stripper's body, and there's a bit of that in there. People just didn't look like that in the seventies—they were scrawny teenagers. But there are others where you can't tell if they're boys or girls, which is what I wanted.

It didn't look so good at first. But we kept darkening it and making it greener, so people have a lurid pallor to their skin, and it also made little bits of cosmetics pop out against the green. Like where Emily Woof is being kissed by Eddie Izzard and her face is all red and raw. It needed that slightly ugly quality.

**NJ:** What happened with the songs?

**TH:** The two featured songs are by a New York–based band, Shudder To Think. I didn't know their music at all until they sent me a demo tape. There were a bunch of Bowie songs that we wanted, and I needed to produce all those tracks before we could shoot. It was taking Bowie a long time to get back to us—and he decided in the end not to let us use the songs. It was crushing at the time, but I think it gives you a slight chance not to read Brian Slade exclusively as Bowie. And it was a nice opportunity to feature songs that had been forgotten.

**NJ:** How has making *Velvet Goldmine* left you?

**TH:** I don't want to touch another film for a few years. I was miserable, and it was largely due to how little money we had and how much I was demanding of myself. I didn't have much fun making the film, and that's sad. It's made me think about the way I work, and what I might want to do differently. Having a real budget would be the first step.

I don't have a lot of good ways of releasing the enormous tension all directors feel. Often they get rid of it in cruel ways that aren't fair to the people around them—I don't like hearing that about directors whose work I love, but I have a feeling they have more fun. When you're a little more sadistic, you get it off your chest.

**NJ:** Do you enjoy talking about it now?

**TH:** It was never pure misery. It always seemed there were four amazing things happening at once, and also seven huge crises that had to be dealt with. And what do you deal with first? The crises, obviously, and the good stuff is just, "OK, great, great, that's set." Then there was always so much to look ahead to—"What about this, what are we going to do about that?"—and running behind. It was stressful. But I knew the actors were having an amazing time and most of the crew were having an amazing time, and there was a great spirit on the set which was captured on film. So I was vicariously having a good time.

# Flaming Creatures

John C. Mitchell / 1998

From *Filmmaker Magazine*, Fall 1998. Reprinted by permission of *Filmmaker Magazine*.

Few current seventies revival films recall that period as flamboyantly or poignantly as Todd Haynes's glam epic *Velvet Goldmine*. John Cameron Mitchell talks with Haynes about creative impulses, Hollywood musicals, and their first time with Bowie.

Emotion—dissected, dramatized, suppressed, and expressed—is at the heart of Todd Haynes's films. Often thought of as a "cool" filmmaker, Haynes actually dramatizes in all of his films the ways in which our thoughts and feelings are constructed by the cultures we live in. Works like *Superstar*, *Dottie Gets Spanked*, *Poison*, and *Safe* form precise social critiques but they also construct characters—like *Superstar*'s Karen Carpenter and *Safe*'s Carol White—that are contemporary archetypes but tremendously affecting nevertheless.

In Haynes's stunning new film, *Velvet Goldmine*, the world of glam rock, with all of its wild costumes, ornately composed music, and sexual fluidity, is recreated with loving care. Employing a *Citizen Kane*-like structure to the tale of a Bowie-esque rocker, Brian Slade, who fakes his death amidst personal crisis, the film references glam-relevant films like *Performance* and *The Man Who Fell to Earth* while, like the sixties works of Alain Resnais, using memory and desire to advance a complex narrative. Boldly riffing on the past lives of a string of famous musicians—Bowie, Lou Reed, Iggy Pop—the film's heart lies not in its exploration of rock star decadence but rather in the dreams of an outsider fan, subtly played by Christian Bale, whose own journey lies in unraveling the meanings these cultural icons are creating for him. Employing this fan's perspective in complex ways—the film often advances its narrative solely through specific and canny period music selections—*Velvet Goldmine*, which, by the way, has nothing to do with music videos, contrary to some Cannes critics' beliefs, throws us back to the oversized passions of American movie musicals while also exploring how pop music machinery can create liberating, powerful dreams within all of us.

We asked John Cameron Mitchell, the creator of Off-Broadway's *Hedwig and the Angry Inch*, which also draws its inspiration from glam rock, to discuss glam, art-making, and concert-shooting on the eve of his own movie deal with Jersey Shore.
—Scott Macaulay, editor

**John Cameron Mitchell:** You're an inspiration for so many people in film because, and I can't think of anyone else who is doing it right now, you're willing to learn new languages to tell different stories. Some of my favorite directors have done that, like Sidney Lumet. *Dog Day Afternoon* and *Network* were made within a few years of each other.
**Todd Haynes:** And they couldn't be more different in terms of style and tone and language.

**JCM:** So many artists are suspicious of trying to change their style. Like, why aren't you doing a Rauschenberg, Mr. Rauschenberg? What was the first moment in which you thought that filmmaking was what you wanted to do?
**TH:** I'm not sure if there was a singular event. It's always been a bit of a struggle between intellectual reasons and a much more instinctive, direct, physical creative need. Being a filmmaker, that need may never get directly satisfied, because of the way that a film gets made. [Making a film involves] such a distended amount of work—taking apart the idea into pieces, producing and materializing each piece, and then trying desperately to piece it back together to something close to what the original instinct was. I don't really think one should make films to satisfy a blind need to be creative.

**JCM:** No?
**TH:** No. Or one shouldn't make narrative films for that reason. Because when you don't think about you are doing, for the most part you replicate all the worst conventions that exist.

**JCM:** It becomes therapy.
**TH:** Yeah. I came to understand the distinction when I was painting. There was a certain style of painting I would do that was based on getting stoned, playing loud rock and roll, and just having an amazingly

intuitive relationship to the work. It would be the most physically drain-ing and satisfying experience. The work though, would end up being not as raw as one would like it to be.

**JCM:** Like, I'm so rock and roll, but . . .
**TH:** But, I'm making choices about this line and this splotch of color. My painting then became more self-reflexive, more "deconstructive." I would start with issues that I wanted to deal with; often it was about almost taking on representation in a semi-antagonistic or investigatory way. A lot of feminist ideas or questions were played out against images of women. And I'd use materials like lace, velvet, and silk and muck them up. The paintings would be investigations into femininity or masculin-ity. And I think that's what my filmmaking ultimately became.

**JCM:** Did you ever take those conceptual ideas and apply them to a more "rock and roll" intuitive process?
**TH:** The making of these paintings could still be pleasurable, but the process was much more workmanlike. It was like, I have a blueprint, a concept, an idea. And though the final result might differ slightly from the image in my head, the act of making it wasn't a "tripped out, creative freedom" kind of thing. It was more about "working it out," much like the way I make films. There are two different modes. Look at *Safe* and *Superstar*.

**JCM:** The "women's" films.
**TH:** In a way. Films like *Superstar* and *Safe* were more conceptually con-ceived, and the process of making then was a process of learning how ideas that seemed external to me were actually internal for a lot of per-sonal reasons. Like anorexia in *Superstar*—the kind of behavior it pro-duced was something I identified with even though I'm not an anorexic, but it took making the film to figure out why I identified with it. Whereas *Poison* and *Velvet Goldmine* are films that come out of a less intellectual, more emotional connection to material that pre-exists, like Genet and glam rock. The process of making these films was a way to start distin-guishing myself from this material as opposed to finding myself within it. And in a way these films are gayer, a little messier—sort of trippy mov-ies. In some ways I think *Safe* and *Superstar*, which are cleaner and more formal, may be better films.

**JCM:** You said in an interview in *Index* magazine that you feel at times you're an overcognitive artist—and that in *Velvet Goldmine*, you were try-ing to draw out the emotional side of your storytelling.

**TH:** The emotional side of *Velvet Goldmine* is very elusive, because in many ways the entire project was an attempt to avoid traditional ways of communicating depth and character psychology—much in the same way that the American movie musical or the melodrama goes for a hy-perbolized notion of emotion and depth. In *Velvet Goldmine*, the emo-tion is often communicated in the music. In the plot of a musical, what happens between the characters is often a bit extreme, almost operatic. It's never about real life in a gritty way. Identification of characters just isn't done in the same, classic Aristotelian manner of most dramas. I was trying to communicate in this film in broader, more stylized terms. The characters are in a way little distillations of real life that people wove around themselves in their stage personas. The biographies of David Bowie and Oscar Wilde blended together.

**JCM:** I know you're quite the "edit-in-the-head" guy. Did you know how all the sequences in the film would cut together before shooting, or did you find it in the editing?
**TH:** No. It had to be pretty nailed down.

**JCM:** Even in those major cross-cutting musical sequences.
**TH:** Yeah, for the most part. Literally, written into the body of the script are where the sections fall in, what kind of camera movement you're coming out of and going into. Songs were being recorded in the studio before we would shoot them, obviously; we needed to have the songs to play back. And some songs, like "Bittersweet," compile numerous scenes. I had to time out phrases of the song, and figured out that I'd have to repeat the intro twice because the scene with Brian and Curt at the window couldn't possibly fit into the single intro, and I knew by the first verse we needed to be into the next scene. So there were meticulous amounts of timing issues and trying to imagine how many shots could tell what I was trying to communicate.

**JCM:** How did you shoot the concert scenes in the movie?
**TH:** It was a matter of just setting up three cameras, two 35mm, one 16mm.

**JCM:** Like shooting an explosion.
**TH:** Exactly, like shooting a stunt. And often stunts were included in

those scenes, like the flame thing. Those were the scariest things to shoot because I've never done that before. I've only made films on minimal budgets where I've approached the lack of money by being absolutely prepared, planned out, storyboarded. I thought that I was never going to get close to being spontaneous with the camera. But with a live performance, you have to be prepared so you can catch the moment. There would be two cameras, one with a track in the audience, often laterally, with heads passing, and then sometimes a track along the side of the stage to get some movement that way. And those two cameras could avoid being in each other's proximity with those two angles. We never did a complete take of a whole song. We would break each song down into verses and change camera angles accordingly. But it was amazing how when morale was low and Christine [Vachon, the producer] was going nuts and Maryse [Alberti, the d.p.] was freaking out and everyone was thinking we'd never finish in time, we'd say "Action" and there would be this amazing song banging through the speakers of the Brixton Academy, and everyone would perk up. It was those moments that really got us through.

**JCM:** How did you connect with glam rock in the first place? For me, it started because I was in Scotland in 1973 in boarding school.
**TH:** You actually lived it in a way I never did.

**JCM:** I was a little sissy boy in a Catholic boys-school world, and not even pubescent to enjoy that it was a boys school.
**TH:** Only straight boys enjoy homosexual sex in boarding schools!

**JCM:** Music was not allowed. I was in charge of the library, and there was a little record player. This was like '73, '74. Bowie was still a scary figure—he scared the shit out of me on *Top of the Pops*.
**TH:** Me too, me too!

**JCM:** I was more into Wizzard, Slade, and Sweet. I smuggled in "Fox on the Run" and played it on the headphones on the tiny library stereo. Blasted it. Danced around in the library, locked the door, knocked over all these books about the lives of saints. That record totally saved my ass at that moment. So how did you come across glam since it never really became a big thing in America?
**TH:** You and me both got to it through surrogates, semi-spokespeople. For you, the most interesting was Sweet. For me it was Elton John,

*Goodbye Yellow Brick Road*, which I loved when I was in junior high. I loved "Benny and the Jets," which I didn't know was a kind of artificial Ziggy Stardust.

**JCM:** So when did you get into Bowie and the glam rock bands in *Velvet Goldmine*?
**TH:** I remember seeing the face of Bowie in the record store on the cover of *Aladdin Sane*, and being completely haunted and disturbed by it. I thought it was going to be really hard acid rock that I wouldn't be able to handle. I remember Alice Cooper and Bowie as sort of really extreme and horrific but also sexually provocative. I put it in my mind that I'd get back to this later. I couldn't handle it then—it was just too disturbing.

**JCM:** I felt that way about be-bop. It's fascinating, but for later—when I'm old and black.
**TH:** And then in seventh-grade drama class we did lip-syncs. I was thirteen, so that was '74. One girl did "Changes," and dressed up just like Bowie with the lightning bolt across her face and a skin tight tunic. She actually looked really pretty and like him. I thought, oh, this is Bowie, I could get into this. This isn't so bad.

**JCM:** I just went back and listened to the first Roxy Music album, and I was just blown away. Unbelievable.
**TH:** I think it's my favorite album, period.

**JCM:** I didn't realize, it's a mini-cinematic epic on disk.
**TH:** Complete melodrama.

**JCM:** Why didn't it work in America?
**TH:** I think it's that there is an intense investment in notions of authenticity here.

**JCM:** British culture glorifies artifice.
**TH:** Yeah. There's a great emphasis on surface, on self-presentation, in style, in the pose, that's all very complex. As soon as you say those words in America, it seems to be an invasion of something underneath the surface. But I think, if you read Oscar Wilde, that notions of depth are just as constructed and prescribed. This refusal to look at the surface of things is a very American thing. Music has always been defined here by the R&B tradition.

**JCM:** It's about getting real.

**TH:** Being truthful and playing raw on stage. And the age-old critique of Americans as being irony-less–

**JCM:** —is pretty true.

**TH:** I think there's some truth to it. I think what you see now in America is cynicism.

**JCM:** Dumb cynicism.

**TH:** Dumb cynicism, but also real cynicism that came out of things like Watergate, and the covers being blown off things in the twentieth century.

**JCM:** Doesn't that cynicism open the door for irony?

**TH:** I guess you're right. I find it uncomplicated, the cynicism I see—particularly in big Hollywood films. Now there's a kind of sarcastic knowingness about genre. It's all about conventions that are flip-flopped around—it's not about ideas. I guess what's at stake is emotional investment, or political investment, or investment in any kind of ideas. And that may be a question for this British tradition as well. If it's all ironic, what do you believe in? But I think with Oscar Wilde, Roxy Music, Bowie, and the more sophisticated strain of this dandy tradition, there's a great deal at stake. It's about questioning dominant ideas about masculinity, identity, art, and the whole ability to communicate something from the gut with no meditation whatsoever.

# Interview with Todd Haynes

Keith Phipps / 1998

From the *A.V. Club*, November 4, 1998. Reprinted by permission from the editor, the *A.V. Club*.

After co-founding the nonprofit Apparatus Productions in 1985 to support new filmmakers, Todd Haynes made one of the most talked-about, least seen films of the eighties. Using Barbie dolls, *Superstar: The Karen Carpenter Story* recounts the life of the light-rock musician. A court order from Richard Carpenter has kept the movie out of circulation, but that didn't stop Haynes from making news. His 1991 film *Poison*, based on three stories by Jean Genet, served as one of the focal points of the debate over the National Endowment for the Arts, outraging conservatives with its explicit gay content. What they overlooked, naturally, was the fact that *Poison* signaled the coming of age of one of the decade's most compelling directors. Divided into three stories—"Hero," "Horror," and "Homo"—told in wildly divergent styles, *Poison* demonstrated Haynes's multi-faceted directorial skills and spearheaded the important, if ill-defined, New Queer Cinema movement. *Safe*, starring Julianne Moore, followed four years later. In it, Moore plays a privileged California housewife who develops "environmental illness," making her highly allergic to the everyday toxins of modern society. Her condition ultimately takes her to a New Age–like retreat, separating her from her home, friends, and family. A memorable and disturbing film, *Safe* touches on many of the central issues of contemporary consumer culture, its profound ambiguity making it that much more powerful. The sterility of *Safe* is far removed from the environment of Haynes's latest film, the semi-fictional glam-rock spectacle *Velvet Goldmine*. *Goldmine* follows the efforts of a journalist (Christian Bale) in a dystopian version of the year 1984 to track down the whereabouts of the David Bowie–like rock star he idolized during the early-seventies glam era. Haynes recently spoke to the *Onion*.

**Onion:** I'll start with a question you've probably heard many times.
**Todd Haynes:** Okay.

**O:** What prompted you to make a movie about glam-rock, and do you think it has any special resonance now?
**TH:** That's sort of like a lot of people's first question and a lot of people's last question together.

**O:** Well, the rest will be a surprise.
**TH:** I think one of the main things that spurred it off was that I love the music, even though I got to it a little bit after the fact, after the initial period in which it happened. It's such an incredibly visual period of rock 'n' roll, and film is a visual medium, as we're told. It seemed sort of inconceivable that it had never been the subject of a film at all. The closest I can think of, I guess, was *Rocky Horror Picture Show*, which incorporates a lot of the themes and has a kind of following like no film ever made in the history of cinema. Which is strange: You still can't quite put your finger on why. But it certainly tapped into something.

**O:** That movie, I think in part because it takes a lot of glam-rock's themes, became sort of like a coming-of-age ritual—to go downtown and see *Rocky Horror*, with all the sexual ambiguity of it.
**TH:** Exactly. And you play along. It invites you into the process. You react in a great way. In many ways, I think that's what I love about glam-rock. It invited you to participate. It asked you to change yourself in all these different ways, or offered up all these options. It's a very different world politically and culturally today than it was in the early seventies. And one of the reasons I wanted to make the film was to say that progress doesn't just mean we become more progressive as we move forward in time. There's a lot of back-stepping that goes on, and a lot of repression and burying of ideas all the time. So that was another reason to sort of look back and learn from the past, kids. Not that it's accessible to us the way it was then.

**O:** You've referred to the seventies as the last progressive decade of this century. What do you mean by that?
**TH:** I mean compared to the eighties and nineties. In so many ways. Obviously, the political climate was one in which there still was a Left in existence, and there was a great openness to the. . . . I think many of the

ideas that opened up in the sixties got implemented in the seventies, and that certain minority voices that were not being heard in the sixties, like women and gay people, were being heard in the seventies. Black civil rights had also found its foothold, and those ideas were also very pertinent. All you have to do is read *Easy Riders, Raging Bulls* and look back at the kinds of films that were coming out of that period, as well, and you realize that it's an amazingly rich period of filmmaking, particularly the first half of the seventies.

**O:** In the film, the David Bowie/Brian Slade character has himself sort of killed on stage, and Bowie sort of did the same thing when he announced that he was ending the Ziggy Stardust thing in one of his concerts. And then there was the "end of glam" concert. It's the only movement I can think of that killed itself. Why do you think that is?

**TH:** I don't know if it was conscious. But, nonetheless, there were all of these examples. . . . There was a self-consciousness about it all along. It was very much in the head. It was physical and pleasurable, and it was about having fun. There were some elements of pretense to the art-school aspects of it. It was basically about celebrating what was theatrical and fantastical about performance and maybe just about identity, period. But I think there was a lot of awareness at a certain point of its own decadence, too, and a lot of discussion about it in the press at the time. That might have just been it: realizing that it couldn't last, because it was decadent to be pushing too many boundaries and going too far. It was going to end. But whatever the case, there was just sort of a sense that the future was going to be very different, and not in a good way. You had Bowie's *Diamond Dogs* record, which was influenced by *1984*. And that's definitely why the film is framed by [the year] 1984. There were a lot of predictions of a doomful future all around. The movie *Cabaret* was really popular in 1972, and, although the decadence of Weimar Germany fit right into the glam decadence, I think it also was informed by the sense that there was a catastrophe looming in the future, like in the late thirties. It informed this idea that it was all going to end, so they just started to end it in all these different ways, both conscious and unconscious.

**O:** I was going to ask you about *Diamond Dogs*. How did that play into your depiction of a fictionalized version of the year 1984?

**TH:** It was all of these things, actually—all these senses of a doomful future, or an apocalyptic future that sort of flanked the glam period. As with everything in the film, I wanted the framing scenes to be half fiction and half fantasy, as well. Part of it is what really did happen, which wasn't too far from their expectations.

**O:** Tommy Stone [the ubiquitous, universally loved rock star from the 1984 section of the film] looks a lot like David Bowie did during that period.
**TH:** Yes, I know. [Laughs apologetically.]

**O:** You couldn't get David Bowie's songs for the film. I actually thought that ended up helping things.
**TH:** Yes, I definitely do. I did want it to be able to be read as fiction. It's a parallel universe to the real history. I think that would have been virtually impossible, at least around the Brian Slade character, if he were also singing Bowie songs.

**O:** The Tommy Stone character seems to be a very heterosexual character, and David Bowie has pretty much abandoned any pretenses, or whatever, of homosexuality. Would you say that's part of the disappointment of what happened after glam?
**TH:** Well, yeah. It wasn't just denying homosexuality; it's that everything went back into little categories. What was so interesting about the glam era was that it was about bisexuality and breaking down the boundaries between gays and straights, breaking down the boundaries between masculinity and femininity with this androgyny thing. It was about breaking down barriers, and in the eighties, for all kinds of reasons, [there was] a lot of fallout of sixties excesses: the drug culture and AIDS, and all the sort of costs of that period. People got scared again and went back into the old-fashioned definitions. But it's not meant to focus the blame on Bowie. Who didn't change after the seventies? Almost every artist involved in the period, except Gary Glitter, drastically changed, or drew back, or reverted to something very different, or went into hibernation. It was more of a culture change, and I think it was hard to escape.

**O:** I really liked the portrayal of Christian Bale's character and his relationship to rock music. What did that come out of, and how much of that is from your relationship to music?
**TH:** Of course it's my experience. But I felt pretty secure in knowing that it was most people's experience—of our generation, or people from Baby Boomers on, since there's been rock 'n' roll. The film is always going to

be much more about the adulation of the fan, what the fan does with those little pictures that get reproduced in magazines and newspapers that give a little sense of what the icon up there is like, that we never know. We never really know what they do in bed. We never really know who they take home. But we have clues, because they flirt with us in that way, and they kind of drop hints. And everything is kind of constructed in our imaginations and in our fantasies and out of our desires. That's almost more powerful than making it real, in a way. So that was always going to be more the focus of the film. And Christian . . . I can't tell you what an amazing actor he is, really the finest actor I've ever worked with.

**O:** It seems like he's been around for such a long time, but he's just now starting to get noticed.

**TH:** He's so good, and so subtle, and so serious about his work. His time is due to really get the attention he deserves. But all the actors in that film blew me away. I feel like I just really lucked out. In a way, [Bale] had the hardest and least fun role, the least glamorous role. But he really carries the film on his back. It wouldn't really work without him.

**O:** You had Ewan McGregor playing an American [as the Iggy Pop/Lou Reed surrogate Curt Wild]. What was behind that decision?

**TH:** When I saw *Trainspotting*, I just could not think of an American actor in his age group with that kind of energy and that kind of physicality. The Johnny Depp generation has this kind of brooding, weighty, introspective quality, very James Dean-ish. Which is nice, great for a lot of characters. It wasn't what I wanted for Curt. I wanted something very volatile and flame-like, almost. There was just nobody else I could think of. I just thought he was so great, and I wanted to work with him. He's not a super-technical actor. He's a very instinctive actor, but we surrounded all the actors with whatever tools they needed: voice coaches or singing coaches or choreography advice. And ultimately, they just had to take it inside and do their own thing. He listened to tapes of Robbie Robertson from *The Last Waltz* just talking, and it's like a rock 'n' roll voice.

**O:** Glam uses camp a lot, and so do you—not with *Safe* so much, but certainly here and with your other films. And camp often isn't taken seriously. What's your approach to camp and using it in an effective way? It can come off as cheap if you don't do it right.

**TH:** I think camp is a really fascinating thing, and it's hard to define and hard to apply consciously. It's almost something you take from material that's already existed in the world, a reading of the world. But I think it speaks of a long tradition of gay reading of the world, before gays were allowed to be visible. And it's invariably a different beast now that we have a presence post-*Stonewall*, I guess. Now, post–*In & Out*. That'll probably be the new gay marker on the calendar. I mean, this new level of mainstreaming gay characters in Hollywood . . . I just think it's changed our relationship to dominant culture in a way that doesn't settle well for me. I guess I feel our resistance is at stake. Because it seems like we're being embraced everywhere, and yet, are the images that are being seen everywhere real? It begs questions like, "Do you really want to be comfortably situated in the living room of everyone's house in America? Do we really want to be sort of declawed?"

**O:** It's like a new set of soft stereotypes.

**TH:** It's like the Sidney Poitier films of the sixties, with this gorgeous, handsome, incredibly safe depiction of black America that every liberal white person could love and embrace and put on their mantle. And again, the gay characters like Rupert Everett in *My Best Friend's Wedding* are these charming, handsome, perfect, kind of sexless characters who charm heterosexual characters left and right. But in both cases, both depictions of these minority characters are basically denying the deep conflicts of ambivalence that the country feels about those constituencies, respectively. The sixties were a very brutal time for blacks in America, but we had this perfect image from Hollywood. It's similar now. It hasn't really changed gay-bashing and homophobia in this country to have *Ellen* on television.

**O:** Getting back to camp, part of what's interesting about it is that it sends up something that it embraces at the same time.

**TH:** In a way, I think Roxy Music is high camp, in a brilliant way. It's what I wanted the film to be; I wanted the very language of *Velvet Goldmine* to be something like that. It's music that is so full of references and little nods and winks to other artists—from Noel Coward to Warhol to literary references, mythological references, whatever—excessively presented, posed, and coifed, with the record albums, the clothes, and the hair. And yet the music is ultimately, despite all of that, for no good reason, incredibly moving.

**O:** Yeah, you can laugh at Bryan Ferry's excesses, like a line on the first album where he sings about "growing potatoes by the score."

**TH:** Oh, God!

**O:** You can laugh at it and be moved by it at the same time.

**TH:** It's like Douglas Sirk films: things that can work on both levels, that are both over-the-top and excessive. And you're aware of the language and you're aware of the references and you're aware of the lack of reality or whatever, but you're moved at the same time, despite yourself. To me, that's the most interesting work.

**O:** You reference Oscar Wilde a lot in this film.

**TH:** Well, in my research, all roads led back to Oscar. It's definitely in a way trying to understand the truly English element to glam-rock. It really does not come from American culture. I got the Lou Reed/Iggy Pop stuff; that I understand. I get Warhol. But it was really trying to understand it that, in a sense, made me want to make the film. And that particular tradition of effeminacy in English culture, the androgynous dandy, the camp esthete who can fully articulate his relationship to society—and often in a way that's very much against the tradition of nature, authenticity, and truth—is very much about constructing notions of the self and culture as artifice and a celebration of that. A refusal of nature as a model is a tradition that goes right back to Oscar Wilde. And the ways in which Oscar Wilde was attacking the Romantics that preceded him, and the Romantic ideas that preceded him, were very similar to what the glam-rockers, particularly Bowie and Bryan Ferry, were attacking in the earnestness of sixties culture. Trying to shock, but with wit, cleverness, and homosexuality.

**O:** Do you find the notion of self-construction kind of limiting? Because how long can you go on constructing yourself? Maybe not for the artist, but for the audience.

**TH:** Well, we're always constructing ourselves, so I don't think there's an end to it. In fact, to me it's liberating to not think of identity as some organic property that we have to find and stick to, but actually something that is constructed, or that's imposed, that we can then counter by taking a different route and re-dressing it, and then re-dressing it again, and then re-dressing it again. It's like having every possibility at your fingertips, as opposed to some natural sense of who we'll be imprisoned by for the rest of our lives. Maybe dad dresses up as dad every day. I find that to be a liberating thought, even if it's just for teenagers for whom instability is at a maximum level. When you really do feel like an alien, and you really do feel like a space creature, and you really do feel you want to experiment and dress up and be different every day, to find what looks best but never stick to one thing. . . . Just the fact that that was offered to those kids during that time is pretty remarkable.

**O:** And that gets back to why *Rocky Horror* is still popular.
**TH:** Exactly. Obviously, it touches the core.

**O:** The Maxwell Demon character [the film's version of Ziggy Stardust] makes Ziggy Stardust more English than David Bowie's creation by tapping into this specifically British tradition of the occult.
**TH:** It was the name. . . . I forget where it originally came from, but I heard it was the name of Brian Eno's high-school band, Maxwell Demon. I thought it was a great name, so I nicked it, like everything else in the movie. I forget what it actually comes from.

**O:** There are a lot of films coming out now about the seventies. Are you afraid of being lumped in with this general movement of nostalgia for the time?
**TH:** No, not necessarily. It seems like the project in most of the other films that came out is so different from *Velvet Goldmine*'s. Often, it's kind of a good-natured look at the seventies and the sort of disposable aspects of seventies culture—with a slight arrogance to it, where *Velvet Goldmine* is fully honoring something truly radical that should shame us by comparison today. In many ways, that's much more extreme than anything we can look at today, except for the fact that a lot of those images were introduced then, so they're "available" in ways that make it seem like, oh yeah, we have access to all of that still. But out of the cultural context that made it happen, we don't. I also think that *Velvet Goldmine*, whether you like it or not, is not going to be like any film you've seen before.

# Fanning the Flames

Amy Taubin / 1998

From the *Village Voice*, November 3, 1998. Reprinted by permission from Amy Taubin.

Todd Haynes's *Velvet Goldmine* is a big, bursting piñata of a movie—a glam-rock opera à clef that, mixing fact with fantasy, swings backward and forward in time as fluidly and disconcertingly as a dream. Though kaleidoscopic in structure, it's anchored in a fan's point of view.

The fan within the film is Arthur Stuart (Christian Bale), a British journalist living in New York in a grim 1984. Arthur is working on a story about Brian Slade (Jonathan Rhys Meyers), a glam-rock idol who disappeared ten years earlier after faking his own murder. The story takes Arthur back to his own adolescence, awakening the memory of his infatuation with Brian Slade, and the intoxicating, ephemeral, sexually subversive glam-rock moment. If glam didn't transform the world into the polysexual paradise it fantasized but never promised, it did give fans like Arthur a taste of freedom ("a freedom you can allow yourself, or not" is how the film puts it) that changed them, more than they might later want to admit.

Arthur is something of an alter-ego for the filmmaker, who views the seventies as the last truly progressive decade, and glam, in "its inversion of sexuality, performance, and identity," as part of "a long history of underground gay culture, dandyism, and camp that stretches from Beau Brummel to Oscar Wilde to Jack Smith."

Haynes remembers his first encounter with glam as an eleven-year-old. "In California, where I grew up, there were these tough, cigarette-smoking glam girls. They were my age and they were really into Iggy and Elton. On the school bus, I heard one of them say, 'Bowie's bi.' That was scary to me, it thrilled and repelled me at the same time. And I remember going over to a friend's house and listening to *Diamond Dogs*. But I didn't really get into it until I was in high school."

Haynes started working on *Velvet Goldmine* in 1990, just after he finished his first feature, *Poison*. "There were many years of accumulating material and then distilling it into a script. There's a messiness to *Velvet Goldmine* but it's also a tightly constructed puzzle. It's all taut and interconnected. I know it doesn't feel that way when you watch it, but it is."

Haynes's description of his work process brings to mind the scene in *Velvet Goldmine* in which the teenage Arthur is in his room poring over music mags, surrounded by album covers and posters depicting Brian Slade near naked or in some outrageous drag costume. You can find similar scenes in thousands of coming-of-age movies, but few in which the attention that the teenager lavishes on his sacred artifacts is quite so fetishistic and fewer still where the fetish object is so subversive. (The reason that Arthur's parents are flipped out is not merely that he plays his stereo too loud, but that his idol is a flaming faggot, pansy, queer.)

To a susceptible viewer, the scene is like a hall of mirrors where one's own fantasy, and Arthur's fantasy, and the fantasy behind the film (Haynes's fantasy) reflect one another. Crudely put, that fantasy goes: what if David Bowie and Iggy Pop had fallen madly in love and then had broken up; and what if, in the cataclysm of their breakup (signaling nothing less than the destruction of glam itself), a space was opened where I could enter, where one of them would notice me, would say to me, "Come with me, don't be afraid. . . ."

That fantasy already has certain rock critics protesting about the film's "lack of authenticity" (as if that wasn't an absurd standard to apply to glam) and about Haynes's totalizingly queer vision, in which drag isn't merely an act. "They're particularly upset about Iggy, the sacred Iggy," says an amused Haynes.

But *Velvet Goldmine* isn't a biopic, though there's a lot of Bowie in Brian Slade, a lot of Iggy in Curt Wild (Ewan McGregor) and a bit of Bryan Ferry, Lou Reed, Brian Eno, and the New York Dolls floating around. It's couched as a fan's memory of glam and of the fantasy that glam produced in him. ("Your memory stays, it lingers ever, fade away never," Bryan Ferry sings in "2HB.") For all its density and pyrotechnics, it's as personal a film as Haynes's *Superstar: The Karen Carpenter Story* or *Dottie Gets Spanked*, which also deal with pop culture, memory, and youthful formative experiences.

"*Velvet Goldmine* is ultimately about the active role the fan takes in this kind of pop moment, and it speaks by association to films and music that give you a role to play, that encourage your fantasies and your embellishment," says Haynes. "The whole act of looking was foregrounded in the glam era in ways it hadn't been before in pop music. The lyrics, the melodrama of the music, the staging are all about the act of looking. So that the roles we all play in life are highlighted by the roles they play on the stage. It offers you the invitation to become the thing you're looking at, to dress up, to experiment."

Haynes is extremely skeptical about the possibility of a glam revival. "Glam established a preoccupation with image and the look of the artist that is now very commonplace—in the Boy Georges, Princes, and Madonnas—but has lost much of its arresting power. It made you think about who you were in ways I don't think it does anymore. Glam isn't an option now, mostly because the culture we live in is so much less progressive than the culture that produced it. And the meaning, energy, and potential glam gave to the act of looking isn't possible in a culture where every image is available to us immediately and outside its cultural context. In a way, glam saved itself from that horrible recycling process that most other significant chapters in the history of rock undergo by predicting its own end in various ways and killing itself off—Bowie killing Ziggy, Eno leaving Roxy. I wanted the whole film to be a reflection of the Roxy Music experience I had, rather than the Bowie experience. Roxy Music has this elegiac, mournful melodramatic quality, this spilling out of emotion, but it's brought to you with such an excess of references, winks and nods, and posturing. The duality of being so emotional and so tongue-in-cheek is always what moves me. It's Sirk and Fassbinder and Oscar Wilde, too. They let you feel the feelings and think about the structures at the same time."

In inviting the fan to become what he or she looked at, glam blurred the distinction between identification and desire, just as it blurred those between masculinity and femininity, heterosexuality and homosexuality, fact and fiction, form and feeling. In *Velvet Goldmine*, the thrill of blurring is specifically tied to the adolescent experience.

"Maybe it suggests," says Haynes, "that the period when we're most vulnerable and impressionable is limited, and that to become part of society, to submit to a single identity, a career, responsible choices inevitably cuts us off from everything glam rock stands for. *The Rocky Horror Picture Show*, which is the only other film I can think of that deals with the themes specific to the glam era, is the film that successive generations of teens cannot let go of. Jim [Lyons, *Velvet Goldmine* editor] and I saw it again a few years ago and we were shocked that the audience's reactions were still the same—the perversions were hailed and the conformity ridiculed. It can only be that there's this brief time before you have to settle on a life for yourself when you're invited to dress up, interact, and engage, to wear the lipstick and the garters, to be faggoty."

And it's not just a boy thing. In *Velvet Goldmine*, the most explicit sex scene between Brian and Curt is enacted with Barbie dolls that belong to girl fans.

"I wanted to show that it wasn't a problem for girl fans to enter that world and play out their desires with two boys instead of a boy and a girl. But ultimately, the little girls holding up their Barbies and speaking through them is exactly what I'm doing in the entire film. It's not the story of Bowie and Iggy. It's what we do with what they put out there. That's the work of the fans."

So, perhaps, it's not surprising that when Miramax, *Velvet Goldmine*'s North American distributor, test-screened the film, it found that it scored highest with female audiences under twenty-five. "I always knew," says Haynes, "that the perfect boy is a girl."

# Heaven Sent

Dennis Lim / 2002

From the *Village Voice*, October 29, 2002. Courtesy of the *Village Voice*.

"I really wanted people to cry," Todd Haynes says of his new movie, *Far from Heaven*, a domestic weepie set in 1957 Connecticut and swaddled in the Technicolor opulence of the period. From the delirious palette to the prim, italicized performances, Haynes's meta-melodrama (in theaters November 8) pays homage to German-born maestro Douglas Sirk. A Weimar stage director who emigrated to the States in 1940, Sirk went on to make a string of Brechtian soaps in Hollywood, wrapping up his film career as resident tearjerker at Universal Pictures. Resurrecting *All That Heaven Allows* (1955), Sirk's attack on bourgeois repression, and *Imitation of Life* (1959), his tempestuous saga of race and identity, Haynes revels in the ebullient artifice of the originals. *Far from Heaven*, pace Courtney Love, fakes it so fake it is beyond real.

There may be no filmmaker better equipped than Haynes to navigate a Sirkian simulacrum. Having cast a Barbie doll as an anorexic chanteuse (*Superstar: The Karen Carpenter Story*), anatomized the existential panic of a blank-slate SoCal housewife (*Safe*), and wreaked semiotic havoc with glam rock's cut-and-paste identikit (*Velvet Goldmine*), he's well acquainted with the pleasures and perils of inauthenticity.

*Far from Heaven* doesn't remake the Sirk movies in question so much as direct their mirrored surfaces at each other—transposing signs, exposing subtexts, renewing resonances. As in *All That Heaven Allows*, a middle-class heroine scandalizes her community by getting too friendly with her gardener. But Haynes's ill-fated pair, Cathy (*Safe* star Julianne Moore) and Raymond (Dennis Haysbert), face a taboo more virulent than the age and class differences that keep the earlier film's Jane Wyman and Rock Hudson apart: Cathy is white, Raymond black. (The skin-color conundrum allows Haynes to acknowledge *Imitation of Life* as well as Rainer Werner Fassbinder's *Ali: Fear Eats the Soul*, in which Sirk's most ardent acolyte updated *All That Heaven Allows* to seventies Germany as a tale of verboten interracial love.) Haynes engineers a further complication: Cathy's husband, Frank (Dennis Quaid), is trying furtively to suppress his homosexual impulses—a twist that locks the three characters into what Haynes calls "this almost beautiful diagram of residual pain" (and effectively springs Rock Hudson from the celluloid closet). He explains, "There's not necessarily a bad or evil character, but when one of them steps toward their needs or desires, it ends up harming everybody in that tangle."

Venturing into a gay bar, a black neighborhood, and even a therapy session, *Far from Heaven* makes explicit some of what was pointedly excluded in fifties melodramas. But Haynes says it was important not to create a sense of anachronistic rupture: "I think about Chantal Akerman's *Jeanne Dielman*, which is so much about the power of the small action. I was trying to do that with *Safe*—reduce the level of activity and crisis, so that smaller things would have a bigger impact. Before *Safe* becomes a film about illness, it's a film about a couch, or a film about the absolute blankness of the things that make up people's lives. With *Far from Heaven*, I set myself a similar challenge: How can you make the word fuck a shocking event again? It made sense to use that as an overall strategy, to keep everything at the minimum. It helped to balance out the grand themes."

Ironically, Haynes first thought of *Far from Heaven* as an attempt to work on a narrower canvas. "I said to myself after *Velvet Goldmine*, 'Dude, you don't have to put the universe into every movie.' Maybe it's OK to do a small domestic drama. But it ends up like, Race! Sexuality! Gender!"— albeit as configured by an alum of Brown's art and semiotics program. "I do believe in the limits of representation," he continues, "and I think they define all three themes. It became clear as I was writing the script that the themes of sexuality and race were counterbalances, with the woman as the force separating them. One was condemned to secrecy and the other to a public backdrop; one was buried within the domestic setting and the other was unavoidably visible and open to rampant projection."

He toyed with several scenarios involving race and sexuality and even considered a fifties gay Hollywood milieu, but never deviated from his goal of making a woman's picture. "Male homosexuality, even in the fifties, could enjoy a double standard over the role of a woman, who would still be harnessed with the responsibility of appearance and the household and the maintenance of traditional values."

*Far from Heaven*'s flavor of brazen pastiche—at once nostalgic and defamiliarizing—suggests a late-night AMC marathon experienced through a hallucinatory fog. As Haynes puts it: "It doesn't flatter our collective idea of what reality is, based on these codes that we all agree on. There are no securing nods to how much more we know today." Eschewing the self-satisfied perspective of hindsight, the movie actually illustrates how little things have changed. Though Haynes briefly flirted with the idea of setting the story in the present, he says, "I thought it would be interesting to use the fifties as a metaphor for today, to ultimately draw questions back about contemporary society." He adds: "And I also couldn't resist the fabric and color of the fifties"—not least the richly complementary hues of *All That Heaven Allows*. "Visually, it's the most supple and subtle of the Sirk melodramas, and the most surprisingly expressionistic. You're astounded by how intensely the simple, quiet domestic themes are depicted."

Moore, it turns out, had a hand in the chromatic choices as well. Haynes, who conceived the film with Moore in mind, had written Cathy as a redhead. But the actress, thinking of "Doris Day's voice and Lana Turner's blondeness," convinced Haynes that she should wear a wig. "A redhead is marginal," Moore explains. "We're 4 percent of the population. We're the best friend, the sexy one, or the funny one, but Cathy's the classic American ideal. I wanted her to be the perfect blonde with the perfect family. I wanted to see that person transform. Watching it, I realized I've never smiled so much in a film—I smile all the way through. I thought, oh my god, Cathy is the ultimate American optimist—and Todd has made a movie about the failure of American optimism."

*Velvet Goldmine*, the most optimistic and celebratory of Haynes's films, left him "bummed out and exhausted," he says. "I tried to take a break and paint and travel—I went to Hawaii alone and finished Proust. But I wasn't very inspired." He embarked on *Far from Heaven* "almost as a last resort—going back to film as a way of working through other things in my life."

After he lost his Williamsburg apartment in the summer of 2000, Haynes moved to Portland, Oregon—"a great physical, emotional, psychological change," he says. With "the absurdity and innate arrogance" of the film world at bay, what was intended as a rest cure ended up being a highly fertile work period. The writing process proved unusually painless: "I did a sketch of Julianne as Cathy, in sunglasses with a scarf and a little basket, pinned it up, and I wrote it in ten days. I was listening to a lot of sad music, like *The Thin Red Line* soundtrack, but it was almost like

I was in this . . . playland. I hate when people say, 'The script wrote itself,' but I felt like I was a bit of a spectator to my own process.

"Constraints are the most inspiring things in a creative process if you trust them," Haynes continues. "A set of rules can be exhilarating." The challenge was not merely to adopt Sirk's rococo style but to wholly internalize his brashly synthetic tone—in other words, to imitate an *Imitation of Life*. "From the outset, I think it was about embracing this beautiful, almost naive language of words, gestures, movements, and interactions that were totally prescribed and extremely limited—not condescending to it, but allowing its simplicity to touch other feelings that you can't be over-explicating."

Moore concurs: "There's a trend now of a so-called naturalistic acting style, with content that's less emotionally realistic or is somewhat heroic. But I prefer it the other way around, like it is in this film. I love the artifice of filmmaking. I love nothing more than working inside, on a fake set. I always think, Why do we have to be in somebody's house? Just build it if you can." (And build it they did: Heaven is a soundstage in New Jersey, where a quintessentially over-appointed Sirk home was re-created, complete with split levels, strategically placed mirrors, and a curved staircase.)

The *Far from Heaven* diorama induces a vertiginous disorientation— what Haynes calls "an ignited, electrified distance that can happen with a certain kind of representational experience." He likens it to watching performance artist John Kelly as Joni Mitchell: "He sounds just like Joni Mitchell, he imitates her stage banter, he's in drag and looks like a ghoulish version of the little pixie Joni Mitchell from the sixties. You're laughing, but you're laughing at yourself, at your own intensely serious investment in Joni Mitchell when you were in high school. But you're also crying, at the beauty of the music, and for that person in high school who loved those songs and who you feel rekindled. There's this freedom to go from one emotion to the next, neither one undermining the other. If the real Joni Mitchell was up there, you'd be going, oh god she's older, oh she can't hit that same note—you get caught up in all the discrepancies of the real. There's something about a beautiful surrogate that opens up this wealth of feeling that you wouldn't have with the real thing. And to me, the best kind of cinema is not about the real—it's about a distance that you fill in, participate in with your life experiences, your memories, and your associations."

Viewers haven't always been willing to bridge that gap. Though he has long been a critics' favorite (*Safe* was voted best movie of the nineties in the *Voice*'s poll of film writers), *Far from Heaven* is his first release to premiere amid a crescendo of ecstatic, across-the-board acclaim. Moore won the Best Actress prize at the Venice Film Festival, and a media mob descended on the film's Toronto press screening the following week (causing irate shutout Roger Ebert to throw what the Canadian press termed "a hissy fit"). An *L.A. Times* Oscar odds article last week ranked it among the early front-runners (Moore is already a two-time nominee for *Boogie Nights* and *The End of the Affair*). Haynes seems somewhat bemused by the decidedly alien notion of award-season prospects: "Maybe I'm not enjoying it as much as I should be." He adds, a little nervously, "I don't know what all this is going to do to me."

One likely side effect: heightened expectations for his next project, a Bob Dylan movie that he describes as "an untraditional biography, where the multitude of changes that he's gone through are literalized by separate characters whose stories are being told simultaneously." He elaborates: "There's a Dylan quote that best describes it: 'You've got yesterday, today, and tomorrow all in the same room, and there's very little you can't imagine happening.' None of the characters really are him; they don't look like him. One's an eleven-year-old black boy. The closest I'll come is a woman who'll play *Don't Look Back*–era Dylan and look the most like the real Dylan."

On the subject of what-nexts, both Moore and Haynes report that post-screening discussions have revolved around possible future scenarios for the film's heroine. "It's so funny how people want to talk about what happens after," Haynes says. Moore, who once again dons mid-century domestic drag in December's *The Hours*, notes, "People have told me, 'It'll be OK—the sixties are just around the corner!'" Haynes says, "Movies today have to show the cathartic articulation of what a character has learned. It's the Aristotelian thing. But these melodramas are in some respects pre-psychological. The characters are moved around by the society, and there's never a point where they master those experiences and articulate them. That burden passes to the viewer, and I think that's why people are almost possessed by it. You have to do something with what she's experienced, on her behalf, and in a way it's really moving, just to be her articulation."

# Imitation of Film: Todd Haynes Mimics Melodrama in *Far from Heaven*

Anthony Kaufman / 2002

From *Indiewire*, November 2002. Reprinted by permission from Anthony Kaufman / *Indiewire*.

Any director who can make Barbie dolls tragic knows how to tread the delicate line between stylization and sentiment. From his all-doll debut *Superstar: The Karen Carpenter Story* to his sophomore masterpiece *Safe* to his most recent *Far from Heaven*—all in a sense heartfelt stories of Barbies gone awry—Todd Haynes has created stories that straddle the poles: on the one hand, you have dolls singing pop songs, an absurdly phobic L.A. housewife, and a laughably perfect fifties homemaker, and on the other, you have the ravages of anorexia, millennial paranoia, and the sexism, racism, and homophobia central to American society. Even in his 1991 Sundance winner *Poison* and the 1998 glam rock extravaganza *Velvet Goldmine*, Haynes shows a deep affection for the worlds he creates, no matter how seemingly surreal or superficial.

Along with longtime producing collaborator Christine Vachon, Haynes's name is synonymous with American independent film. And looking back at the last ten years of his career is to see how far the movement has traveled—and in many ways stayed the same. (James Schamus, one of the producers on *Poison*, will now distribute *Far from Heaven* as co-president of mini-major Focus Features.) The day after presenting Julianne Moore, his self-described "muse," a special acting prize at New York's Gotham Awards, Haynes met with indieWIRE's Anthony Kaufman to talk about his latest film *Far from Heaven* (opening November 8), a 1950s-set melodrama that remarkably reproduces the style and feel of the "women's weepies" of the period, in particular the color-saturated, enamel-coated work of Douglas Sirk (*All That Heaven Allows*, *Written on the Wind*, *Imitation of Life*). Here, Haynes speaks about finding emotion in artifice, overcoming low budgets, and taking risks.

**indieWIRE:** I feel that *Far from Heaven* may be one of the biggest, most experimental mainstream films of all time. Do you think it's fair to call it experimental?

**Todd Haynes:** Yes, because it refuses a lot of familiar narrative touchstones that makes us feel like we're watching a genuine drama: contemporary codes of naturalism, psychological realizations, redemption, and any sort of heroic victory. So it refuses all of those things and maintains a completely synthetic language that comes directly out of the world of film. And yet it's done in complete faith that that language in some way embodies more potential for emotional feeling than anything that mimics what we think of as reality. In other words, people talk about this film in relation to sincerity versus irony. And I think it's different. I think it's about the intense feelings that only come from synthetic film language, that only come from artificial experiences that we know from film, but we nevertheless invest with intense feeling.

**iW:** How do you see irony not coming into the picture? Just the fact that it's made today makes it quite self-conscious.

**Haynes:** I think one of the reasons why it comes across as having emotional integrity is that we were enjoying it while making it. There was an amorous feeling towards the material. Even when there are lines like "Oh, jiminy," it was with incredible respect and I think that comes through.

**iW:** There is this line, "Do you think we can ever see beyond the surface of things," which I think again brings the issues of the film to the forefront. Do you think it's dangerous to put a line of dialogue like that, which in a sense broadcasts your project?

**Haynes:** I am not sure if it is any more obvious than most of the lines in the movie, which are always on the verge. It's movie dialogue. Movie dialogue has always showed its thematic thesis statements.

**iW:** Financially speaking, this project could not have been made earlier in your career.

**Haynes:** All of my films mirror each other economically, because we've never really had enough money to make any of them. It always takes a huge amount of work, if not criminal acts, to make it look like it was shot for more. *Safe* cost just under a million dollars. *Velvet Goldmine* cost around $7 million and this cost $14 million, so these are incredibly low-budget movies for what they are. Big budgets come with bigger unions, so it often feels like when you have more, you have less.

**iW:** So how did you do it for such a low budget?
**Haynes:** It was really, really hard. When I'm working, I work harder than anyone I know. I'm obsessive, I'm self-abusive, and I don't sleep. In this case that working style was supported by so many successful creative alliances. I remember one day when we were knocking stuff off pretty quickly the first week. And it was Cathy's angle, and we did one take; it was perfect and we did a second for a backup, and I was like, "We got it!" And Julianne was like, "Yeah, let's go!" And the whole crew picked stuff up and we ran to the backyard for the next shot. It was just this great, exhilarating feeling and everybody—no matter what their production background—got into the crazy speed of it all.

**iW:** Your opening shot seems to exactly recall the beginning of *All That Heaven Allows*. How many hours of close shot-by-shot study did you do of Sirk's films?
**Haynes:** Some of the parallels are evoked more than they are literal. In *All That Heaven Allows*, it's just a simple pan, but it has a similar feeling. Whereas when Cathy cries on her bed in the end, it's the only shot that's literally a facsimile of the shot in Max Ophuls's *The Reckless Moment*, when Joan Bennett breaks down and cries at the end.

**iW:** After I saw the movie, there were some people in the audience who had never seen a Sirk film and some who had. How do you see these two different audiences experiencing your movie?
**Haynes:** I am eager to know that as anyone. In Venice, there was a very well-attended press screening and we heard afterwards it was filled with a lot of appreciative laughter. I realized in the laughter, there is some interaction with the codes that we're obviously playing with—and ultimately embracing. And then we had the official screening and they were dead silent through the entire movie. It was weird. And then they all stood up afterwards and applauded and then Julianne won the Best Actress award, so it's beginning to dawn on me that for certain viewers it's possible to watch the film with absolutely no framework whatsoever and get right into the content immediately.

**iW:** Perhaps those who aren't familiar with Sirk appreciate it in a more primal, emotional way?

**Haynes:** My favorite classic Hollywood films have always been the ones that play at a popular level at the time they were released—with some exceptions like *Night of the Hunter* and *Ace in the Hole*—like Hitchcock's and Billy Wilder's films. They were absolutely popular, but they also have so many layers. Hitchcock is the best example, because he was dismissed as a purely popular filmmaker, but only later, received a following of cineastes. But I've never made a film before that was ever eligible for that possibility.

**iW:** The lighting of the film, of course, is so incredibly vivid. How much were you relying on gels verses getting those lights right in post-production?

**Haynes:** It was all in production. We didn't have any money to do any fancy stuff in post. If we had any money, I would have struck one Technicolor print of the movie. I had meticulous conversations with [cinematographer] Ed Lachman and Ed's team. I made color charts for every scene in the movie. There was a spectrum of about twenty different colors for each scene to describe the mood that I was looking for. And then all the departments would gather around my swatches, and then we had tons of stills from Sirk's films to discuss, in regard to framing, color, angles, clothes, sets. We'd sit and talk about colors for days, literally.

**iW:** How do you feel that the color creates emotion?

**Haynes:** In the Sirk films, you realize how extreme the color palettes were, and how complex they were, in terms of warm and cool spectrums. Many movies today are dumbed down, in terms of color—a whole movie will be honeycomb gold colors if it's set in the past or all icy blue if it's a suspense thriller. But these films use complex interactions of warm and cool in every single scene. And emotions are multi-colored. Color, lighting, costume, all the visual elements are supplementing what can't be said in these films.

**iW:** When making movies, one can think they're doing something over the top when you're doing it, but to the audience, it doesn't seem over the top.

**Haynes:** There can be a fine line; I agree with you. But we never thought we were going over the top when making *Far from Heaven*. I kept saying to Ed, "I don't want to look at the Sirk films and say they were bolder than we were." They were radical. I wanted that to open us all up to things. You know why I wasn't so panicked about pulling this off? Because the people who read the script got into it emotionally, and that's without the visuals and the performances. We know these forms so well and they have resonance.

**iW:** Now that you've made a few films, do you feel it's easier or harder to take risks?

**Haynes:** I think the worry is you get older, and you stop taking risks. That's more of what you see in the world, politically and creatively. Successes, especially, fuck you up. But I've always felt successful because I've always made the films I wanted to make and I'm really lucky to have a body of press that's been interested in my work. They've never made money and they've never reached a large audience, but that's not why I made them.

**iW:** Do you know what you're next project is going to be?

**Haynes:** I'm going to do a movie about Bob Dylan, but it's going to be weird, not a traditional narrative by any means. I'm still writing it. I've had a bad career acquiring music rights, from Karen Carpenter to David Bowie, but [Dylan] was pretty receptive, which has never happened before. So it's exciting. And I bet it won't be what people expect from me after *Far from Heaven*, such as something suddenly very accessible.

**iW:** I see super 8mm.

**Haynes:** Maybe. Yeah. Could be. (Laughs)

# Past Perfect

Geoffrey O'Brien / 2002

Seen from one angle, Todd Haynes's *Far from Heaven* is a cunningly precise pastiche of a movie Douglas Sirk might have made in 1958—if, that is, Universal Studios had been prepared to release a movie bearing on homosexuality, interracial romance, and the civil rights movement. Right from the start—as the camera descends through autumn foliage toward an overview of a serene street in what is meant to be Hartford, Connecticut, to the sweeping, plangent accompaniment of Elmer Bernstein's score—we have the vertiginous impression of being dropped back into a past all the more welcoming for having never quite existed in the first place. As Haynes explains, the film is built out of "the language of fifties cinema, not the fifties." But if this point of departure suggests either a wan conceptual exercise or an attempt to satirize the foibles of a long-gone social order, the result is strikingly different: a movie whose period stylization taps into reservoirs of powerful emotion. Through an unexpected alchemy, *Far from Heaven* ends up becoming the object it contemplates, and its path of conscious artifice leads toward a tragic sense of reality.

"Everything about film is always artificial," Haynes remarks. "You can come to something far more surprisingly real by acknowledging how much of a construct it is first. It always feels so much more false to me when you set out to be real." *Far from Heaven* signals its artifice at the outset by its unmistakable links to Sirk's 1955 masterpiece *All That Heaven Allows* (a work that, after *Far from Heaven* and Fassbinder's 1974 *Ali: Fear Eats the Soul*, should be recognized as not only a great film but the cause of other great films). Here it is not Jane Wyman but Julianne Moore who falls in love with her gardener, here not a Thoreau-influenced Rock Hudson but Dennis Haysbert as an African American intellectual who wins

115

Moore's heart partly through his eloquent commentary—at a suburban art show where his mere presence creates ripples—on the religious implications of abstract art. Where Wyman in the Sirk picture is recently widowed, in the Haynes film Moore finds herself abruptly estranged from her business exec husband (Dennis Quaid) when his long-repressed homosexuality comes vividly to her attention.

The husband's sexual crisis is handled with an aura of hysteria and pseudoscience appropriate to the period—his anguish and shame call to mind Grant Williams as *The Incredible Shrinking Man* (1957) angrily rejecting his wife when she attempts to comfort him for his mysterious loss of masculine pride. In these early scenes—a pickup in a gay bar, an interrupted assignation in an office, a session with a therapist offering the latest theories on curing homosexuality—one has the sense that Haynes is having fun by messing with the proprieties of fifties cinema, showing what could not have been shown, somewhat in the manner of those "Scenes We'd Like to See" that used to be featured in *Mad* magazine. Here is a way to reinvent the past, to travel back in time and insert forbidden episodes, taboo locations, into the history of cinema.

The sense of risk is palpable, since at any moment the movie might founder into the ridiculous or caricatural. But Haynes isn't interested in the kind of easy satire of suburban conformism encountered in a movie like *Pleasantville* (1998). "When most people see films set in the fifties today," he says, "there's an immediate sense of superiority. It's all about the myth that as time moves on, we become more progressive. Oh wow, they didn't know what sex was until we started to give it to them from our contemporary perspective. So the fifties become a sort of earmark point of oppressive politics and climate, which is very flattering to us as we look back."

Rather than imposing the enlightenment of latter-day opinions on its version of the fifties, *Far from Heaven* adopts the perspective of characters who can see no clear way out of the dilemmas their world forces on them. There are no villains here: "To me the most amazing melodramas are the ones where when a person makes a tiny step toward fulfilling a desire that their social role is built to discourage, they end up hurting everybody else. It's like a chess game of pain, a ricochet effect where everybody gets hurt but there's nobody to blame." To find pain at the heart of the lushest cinematic pleasures is the film's peculiar accomplishment.

Those pleasures are associated with a past as alluring as it is ultimately unreachable: the mythic fifties of precisely this kind of psychological melodrama, an era that (like the Old West, where sheriffs and outlaws play out their confrontations) starts as a historical period—after the depression and World War II, before the eruption of social unrest and personal liberation in the sixties—and turns into a region outside time, an operatic space where emotions, hemmed in, finally prove irrepressible. "I love these films," says Haynes, "because they were always more about the smaller domestic limitations of possibility and experience than the genres associated with men, like the western or the gangster film, which are about the limitless frontier that you can discover and take over." In the *verismo* of fifties melodrama, the climax comes not with an explosion of gunfire or the advance of cavalry down a hillside but through a blossoming of inner feeling, gently assisted by a full-bodied color palette and an orchestra alert to every shift in mood.

After the air-conditioned, invisibly toxic contemporary wasteland mapped in *Safe* (1995), Haynes's unsettling, deadpan account of a woman's gradual withdrawal from a world to which she has unaccountably become allergic, *Far from Heaven* might seem like a turn toward a warmer, more inviting past, with Julianne Moore playing something of an ancestor to the damaged self she embodied in the earlier film. With the road to the future seemingly barred, a certain nostalgic retreat could be understood, and we are given at least the materials for such a nostalgia. For a product of fifties suburbia like myself, the film's early frames feel like the sort of strange homecoming that dreams sometimes offer; and those opening shots, as it turns out, ultimately provide just as little solidity. The accoutrements, though, are solid enough. The creature comforts of the fifties—fabrics and furnishings, clean machines and verdant streetscapes—are re-created here with a nearly fetishistic devotion that makes every frame look like a hallucinatory extrapolation of an advertising layout in *Life*. "I wanted every car perfectly polished and clean," Haynes recalls. "We had to take gritty New Jersey exterior locations and clean them up. We had buildings cleaned because they had bird shit hanging off the edge or they had too much dirt, and we had to make it look as much like a back-lot soundstage as possible."

In these resonantly colored interiors and well-tended gardens we can trace the contours of a paradise spoiled only by the conflicted emotions of those who inhabit it. If only they didn't have to feel, what a life they could live among these structures, illuminated by the eerily otherworldly lighting that makes even the upholstery seem ghostly. The classicism of *Far from Heaven* is architectural; here décor—the décor that women spend their lives trying to get exactly right—is destiny. Haynes quotes Fassbinder quoting Sirk: "You can't make films about things, you can only make films with things, with people, with light, with flowers, with mirrors, with blood." As I contemplate the cast-off furniture from *Far from Heaven* that has found its way into Haynes's 1909 bungalow—here the sprawling sofa where a marriage definitively unravels, there the gardener's wooden workbox that suggests a natural serenity just out of reach—I am reminded of the determining presence of interior decoration in all his films, whether the bedroom of the child murderer's schoolmate in *Poison* (1991), the gyms and shopping-center restaurants in *Safe*, or the makeshift luxury enjoyed by the glam rockers of *Velvet Goldmine* (1998). His grandfather, he tells me, built sets for Warner Bros. in the forties; perhaps that's one reason why his work recalls a time when movies were not so much filmed as constructed, little worlds with their own rules and their own specific boundaries.

The unbridled optical pleasure of the world he constructs here is the necessary corollary of its emotional dissatisfactions. Haynes mentions Max Ophuls as another guiding influence on the film, singling out *The Reckless Moment* (1949)—another near-tragic story of a desperate housewife—as a particular favorite. The debt to Ophuls can be felt in the way the film makes poetry out of a car pulling out of a parking lot, a train leaving a station, a woman looking out a window, the wordless communication between two almost-lovers as they walk in the woods: the kind of images that translate the commonplaces of romance novels into the cinematic sublime. Falseness is no more an issue here than in, say, the last act of *La Boheme*. There is simply a vocabulary of apparently banal acts and gestures and objects that, properly deployed, can express what would otherwise be unsayable. You can regard it through whatever prisms of irony and complication you like, but the forms themselves remain the same: A glance is a glance, good-bye is good-bye.

There is an essential realism that has nothing to do with naturalistic trappings. Behavioral truth can as easily be found in the most convention-bound melodrama as in a pseudo-documentary slice of life on the street. Films today tend to look superficially lifelike at the same time that they promulgate wish-fulfilling fantasies even more shameless than those that flourished in the era of the Hollywood ending. It is not the least of *Far from Heaven*'s paradoxes that in embracing the structure of the classic weepie it asserts a rigor utterly alien to the feel-good dynamics of movies in which, as Haynes says, "every character has to come to some kind of redemptive knowledge of who they are and what they've done wrong. The father who can't deal with his family because he's so ambitious at work has to go through a series of changes that make him realize the value of the family and the wife and the kids, and go home whole-heartedly at the end. It's such an amazingly uninteresting trajectory. . . . The onus is on the individual to fix it, in a weirdly open-market sensibility of resolution." As against movies in which an emotional break-through can solve any problem, *Far from Heaven* is bound by rules—rules of society, rules of genre—that make a happy ending improbable, if not impossible. The lovers cannot even make love: This is one of those rare contemporary movies—like Scorsese's *The Age of Innocence* (1993) and Wong Kar-Wai's *In the Mood for Love* (2000)—that hinge decisively on unconsummated passion.

The rules are both a matter of historical fact and an arbitrary system of aesthetic controls. Haynes needs to work with "a set of constraints within which I have to construct a narrative, constraints that conversely give you a certain freedom." He sets up arbitrary limits, like those writers of the OuLiPo school who write novels without using the letter e or po-ems in which every line must be interchangeable with every other line. Here the constraints are a derivative of those that Douglas Sirk encoun-tered in making films for producer Ross Hunter in the fifties: There were things that couldn't be said, places one couldn't go. From those original constraints came formal choices that Haynes has now broken down into their components.

He shows me some of the preparatory books from the early stages of *Far from Heaven*'s development: scenes from Sirk films reduced nearly to sequences of stills. He comments on a frame in which a vulnerable Lana Turner (in 1959's *Imitation of Life*) enters the office where she is about to be rudely propositioned: "It etches every bit of the content with a fatal inevitability. It's a wide shot, but she seems completely boxed in. You don't feel like you're wide; you don't feel a sense of expanse and space. It feels like the walls are actually closing in on the characters, even if you're seeing them from a distance." He talks as well about Sirk's use of color—"color is the keynote, color is everything"—so different from cur-rent practices. "Today's use of color is totally reductive. Happy scenes are warm, sad scenes are cool; sometimes an entire movie, if it's set in the past, will be shot through honey-colored gels. The Woody Allen period films are just gilded gold, warm butterscotch. What's beautiful about Sirk is that every frame is a complementary palette. Every single scene, regardless if it's happy or sad, plays with an interaction of warm and cool colors. It's so powerful."

It becomes apparent that in this context, for practical purposes, "Sirk" does not denote a mood or a philosophy or a set of plot elements, but rather a repertoire of technical decisions. With that lexicon of effects, new sentences can be written. Haynes recalls how the color schemes for each scene in *Far from Heaven* were worked out, the spectrum of tones playing a determining role in the scene's development: "I would sit down, close my eyes, think of a scene, and go through swatches and put together a range of colors that communicated a mood. The gay bar, for instance, utilizes a very specific palette of puce green and a very intense magenta that's very unnerving and strange. Ernie's bar also uses purple and green as its color sources, but it's a very different purple and a very different green: And yet they're the same two families of colors, contrasting, clashing against each other."

This transmutation of melodramatic narrative into a play of colors reminds me of the pivotal scene where Dennis Haysbert delivers his impromptu remarks on a Miro painting to a visibly impressed Julianne Moore. Structurally the scene corresponds to one in *All That Heaven Allows* in which Jane Wyman is made aware of the importance of Thoreau's *Walden* to Rock Hudson and his friends. For Sirk to invoke the return to nature in the midst of Universal glossiness is perhaps an irony comparable to Haynes's invoking, in a movie so thick with historical and cultural markers as *Far from Heaven*, the notion of abstract art as a search for the divine.

The character so remarkably incarnated by Dennis Haysbert is himself a nexus of tensions: an African American so overqualified with virtues and credentials that—apart from race—not even the bourgeoisie of the film's fictive Hartford could find any fault with him. As with all the roles in the film, psychology has nothing to do with it. They are types, abstractions, creatures of circumstance: characters for a seventeenth-century novel or a Kabuki play. That the absence of psychological explanation makes them no less human is a further vindication of Haynes's formalism: "It's the shorthand of psychobabble that we require a sense of depth of character in movies today. The person is fucked up because the mother did this to them when they were a kid; you have to show maybe the flashback to childhood. When you really analyze it you realize how flimsy and silly it is, how it's just another narrative code."

Take that layer away and you have a movie not about motivations but about situations. Motivation can be assumed: Everybody wants love, everybody wants to be happy. The devil is in the trapdoors and dead ends of social regulation. This is where aesthetic formalism merges with subject matter: The characters themselves operate according to a predetermined script, a limited vocabulary of possibilities, exactly as if they were conceptual artists, the catch being that the concept is not of their own choosing. "We all speak a script that's conducive to the world we live in, that is always a translation of a wild mass of instincts and desires," says Haynes. "I've always had a hard time depicting the experience of radical revolt from culture, truly transgressive experience. That kind of experience is ultimately everybody's own job and work to do; you're cheated when it's given to you intact. In a way I'm more comfortable showing the limits that make that kind of response necessary."

That sense of limits is what makes the film seem increasingly real as it progresses. But it is, again, not a realism of surfaces: "What people seem to want is the opposite of what this film does; they want something that seems naturalistic on the surface, according to today's codes of naturalism, but that inside is actually incredibly heroic and false. In movies like this, on the other hand, the external experience is very synthetic and highly stylized, but it's actually about people who are much more like us, fragile and afraid, and who cave in when society tells them to." The stylization is thoroughgoing and for the crew meant reinventing every procedure, from the camera's distance from actors (much greater here than in contemporary TV-style framing) to the expressive, non-naturalistic lighting. "All these things that we come to today with a sense of naturalism, we had to break every one. People started to think differently."

To stay within such prescribed boundaries creates an air of brittleness. At any moment a single false step might bring a world of agreed-upon responses crashing down. The difficulty of sustaining such a world can be felt from moment to moment, especially in the acting. Contemporary actors find it nearly impossible to empty their performances of the Method-derived mannerisms we have come to think of as lifelike, to return to an earlier, flatter style of line reading, the sort of guileless performance that served Rock Hudson for a whole career. Nowadays we expect actors to project a knowing quality, whereas in old Hollywood movies it was often more a question of their just being there: sometimes with tremendous art, sometimes merely with an ability to seem absolutely at home in the counter world of cinema.

*Far from Heaven* might best be thought of as parody in the oldest sense, an imitation undertaken for wholly serious purposes. If this is camp, it is that highest camp—"something that uses artifice to bring you to a place of heightened emotions that you couldn't get to any other way"—which finally is indistinguishable from the "real" thing, whatever that might be. In the end, all questions of real and unreal dissolve in the fragility suggested by Julianne Moore's remarkable performance. She plays her part as someone who reads the lines she's been given as if she senses their falseness but can't come up with an alternative, and who undergoes onscreen a moral evolution that still doesn't guarantee anything like happiness. Even in the movies—even in a movie consisting of nothing but the language of other movies—there are still realities that cannot be dislodged or evaded. But then, as Todd Haynes summarizes: "Just to know what you love is so important."

# A Scandal in Suburbia

Jon Silberg / 2002

From *American Cinematographer*, December 2002. Reprinted by permission from Jon Silberg.

When writer/director Todd Haynes set out to create his own take on the Douglas Sirk melodramas of the 1950s, he wasn't interested in giving the genre a hip or ironic twist. As a result, *Far from Heaven*, shot by Edward Lachman, ASC, is as earnest and straightforward as Sirk's *Written on the Wind* or *All That Heaven Allows*.

Sirk was among many filmmakers who emigrated from Germany to the United States between the two World Wars. Like other artists whose roots were in German theater, Sirk used a theatrical visual style to convey political messages, but his Hollywood creations were designed for mass audiences—they were studio melodramas, the "chick flicks" of their day. His films illuminated the social, racial, and sexual tensions that defined postwar American life, but the stylistic conventions he employed were mocked by some for their artifice.

Haynes had no intention of joining in the mockery. "People attribute to me a kind of gay brand of easy irony," he says. "But what always surprises the people who like my films is that they find themselves very emotionally engaged."

Haynes says that in some ways, *Far from Heaven* resembles his first film, the short *Superstar*, in that it has all the trappings of satire but is actually something quite sincere. *Superstar* used Barbie dolls to tell the story of self-destructive 1970s pop singer Karen Carpenter. Haynes observes, "The only way *Superstar* works is through an enormous trick: it makes you think you're about to have a laugh riot watching a condescending story, but in fact, the goal of the film is to make you forget you're watching dolls and form a weird, unexpected emotional connection to what is an incredibly sad story."

Set in 1957, *Far from Heaven* stars Julianne Moore and Dennis Quaid as

Cathy and Frank Whitaker, an archetypal suburban couple plagued by the kind of dark secrets and hidden longing that permeate Sirk's most famous films. Cathy discovers that her husband has been a closeted homosexual throughout their marriage, and in her confusion and loneliness, she develops an emotional attachment to her African American gardener, Raymond (Dennis Haysbert), causing a scandal in her segregated town.

Haynes says he wasn't interested in creating an "issue-oriented" film in which strong, admirable characters confront unfair social forces. Like Sirk's characters, the people in *Far from Heaven* cannot rise above their circumstances. "Sirk's films do have artificial elements—exquisitely rendered lighting, the clothes, the décor, and all of those things we think of as archly fake," Haynes observes. "But they tell incredibly simple stories about domestic crises that concern people who are very ordinary, despite how gorgeously they dress and move. They're not heroic; they don't overcome their problems and change the world. They're really victims of their society, and that makes them shockingly real."

*Far from Heaven* was Haynes's first collaboration with Lachman, who is known for taking on offbeat projects (including *Ken Park*, *The Virgin Suicides*, *Light Sleeper*, and *The Limey*). Lachman's work on *Far from Heaven* earned a special jury prize for cinematography at this year's Venice Film Festival. *AC* recently asked Lachman and Haynes to discuss their collaboration.

**American Cinematographer**: Why did you want to recreate a Douglas Sirk melodrama in 2002?

**Todd Haynes:** I think the best movies are the ones where the limitations of representation are acknowledged, where the filmmakers don't pretend those limitations don't exist. Films aren't real; they're completely constructed. All forms of film language are a choice, and none of it is the truth. With this film, we point out at the start that we're aware of all this. We're not using today's conventions to portray what's "real." What's real is our emotions when we're in the theater. If we don't have feeling for the movie, then the movie isn't good for us. If we do, then it's real and moving and alive.

**AC:** Did you try to work within the limitations that Sirk had?

**TH:** We tried to. We used old-fashioned back-projection for the driving shots. Dissolves and effects were all optical, not digital. We wanted to get the rich color his films had. Some people asked me if we got this look using the newest digital technology, but the answer is absolutely not. Ed did it in camera and with gels, the way it was done on the Sirk films.

**Ed Lachman:** We wanted the audience to enter Sirk's world, so we decided to be true to the means he used to create this world of total artifice. We decided not to use any techniques that Sirk and his cinematographer, Russell Metty [ASC], didn't have. We wanted to create a saturated "Technicolor" look, but we didn't want to use digital methods. I exposed the film stocks one to two stops over the recommended exposure to create a dense negative.

**TH:** I also think the lighting style helps to create a kind of intense foreboding and a sense of danger.

**EL:** Sirk and Metty always had their characters kind of edged and separated from their world by darkness. Again, this reinforced a kind of emotional loneliness. They weren't afraid to use strong chiaroscuro lighting. We used lighting that would generally be associated with film noir—more of a black-and-white style, with hard lights coming from up on a grid.

My gaffer, John DeBlau, started out in the sixties as an electrician, so he was very aware of the style of lighting they used back then. We created a grid system and had lighting cues. When the camera follows actors and they move in and out of certain spaces, we had to have somebody controlling the light from a lighting board so the cameras wouldn't create a shadow. Today we usually use softer, bigger sources; we're not usually going through such hard lights.

I used Big-Eye 10K Fresnels through the windows and 2Ks and 1Ks on the set. I tried to use units they would have used in that time period. They might have had different gels, but we got the same kind of rendition by mixing complementary gels.

Also, Russell Metty did something that I found really interesting: he used light bulbs of different color temperatures in the fixtures. In *All That Heaven Allows*, I think he used daylight bulbs in the practicals and then lit the room to be warm, which would be the opposite of what you'd normally do. For the night scenes in the bedroom, I used what are called "bug lights," the yellow lights used for exterior lighting at night. And then the [ambient] night [light] had a blue-purple or blue-green look, so the tungsten lights, even though they burnt out, emanated a certain warmth that worked in contrast to the blue.

**AC:** So your approach was very different from one you'd take to light a contemporary film?

**EL:** Metty lit Sirk's characters in their environment, rather than lighting the environment and then having people move through it. It was more like portrait lighting. I used more backlight on *Far from Heaven* than I normally would. Those films try to separate people from their environment, from the walls. Perhaps it came out of [working with] black-and-white, but they were much more cognizant of key-, fill- and backlight for every shot.

When someone stands next to a lamp in a contemporary film, we try to show that the light is coming from the lamp, that the lamp is the source. But on this film, we decided to have another light over the lamp, so that when the person is standing next to the lamp, the light is edging them from a source other than the lamp.

**AC:** Sirk's films were shot almost entirely on studio backlots, but you shot *Far from Heaven* on location.
**EL:** We shot it in New Jersey, which was standing in for Hartford, Connecticut. We used towns that were in a kind of time warp, but the difficulty for me was recreating the kind of artifice that Sirk achieved by shooting everything on a soundstage. I brought in lights for the day exteriors; I used [color-corrected] tungsten units, not HMIs, to create the look and feel of the units they used then.

Also, we were lucky that we began shooting in the fall, exactly as the leaves were turning. I think the colors of the leaves had a lot to do with creating a sense of artifice, even though we were on real locations. Plus, a lot of scenes were shot late in the day in overcast conditions, which helped me give the colors of the leaves a richer rendition. Interestingly, if you limit the range of highlight and shadow, colors become more vibrant because the film emulsion is able to hold all the information. If it isn't totally gray outside, those highlights come through richer because the latitude of the film isn't so stretched.

I also used 10K Big-Eyes with gels and some large reflectors to accentuate parts of the frame and bring out specific colors. When I saw how well this worked, I decided to duplicate the effect even when we were shooting in bright sunlight; in those conditions, I used negative fill and a lot of 12-by and 20-by diffusion to simulate an overcast look. The idea was to give the scenes shot on location the feel of scenes shot in the studio.

**AC:** In the old days, cinematographers were less concerned about where the shadows were coming from, even outside. Was that a consideration for you?

**EL:** I never consciously tried to create double shadows outside because of my own aversion to them, but if they were there, I didn't fight them.

*AC:* Did you maintain a particular focal length throughout the film?

**TH:** The Sirk films tend towards wider angles and traveling masters that settle a few different times in a scene. They have elegant compositions that incorporate the architecture into the frame, but the effect is claustrophobic in every sense of the word.

**EL:** I watched Sirk's films closely, and I think Metty used 25mm and 32mm lenses a lot. Even close-ups used nothing longer than 40mm. It created a spatial relationship for the character that placed him or her in the environment. I tried to use the same focal lengths on *Far from Heaven*. We never shot a close-up with a 75mm or a 100mm. I used older Cooke lenses, the Speed Pancros, for a lot of the film. I used Cooke S4s at night because I needed the speed, but I used the older lenses when I could.

**TH:** In a weird way, I think wide-angle lenses are more oppressive than long lenses, because everything is visible. There's no escaping the vantage point of the camera. The character is limited by the architecture and the way other people are placed in the frame. When a character's talking to someone else, he or she is never alone in the frame; it's always an over-the-shoulder shot.

There's one point in the film when we track in past an over-the-shoulder to Julianne Moore alone in the frame. Even then, she's not framed like women are today. Women today have a sturdy dominance of the frame, whereas women in Sirk's films are framed with headroom—they're diminished by the frame. They don't own their own frame.

**EL:** The framing was totally alien to me. In those medium shots, they'd sometimes cut off people's hands or feet. I know they did it for the geography and because they needed certain information from a two-shot or a three-shot, but it was awkward for me to create those types of compositions.

*AC:* How did you approach camera movement?

**EL:** The Sirk films have a lot of moving masters. Maybe it was to complete the day's work—they shot those films in eighteen to twenty-four days! But I noticed that the camera wasn't as much in people's eyelines as it would be today. The camera is often off the eyeline in a two-shot or a single because it was moving, and they thought it had to see both characters. I think this helped the audience look at the characters with a kind of distance, which is a Brechtian idea.

**TH:** Even in big crane shots on Sirk's films, there's always a sense that the character is trapped in a space. [Camera movement] never liberates them.

**EL:** On this film, we used a ninety-foot crane called the Strada. It comes from Oregon, and it was the only one like it on the East Coast. Our key grip, Jimmy McMillan, is the sole distributor for it in the East, and we used it a lot. There's one shot in which Cathy walks around her house, and the crane rises up and gives us a perspective looking down at her. It's all about entrapment—the character is never able to leave the frame.

*AC:* Sirk's dramatic use of color is clearly another element of his style integral to this film.

**TH:** Every scene in his films has a palette in which complementary warm and cool colors interact. If the scene is predominantly cool, then it has warm highlights, and the interaction is subtle and complex in the way that emotions are complex.

**EL:** I used different combinations of advancing and receding colors to suggest the interplay of characters' emotions. I used cool colors against warm colors to establish the characters' conflicts with themselves and their environments.

**TH:** There are two bar scenes, one in a gay bar and the other in a bar on the black side of town. We used different greens and warm colors in both settings, but to very different effect. One scene is supposed to have a slightly disturbing otherworldliness, and the other is the site of one of the film's peak romantic moments; the same basic colors create polar-opposite moods.

**EL:** We wanted to show that the black bar was closer to nature, which is represented by Raymond, the gardener, whereas the gay bar was viewed at that time as an aberration. That pair of scenes is a good example of using the same colors in different chromas and hues to create the characters' emotional context and space. The gay bar is done in secondary colors of lime green against magenta, whereas the black bar is done in primary colors of nature, forest green and the yellow-orange of the sun.

*AC:* What were your discussions like with the other creative departments?
**EL:** I began prep six weeks before we started shooting. After my initial meeting with Todd, I got together with Mark Friedberg, the production designer, and Sandy Powell, the costume designer, to have extensive design and color meetings. Todd, Mark, and I worked on the color palette and the spatial relationships of the designs in the sets. I shot extensive

tests using 3-by-3 panels painted with the colors intended for the set; I experimented with them by mixing different-colored gels to create the Technicolor effect of deep saturation and hue.

What you get back on film doesn't always look the same as it does by eye. I didn't want to achieve the Sirkian Technicolor look with more contemporary methods, such as using digital color-correction or digital opticals, or by printing onto Vision Premier. Our approach was to retain a 1950s sensibility and use the techniques available to filmmakers at that time.

**AC:** Was your approach to color determined entirely by the Sirk films, or did you take some departures?

**EL:** To suggest the emotional arc of our story, we explored different looks for night. *Far from Heaven* takes place over different seasons, and that's a metaphor for what's happening to the characters emotionally. We changed the color of ambient night light as the seasons changed. For the fall scenes in the beginning, the night is a lavender or periwinkle blue. As the story evolves and we get into winter, as Cathy and Frank's relationship deteriorates, night becomes more aquamarine or green-blue—less warm.

**AC:** You seem to have discovered that hewing to the visual conventions of Sirk's films actually gave you the freedom to create something quite emotional.

**TH:** That's true for every element. It's true for the dialogue as well—there are only certain things the characters could say, and only certain gestures they could make. It's about using a limited set of terms to describe a much bigger set of issues. It's almost the opposite of filmmaking today. Today, we have endless ways of telling a story about a guy who shoots another guy. We can whoosh in and out, and the camera can be with the bullet as it goes into somebody's body. The visual vernacular is overwhelming, but the content—what they're trying to say—seems to be shrinking.

# The Many Faces of Bob Dylan:
# An Interview with Todd Haynes

Richard Porton / 2007

From *Cineaste* 33 (2007). Reprinted by permission from *Cineaste Magazine*.

One of the most anticipated films of the fall season, Todd Haynes's *I'm Not There* was enthusiastically received at the Toronto and New York Film Festivals. *Cineaste* met with Haynes in October 2007, shortly before the premiere of *I'm Not There* at the New York Film Festival. The amiable Haynes is a lucid interviewee. Sharing anecdotes and quips, he discussed the significance of the film's multiple Bob Dylans, his collaborations with actors such as Marcus Carl Franklin and Cate Blanchett, as well as cinematographer Ed Lachman, and his critique of Dylan's sixties macho posture.

**Cineaste:** I saw your rarely screened student film, *Assassins*, a few years ago and, since it deals with Rimbaud, I wonder if you've come full circle now with "Arthur Rimbaud" being one of the Dylan personae in *I'm Not There*.

**Todd Haynes:** I watched *Assassins* again recently with Bob Sullivan, who's doing this long piece for the *New York Times*. It has the Rimbaud figure posed against a wall, as in *I'm Not There*—a very Godardian, or student film . . . or should we say "student of culture" [laughs] device? I don't squirm when I see *Assassins*. I find it very moving and analogous to looking back to the kind of music you listened to in college. It's basically a movie about translation—taking the same poem by Rimbaud and hearing four loose translations on top of one another. So you're hearing the nuances of words and interpretations played out as you're listening. So, yes, I guess I haven't really deviated from my earlier creative instincts.

**C:** You obviously didn't want to make a traditional biopic; fact and fiction are clearly scrambled. But you seemed to choose incidents from Dylan's life—e.g., his speech before the Emergency Civil Liberties Committee, shocking his audience by going electric at Newport—that emphasize his chameleon-like nature.

**TH:** It really does give you all of the "greatest hits" that you'd find in a biopic. But one of the major differences is that the biopic, as it's evolved, is a deceitful genre. And we know it. We know that these films blend fact and fiction in every scene, in every bit of dialog. And we're complicit in this deceitfulness when we go to see these movies—it's fun on a certain level. And it's obviously true of any movie that, on one level, there's reality being captured at that moment on screen as well as a huge apparatus that's turning it into entertainment and a commodity or means of escape.

This film also of course blends fact and fiction, but the difference is that you're in on the joke, you're invited to laugh at this process along with me and push the fiction one step further, so there's no question that it's a creative choice to make a point. Take the choice of making "Woody" a little black kid who calls himself "Woody Guthrie." We all know that's not true to life. But you're forced to think about why that choice is being made—as opposed to the traditional biopic where you're not allowed to think about these choices because that would ruin the entire illusion.

**C:** And your choice of pivotal moments in Dylan's life emphasize his elusive nature, his desire to transform himself from, say, a folk balladeer into a less overtly political singer clearly influenced by Beat poetry.

**TH:** To really get inside the process of a person changing and a person rejecting who he was yesterday, you also have to commit entirely to what he's doing at the time and not treat him as a constantly changing, self-disguised figure. You have to treat him as someone who is following a line of thinking through to its ultimate point, a point of critical mass basically where he can't go further or there are too many obstacles in his way, so the next character is forced into being. The speech before the civil libertarians and the interest in Beat culture are two critical examples, particularly for the Jack character because that's the last time we see Dylan as "Jack." And you're right. He's already fully questioning, if not attacking, a political consensus or "line" he's supposed to adopt and is bristling at feeling straitjacketed by that and has to strike out. It's a prelude to the fact that he's going to reemerge shortly as "Jude," somebody whose entire instinct is to rebel against anything deemed doctrinaire.

*C:* I was looking at some YouTube excerpts of *Eat the Document* recently. The Jude sequences truly capture the manic quality of Dylan during that period, a mania probably spurred on by his heavy use of amphetamines.
**TH:** It's unbelievable, right? I love it! It's really distinct. Besides *Eat the Document*, you really see it in the clip at the beginning of Part 2 of the Scorsese documentary. He's standing outside the store and playing with the words. It's like a jazz riff or a scat performance where he's just giggling with word play. The creature quality of the guy is so pronounced. There are moments when the veneer of any famous performer—it doesn't have to be Dylan—cracks and you see the real pulse or essence of the guy and say, "That's what makes him special." You don't get the icon that hangs on the mantle but an inkling of the real creature that people would have found it necessary to contend with at the time.

*C:* You've remarked that he seemed almost androgynous during this period. Do you think that's attributable to what appears to be his extreme vulnerability?
**TH:** The speed was probably a big part of it [laughs], the skinniness of the body and the hyper-ness. And it was also the cut of the clothes— there was a foppishness to the beat, cool hipster style of that time. That was obviously evident in the Warhol Factory world and this influenced how he dressed and behaved. So that was cool, man. Even if you weren't in a totally queer world, you dressed and acted that way if you were going to be on the cutting edge. And he had a total crush on Allen Ginsberg; they had a kind of love affair of the mind. And who knows what else? In the Robert Shelton biography, which was based on extensive interviews with Dylan, he was sort of showing off. But he said all sorts of provocative things about his sexuality, including the claim that he hustled to get money during the first couple of nights he spent in New York City. That was a cool thing to say. And, again, the veracity of the incident is less important than his instinct to boast about it.

*C:* Of all the Dylans, Blanchett seems most attuned to the way his leg was always pumping and in motion.
**TH:** Yeah, every Dylan in the movie has a moment when his leg is bouncing. We thought it would be a good way to link them all together as a single person although the only ones that remain in the final cut belong to Woody's at the beginning and Jude's later. But we had a scene where Claire looks down at Robbie's leg and notices it's bouncing and, at one point, Richard Gere's leg was bouncing as Billy.

*C:* You of course allude to Godard and explicitly quote *Masculine-Feminine* at one point. This seems appropriate since, like Dylan, Godard has always been a shape shifter who's gone through various phases—the New Wave period, the Maoist period, etc.

**TH:** Yes, and I see them both as interesting and symptomatic examples of the male prerogative of the sixties as well as typical of the inconsistencies and contradictions of even the progressive—radical in the case of Godard—male artists of that era. But there was a double standard; women were not treated as intellectuals and were generally regarded differently than men. And there wasn't a hyper self-consciousness or self-critique of that and in fact it was tied up with the way that women were idolized or serenaded by the camera or the guitar. Ultimately, the poetry of their work is what we carry away from their songs and their films. You can critique them intellectually. But the poetry is still what resounds with me; these are true artists, their blind spots and shortcomings notwithstanding. I can still be moved by "Just Like a Woman" or the way women are photographed in Godard films. The power of what they rendered wins out in the end.

*C:* So does Charlotte Gainsbourg function as your Anna Karina or Chantal Goya?

**TH:** She was—and the coolest thing I heard, and I don't want to overstate it because it's not from the source, but at the beginning of yesterday's press conference at the New York Film Festival I was told that Suze Rotolo [Dylan's ex-girlfriend], who was concerned about a film being made about Dylan, saw the film and loved the Gainsbourg character; it made sense to her that she was made French. So that made me feel good. She's the only person I talked to before making the film, almost by accident, and she was worried about how she would be depicted. Even though she might not be explicitly included in the film, you see this character turning him on to avant-garde theater. They're doing a live performance of *The Threepenny Opera* at this coffee shop. She's reading him Rimbaud and he's learning from this woman. So she's in the film even if she isn't literally cited. In any case, when I talked to Rotolo on the phone I told her that I thought she came off extremely well in every biography. Since she's consistently referred to as a positive inspiration on Dylan, I didn't fully understand her concern.

*C:* I'm not sure Joan Baez would necessarily appreciate your version of her—"Alice Fabian."

**TH:** Why? Do you think we make fun of her?

*C:* Well, yes—a bit.

**TH:** Yes, but not for being a forlorn damsel in distress. I think people laugh because she has sort of an attitude—and an ego. She's not some poor, put-upon folksinger. In a way, she's the sturdiest character that Julianne [Moore] has portrayed in any of my films.

*C:* To get back to your comments on the shortcomings of Godard and Dylan as male artists, it comes through quite clearly that you're formulating a critique of this sort of machismo in the sequences featuring Heath Ledger as "Robbie." It seems as if you don't want to appear totally besotted with the Dylan myth.

**TH:** Yes, and I think that's true of Cate's "Jude" as well, who savages his best friend and plays a game of cat and mouse around this character called Coco Rivington played by Michelle Williams. He definitely wants to have it all ways. He's actually less cruel or malicious to journalists, even if the "Mr. Jones" character seems to really get under his skin. But he's not the little petulant brat to the journalists that you get in *Don't Look Back* and of course the Jones character proves a formidable match for him. But this is stuff I read about and it can also be attributable to the drug use of the period. Amphetamines, which were of course legal then, created a lot of paranoia in social circles, not just Dylan's.

*C:* And even in more explicitly political circles such as SDS, there was a condescension towards women, a feeling that they were there to fetch the coffee for the men. This doubtless carried over to more bohemian sets, such as the ones depicted in the Blanchett and Ledger sequences.

**TH:** Yes, absolutely. And I think people recoiled even more strongly since it seemed like such a contradiction coming out of supposedly hip, informed circles.

*C:* How did you construct the "Mr. Jones" character, a composite journalist representing the Establishment attacked in "Ballad of a Thin Man"? He's not a total straw man and makes some perfectly valid points.

**TH:** Right. That's where the real threat of the press resided for Dylan since he was someone who resisted telling the truth! [laughs] Especially at the beginning of his career when he refused to disclose his background or own up to his Jewish, middle-class origins. You're going to get caught eventually and maybe it didn't even take that much to find him out. Once that happened, the *Newsweek* article that came out—in 1964 I think—really demarcated a change in him. The press was justified in challenging the image he wanted to control of himself, what he wanted to give up and what he didn't want to give up. The press isn't always going to play your game by your rules. That's valid and you just have to kinda go with it. It's amazing he didn't get found out earlier. He felt stripped and violated.

But when you're in the public eye and produce so much extraordinary work that's embraced by so many people (and not all extraordinary work receives so much attention), you're naïve to think you can remain in total control of your image. In a way, "Ballad of a Thin Man" is too easy. It's not even a song that I particularly love because it plays into those easy assumptions about us and them and parents vs. the cool generation. And even if its mode of attack is so complex, and ultimately so sexual, I wanted there to be an equal duel between the two characters.

*C:* On the other hand, you get a sense from the movie and the many biographies that even if he's literally a liar he's connected to this bona-fide and intrinsically American tradition of self-invention. This is of course complemented by the fondness for European avant-garde culture we've already mentioned.

**TH:** This is the galvanizing mode of American craft—how we draw from and combine our own indigenous culture with European traditions. It's always in flux and always affected by a wide variety of influences.

*C:* Was it your conception from the outset to have "Woody" played by a young black kid?

**TH:** Yeah, definitely. The ideas to have Woody portrayed as a black kid, and the '66 Dylan portrayed by an actress, were there from the beginning.

*C:* How did you find Marcus Carl Franklin, who plays Woody?

**TH:** Isn't he incredible? If you read the lines, you don't know how he can pull it off. He's really precocious but he makes it sound completely effortless. And that's a tall order for any actor, let alone a kid. Laura Rosenthal, who cast my last few films and is great, found Marcus. He's a working actor and, at that time, perhaps the only thing he had done was *Lackawanna Blues*. But he was mainly an observer of all of the various cameos in that film and wasn't asked to do anything nearly as ambitious. And the fact that he could sing so beautifully was another side benefit and it was certainly not a requirement for the role.

*C:* Christian Bale originally recorded his own songs, didn't he?

**TH:** He recorded them and they were great but Mason Jennings had already recorded those songs. I ended up going with Mason's work. But it was a hard choice since Christian is so unbelievably gifted. The guy can do anything. I encouraged all of the actors to try some singing. I wanted Cate to try but she was already taking guitar and piano lessons and singing would have been just one more thing on top of that.

*C:* My favorite line in the film occurs when Ginsberg and Dylan/Jude are looking up at Jesus on the cross and Jude blurts out, Why don't you play your early stuff? Where did that come from?

**TH:** I went through so much rampant research and source material that it's now difficult to remember what was taken verbatim and what was adjusted or expanded. But I do think this was part of a conversation that Ginsberg and Dylan did have while gazing up at a crucifix in a church in New Jersey. They spent a day together and discussed religion, among other things. Religion was already coming into his discourse and some people will argue that biblical references were a big part of his lyrics from the start. But it was obviously from a much different point of view when he entered his "born again" phase.

*C:* The research must have been staggering. Even if you go into a modestly stocked Barnes and Noble, there's at least a shelf of books on Bob Dylan.

**TH:** I know, it never ends. I've read most of them and spent a lot of time with those volumes; these books are often part of publishers' Christmas lists. Dylan is still, today, the number one Columbia recording artist! That might be slightly misleading since only members of the boomer generation still buy CDs on a large scale. I don't know if he's the number one downloaded musical artist.

*C:* Did you know from the beginning of the project that you'd be working in widescreen?

**TH:** Yes. I was looking forward to a real reason for using widescreen. Some films are in anamorphic and there doesn't appear to be a valid reason—you just get the impression that the director thought it was cool. But it seemed absolutely necessary in this case, particularly for the landscape shots in the Billy the Kid sequences and the glimpses of trains in the beginning.

**C:** And someone like Ed Lachman is so versatile that he's able to go from one visual register to the next with great ease.

**TH:** Yes, incredibly so. It was such a pleasure to work with Ed again. As well as with John De Blau, his gaffer, who keeps threatening to leave the business, although Ed keeps yanking him out of imminent retirement. He was holding a stun gun on the Beatles when they got off the plane here in 1964 and he's been doing amazing things with lighting ever since then.

Ed's a real artist. He has enormous command of the vocabulary of film, as well as vast experience and technique, in his arsenal. But he approaches each film as a new canvas. That's why, if you look at all the films he's shot back to back as a DP, no two look the same. There are no characteristic motifs. Perhaps, since I know his work so well, I could see certain recurrent elements. But they'd be so subtle—and in a way that isn't even true of the work done by the very best DPs.

**C:** Do you know if Dylan has seen the film?

**TH:** No, we haven't heard yet. But I hope he does and lets us know what he thinks.

**C:** I'd think he'd like it since it's somewhat similar to other nonlinear films he was involved with such as *Renaldo and Clara* and *Masked* and *Anonymous*. He's always seemed interested in experimental film.

**TH:** Yeah, and it's not overly reverent—and not just because of the fact that some of the characters critique him. But the tongue-in-cheek, freewheeling approach to telling a story might, I hope, appeal to him. We'll see. [Laughs]

# Conversations: Todd Haynes

Stephanie Zacharek / 2007

From *Salon.com*, November 21, 2007. This article first appeared in *Salon.com*, at http://www.Salon.com. An online version remains in the *Salon* archives. Reprinted with permission.

With *I'm Not There* (the title says it all) Haynes celebrates Dylan's elusiveness, his refusal to fit into the neat little boxes we try to cram him into. I spoke with Haynes in Toronto in September, where he talked about Dylan as a shape-shifter, a mischief-maker, and a perennial source of astonishment.

**Stephanie Zacharek:** The idea of Bob Dylan is so outsized that when people talk about him they generally break him down into periods—*The Freewheelin' Bob Dylan* Bob Dylan, the *Blood on the Tracks* Bob Dylan. And what you've done is broken him into different people, which is such a brilliantly simple idea that I can't believe no one has done it before. How did this idea evolve?

**Todd Haynes:** It was just plain on the page. When you really decide to look at the biographies and the accounts of him in the sixties, if you just read a few of them, they all line up in that idea. And you hear testimony of people saying that they hung out with him in August of '63, and then in November of '63 he was a different person. Like he had shape-shifted right in front of their eyes.

And you can hear it in the records, and you can see it much more clearly in these radical breaks, like when he plugged in electric [at the 1965 Newport Folk Festival], or when he became a born-again Christian, or when he had his motorcycle crash and ducked out into the woods for several years. But it felt like the only way to really get to some core truths about this fascinating guy.

As you know, there are a lot of people who are constantly trying to get to that truth, kind of scrabbling at it. There are people who really burrow into Dylan lyrics, thinking, "All the secrets must be in the songs!" And who's that guy who went through his garbage? Like, "The truth will be found in the garbage!"

**SZ:** But then on the other end of the spectrum you have people like Greil Marcus, who realize that the music is finite, it doesn't change, but the context around it is changing constantly. That's kind of the approach that I saw coming through in your movie. The music is the anchor, and everything else is moving around it.

**TH:** Yeah, the characters are totally committed to their moment, and their ideas, and the world they're in. And the songs they produce are the total and complete products of that commitment. And yet they are completely in dispute with the other selves and the other songs around them. So there's a kind of dialogue going on internally between all of these absolute and total commitments to an idea or a position or a moment.

But the thing is too, what's so crazy about Dylan today is, that he'll go out and take these songs that are absolutely true to their time, perhaps, and to their inspiration and their moment, and he will reinvent the way they sound. So even the associations that you bring to them, and the desire to preserve something and keep something intact, are once again destroyed by him. Because *he* needs to be invigorated and break out of the Bob Dylanness of himself—break out of the fixedness that everybody wants to attach to him.

I also think the thing about identity that's so interesting is that we strive to be affirmed somehow by identifying with something else. We strive to be rewarded—it's like our own completeness is rewarded by identifying with somebody else's completeness. And Dylan is such a strong presence and voice and articulator that a whole generation, and more, have sought that from him.

But he so refuses to give that completeness back. And it only makes the desire for it all the stronger. I posit in the movie that that's what freedom is. Freedom isn't about being fixed, about finding out who you really are and staying put your whole life, finding out that you have a stable self, a completely cohesive being or something. No, we're always shifting and changing and adjusting and altering who we are, all the time. It's a constant state of creation. And Dylan makes that a life practice. He makes that whole idea of rejecting fixity, of rejecting holism, a gorgeous life work. And it's something that throws that whole idea of identity out the window. But at the same time he so frustrates the desire for that [identity] that it keeps regenerating itself.

**SZ:** And, oh man, those Dylan guys!

**TH:** I know, right?

**SZ:** You go to parties with these guys and they stand around and talk about bootlegs all night, and catalog numbers, and what he was doing on January 14, 1963.

**TH:** Oh God! [Laughs]

**SZ:** I always wonder, with all that information in their heads, do they have any room for the music?

**TH:** Exactly. And how opposite that is from him, the person they love and fetishize so completely.

**SZ:** I felt so exhilarated watching this movie, beginning with the credit sequence. Some of Dylan's music is very serious, and people approach it very reverently. But watching that opening, I remembered there's so much joy and pleasure to be had in this music. He plays around a lot. He's always goofing around—not even just wordplay.

**TH:** Oh my God, totally. There's a mischievousness, and there's incredible wit and humor. I don't think he thinks of himself as some intensely serious guy who's really heavy and should be analyzed and contemplated, and so highly regarded every step he takes.

I really think that that humor is just something that has been so evident from the very first record, with the talking blues songs that are so witty and funny, to the most recent recordings, where it's a whole other Dylan. It's this droll old man, with these wisecracks.

**SZ:** Aleeeecia Keeeys . . .

**TH:** [Laughs] Exactly! But that's been consistent through his entire career. To me, that's a testament to his brilliance and his intelligence—his ability to play around and goof around, to be able to throw things up in the air and see how they fall.

Of course, he's had his moments of intense seriousness and righteousness. I kind of put those together in the character of the Christian Bale story, [where there's] this kind of intense commitment to a sort of doctrine, whether it's that of the New Left in the folk era, or that of the born-again Christian in his Christian period, where all of a sudden he had the answer. And he was going to tell us what it was, as beautifully and passionately and emotively as he knew how. In both cases, amazing music came out of those convictions. There was a fixity, there was a righteousness, there was a lack of humor to both those periods of music. But they were very specifically lived. They do not cast oppressive shadows across his career. They were things he went right into, and then right out of.

**SZ:** It struck me that you've chosen one of the most beautiful actresses we've got to play Dylan in the period when he was the most beautiful. I look at him from that period–'65, '66—and he's such a brat. There's a part of me that resists him. I think, Can't you just be a little bit nicer? You don't always have to be an asshole. But, given the chance to sleep with him at the time, I would have. I know millions of people have felt that way. Obviously, you knew you wanted different people to play Dylan. Was there ever a point where you just decided you wanted to cast a beautiful woman?

**TH:** I do think he's beautiful at that period. But I was really more after the strangeness of what he had become as a man at that moment. How he was androgynous, but not in the way David Bowie would be androgynous a few years later, in the early seventies. It was almost more the way Patti Smith was androgynous. He was just this otherworldly creature. This otherness had crept into him completely by that point.

It's not like he is in [the 1965 D. A. Pennebaker documentary] *Don't Look Back*. It had already progressed to this degree where he was really almost disturbingly skinny. And the hair was wildly outsized in proportion to the rest of his body. And his hands would just fly up in these crazy, fingernail-driven gestures while he'd play piano and talk, and how he was just fidgeting. And I was thinking, What would that have possibly been like to an audience in 1965, '66—when the Beatles were still sweet, and little Munchkins, you know? This guy was dangerous and fascinating and erotic but in a completely unsoft way. He also drew off the hostility and animosity that he'd generated by plugging in electric. It fueled him, and he struck back. The vengefulness of his feelings toward his audience, toward American culture and English culture, only seemed to propel him to do even more great songwriting and incredible recordings. That is just a moment that has become so canonized that I feel we've lost the shock value, and the genuine risk that it must have generated.

On a purely superficial level, I just wanted a woman's body to occupy that place, so that this strangeness could come back. But then Cate does something to it that takes it in so many more subtle and beautiful directions—where you can really watch this character exist on-screen, for his humor, for his unpredictability, as a love object, as an artist. Just the lay-ers of subtlety that she brings to it are so profound and so incredible.

I'm so lucky with my actors, I just can't believe it. I was lucky with my creative team as well—they really rose to the occasion and did so much with so little. But the actors did so much with so little, too. Be-cause they're all on-screen for relatively shorter amounts of time than they usually are, as lead actors.

**SZ:** And trusting you, too, because they had no sense how it was going to come together.

**TH:** Yeah, and trusting a really difficult script that reflects the complex-ity of the structure [of the movie], without any of the fun of the fact that it's music-driven and has a rhythm. But you can't really get that on the page when I describe things so ornately, the way I do. The fact that it re-ally came together this beautifully is miraculous.

# Todd Haynes

Noel Murray / 2007

From the *A.V. Club*, November 20, 2007. Reprinted by permission from the editor, the *A.V. Club*.

When word first leaked out that filmmaker Todd Haynes was making a Bob Dylan biopic that would star Heath Ledger, Richard Gere, and Cate Blanchett as the folk-rock icon, people unfamiliar with Haynes scratched their heads, while Haynes fans immediately circled the film's release date on their calendars. Outside of the popular fifties melodrama pastiche *Far from Heaven*—which confused some with its earnestness—Haynes's work has tended to be arty and obscure, and the Dylan film *I'm Not There* is no exception. Yet few contemporary filmmakers have been as daring as Haynes at recombining familiar pop elements to comment on what they mean. In movies like *Poison*, *Safe*, and the glam-rock fantasia *Velvet Goldmine*, Haynes has advanced a style that's simultaneously intellectual and emotional, producing films that are far more engaging than mere plot descriptions make them sound. Haynes recently spoke with the *A.V. Club* about how he's able to convey such a personal vision while working in a medium as collaborative as film.

**The A.V. Club:** Between *I'm Not There*, *Velvet Goldmine*, and *Superstar: The Karen Carpenter Story*, you've made three films about popular music. Is some part of you a frustrated rock critic?

**Todd Haynes:** I don't think I'm a frustrated rock critic; I *love* this music. I didn't want to be a mean old rock critic to these subjects. You always feel like rock critics are frustrated musicians. I envy musicians their ability to live their art and share it with an audience, in the moment. From a filmmaker's standpoint, that's so rare and pure in a way that I'm sure is way more complicated than it appears. The grass is always greener, right? But music—and I'm certainly not alone in this—has had such a powerful effect on my life. Pop music can get inside us and enter our memory bubbles. It provides those true Proustian moments, unlocking sensations, unlocking our imaginations. Music inspired me as a filmmaker. So no, I don't think I'm a frustrated rock critic.

**AVC:** But there's definitely something evaluative in the way you hold up these artists' work: analyzing it, exploring it, and explaining what it means to you personally. Isn't that what a good critic does?

**TH:** No, you're right. Just as I was finishing my last sentence, I was thinking about Greil Marcus, whose work was clearly an inspiration on this film, and who's now my buddy—which still gets me all excited, that we send each other e-mails. But his kind of creative imagination, and the way he's converted his own medium into something you can't even categorize, is something I do feel inspired by, and something I hope I can do as a filmmaker.

**AVC:** The Richard Gere segments of *I'm Not There* are like a Greil Marcus essay brought to life.

**TH:** Yeah, totally. Marcus's *Invisible Republic* was instrumental in the whole period of rebuilding and rediscovery I found myself in during the year 2000. I read the book before I got my hands on the five-disc *Basement Tapes* collection—the original recordings that include the song "I'm Not There." That was a whole free-play time for me, of discovery and excavation of material I'd never heard before. And Greil Marcus's book was part of the spell.

**AVC:** How much of *I'm Not There* is decodable? Does everything in the movie have an explicit meaning to you, or is the movie more loose and intuitive?

**TH:** People tell me that the more they see the film, the more complete and logical it seems, and not so enigmatic. In my mind, it isn't as complex or strange a movie as it might seem to some people. Each of the stories are fairly simple in and of themselves, and all belong to genre traditions or sixties cinema traditions—things we've all seen before. I felt it was important to have very identifiable sub-stories going on. It's the way they interact with each other that feels different, and maybe not completely clear. But I think when you see the movie a second time, it starts to have the weird logic of accumulated life. There's a lot of jumping around and zany stuff in the first half, and a lot about the freedom to experiment and try things out. Then, particularly in the "Jude" story—Cate Blanchett's section—the free play and wildness start to gain a darker shadow, as those experiments take a toll. At the same time, the marriage starts to unravel [in the Heath Ledger section] and Billy the Cowboy has to come down from his hill and confront society [in the Richard Gere section]. So there's a sense of the repercussions that life brings. And I hope you start to feel the whole piece.

**AVC:** At any point in the development of this script, did you consider going linear, with five separate stories laid end-to-end, or was the film always meant to be jumbled up?

**TH:** It *had* to have that feeling of interconnection. Even though the stories introduce themselves linearly and take their exits linearly, I felt the jumble was a part of the songs themselves, and the complexity that Dylan's narrative style explored over his many songwriting periods. But it's also how we experience our own lives. When we look back, nothing's ever in tidy order. Things jut out, and make connections that aren't consistent or informed by conscious logic.

**AVC:** Were there any aspects of Dylan that you wanted to cover but couldn't find a way to squeeze in?

**TH:** Yeah, there were so many. I never intended to take on his changes and stages much past the sixties era, because I felt that all of these root characters had their origins in the sixties—which to me means the early seventies as well, because I think of the whole Vietnam era as one. Dylan checked out of the spotlight he was under in 1967, when he crashed his motorcycle and settled in Woodstock and found a lot of comfort and inspiration in roots music and traditional music. And even though that would later turn into *Nashville Skyline* in '68 and *Pat Garrett & Billy the Kid* in 1973 and traveling like a troupe of gypsies in '76, the inspiration of those original models would continue to inspire his work, right up to now. It's all rooted in the sixties. So I addressed it all in the context of this very dense period of Dylan's life, even though I saw the strands of those characters going on and recombining as his life went on. My research involved collecting *so* much stuff, and fitting it into each of the characters, almost like they were these containers, or envelopes. And then it was just about reducing, distilling, getting rid of redundancies, and trying to find the best example of this idea or that idea. The whole process was basically about letting go of a lot of stuff.

**AVC:** Having had some limited interaction with Dylan, do you get the sense that there's a "knowable Dylan" that those close to him encounter? A Dylan that's true to who he actually is?

**TH:** Well, I'm not close to Dylan. I've never met him. I've never spoken to him. I'm only a person he gave everything to, for some reason I'll never completely understand, and still feel shocked by. I don't even know if he's seen the film. He's had a DVD of it with him on tour for the last few weeks, but that's the last I heard. So I don't have any more direct first-hand evidence than anyone else. But I almost think that people make too much of this "unknowable guy." I think you find him wherever he is performing, and wherever he is committed to what he's doing. And we happen to have most of those performances recorded. With every studio release, he's made a series of live performances, and he lives and dies in the moment that he's performing his music. So you have these unbelievable, concrete examples of who he is at all of these different stages. How much more can you ask of somebody than that? Especially considering how much of it there is.

**AVC:** You've spent a lot of time around actors. Do you have a similar sense with them, that they're only "who they are" in moments of performance?

**TH:** Absolutely. It's a really profound question, especially given the context of what I was just talking about with Dylan. I'll never be able to totally explain or understand how actors are able to project this moment of absolute relaxation and spontaneity, and to do it with so much technical rigidity and reliability. Musicians have to hit the right chords and pluck the right strings and sing the right lyrics, and that's a form of technical restriction as well, so I guess there's always "technique" at the heart of any creative process. But there's also always an element of surprise and something raw, and I feel like I'm at the furthest end of that ebb. Actors are amazing to me that way, because they really do have to create something alive, which then gets recorded and captured. And they all arrive at it in a different way.

**AVC:** Have you acted much, beyond cameo appearances here and there?

**TH:** Well, I liked to act in plays when I was a kid, and then in college. But that's the last time I *really* acted. I always loved it. But my interests were more in looking at the whole, rather than getting completely swallowed up in a single part of the whole.

**AVC:** How do you direct actors in a movie like *I'm Not There*, where a lot of the characters are symbolic? Do they still deal with their characters like they were real people, with real motivations?

**TH:** Definitely. You break it down to its components and play it out, for real, in real time. And that went for every aspect, including the stylized language the actors had to deliver. In a lot of my films, from *Velvet Goldmine* to *Far from Heaven*, there's often been some stylization to the language, but it still boils down to something absolutely specific and concrete. Flesh and blood. For *I'm Not There*, all the actors got little packages of research, with films, and recordings of Dylan speaking, and collections of the music that inspired their stories, and images I'd collected. That all went into what they did, to provoke something unplanned and untutored. They all used it. It was remarkable to see how that material would keep coming back out, in ways the actors probably couldn't even explain.

**AVC:** Were you surprised by the success of *Far from Heaven*? You've never been a commercial filmmaker, but that film did well at the box office, and was nominated for awards.

**TH:** Of course. I thought it was as big a risk as any of my films, because it was such an outmoded, degraded genre. And the style of acting and the artificial look of the film, we tried to preserve from Douglas Sirk and fifties cinema. They weren't things I tried to soften or minimize for a contemporary audience. I think *Far from Heaven* is the film where I've come closest to making it work like a lot of my favorite movies work. Like the way Hitchcock films work, in an almost diagrammatic way, where you "get" them immediately and they're communicable to a five-year-old child and an eighty-year-old adult. But then you look deeper, and there are all of these other things that come through that only reinforce what the film looked like from a distance. It's hard to describe, but I think it's the truth about popular art, that it has to work toward emotional clarity, and there are all these layers that you can peel off, but ultimately, it also has to function in an immediate way. But I don't think all my films do that, or even try to.

**AVC:** Were you tempted, having had that kind of success with *Far from Heaven*, not to repeat yourself necessarily, but to make another film that could be enjoyed conventionally as well as on those other levels?

**TH:** Well, I think all my films can be *enjoyed*. In fact, they've often surprised me with how they're received. A film that had the hardest time, at least initially, was *Velvet Goldmine*, and it's the film that seems to mean the most to a lot of teenagers and young people, who are just obsessed with that movie. They're exactly who I was thinking about when I made *Velvet Goldmine*, but it just didn't get to them the first time around. Now we have all these different ways for movies to get to people. People can live with them over time and pass them around like special secrets. The movies all live their own weird lives, which is so cool. So no, I didn't feel the need to repeat anything.

**AVC:** If you could have any director's career other than your own, whose would it be?
**TH:** Meaning their actual body of work?

**AVC:** Their body of work or their skill set. What they're capable of, living or dead—which director would you want to be if you weren't you?
**TH:** I immediately always want to say Rainer Werner Fassbinder, because of his body of work and his amazing ability to materialize popular art out of brutally honest social critique and historical critique. The way that work comes out almost as natural as breathing . . . that's just incredible. The way he lived his life, with the terrible afflictions and abuses that are almost movies unto themselves, that isn't necessarily what I would want. But his career blows my mind.

# It Ain't Me Babe

Matt Prigge / 2007

From *Philadelphia Weekly*, November 21, 2007. Reprinted by permission from Matt Prigge, *Philadelphia Weekly*.

The *New York Times Magazine* ran a cover story early last month on the new Bob Dylan biopic *I'm Not There*. The story was titled: "This Is Not a Bob Dylan Movie." When asked if he agrees with the title, Todd Haynes—the film's friendly, well-spoken director, in town for a siege of interviews—replies with a simple, "No."

Well, of course he doesn't . . . right? If it sounds crazy to even consider that a movie concerning Bob Dylan might not actually be "about" him, then you might not know much about *I'm Not There*.

In one sense Robert Sullivan, who wrote the article, is right. The name Bob Dylan appears only in the opening credits, where he's billed as "inspiring" the film. Dylan himself appears in concert footage in the final moment while covers of his songs litter the soundtrack.

But otherwise we jump around six main characters with names like Billy, Jude, John, and Woody Guthrie, played by people like Richard Gere, Cate Blanchett, Christian Bale, and Marcus Carl Franklin—a young black kid playing a train-hopping guitarist. Is it really so out-there for Sullivan to assert that "Todd Haynes's film about Dylan is as much about Todd Haynes as it is about Dylan"?

"I think it's about as close to a Bob Dylan movie as you can get," Haynes explains. "That's not to say there's only a singular Bob Dylan movie that's out there. I think *Don't Look Back* is a Bob Dylan movie. *Renaldo and Clara*, love it or hate it, is a Bob Dylan movie. And maybe *A Face in the Crowd* is a Bob Dylan movie."

That Haynes lumps in *A Face in the Crowd*, Elia Kazan's 1957 drama with Andy Griffith as a folkie turned demagogue, with D. A. Pennebaker's documentary on Dylan's 1965 tour and Dylan's own notorious four-hour surrealist drama says a lot about the discursive, restless style of *I'm*

*Not There.* (Haynes says *Crowd* wound up figuring heavily in constructing the Franklin segment.)

"I knew a conventional, singular narrative would never suffice to tell Dylan's story, so that was something I excluded from my options right away," Haynes explains.

The result? A film even weirder than you've heard. There's virtually no narrative or dramatic throughline. References—from not just Dylanology but culture, music, and films—fly fast and hard. And all the while Haynes intercuts madly between the six sections.

When asked if there was ever a temptation to make the film easier for the audience, particularly Dylan neophytes, Haynes says no.

"I would say the best way to experience the film is how you experience a Dylan song. There are narrative elements that you pick up, but that's not really why you're listening." Still, Haynes claims he didn't try to "mimic" a Dylan song, though he "took to heart the formal experiments he made in his music."

One of these results in the intercutting style. "There came a point when he became consciously interested in time travel within a single song or a single record," says Haynes. "That was most clearly articulated during the *Blood on the Tracks* era, when he was studying with a painter who proposed this idea of art as a single canvas that could contain multiple narratives.

"I think when we look back on our lives, we realize we do occupy certain selves and attitudes and personas at different times," Haynes notes. "Life doesn't come in a nice narrative package with a culmination of meaning. It comes in a jumble."

But with Dylan it was a little different. "This is someone who kept producing material—massive amounts of it with every step he took. So there are embodiments of who he was left over. There's evidence that he was a protest singer in 1964. But that's not him anymore. That's a curious out-of-body experience that artists have to contend with as they move forward—all the echoes of what they left behind."

Though he's best known for 2002's *Far from Heaven*, Haynes, forty-six, has a history with radical musical biopics. His 1987 short *Superstar: The Karen Carpenter Story* tells the anorexic pop star's story with an all–Barbie doll cast. In 1990 *Superstar* was hit with a copyright infringement suit by the Carpenter family over the use of their songs, though Haynes says he hasn't checked in with them in nearly a decade.

"I think maybe it's time to try again," he says.

*Velvet Goldmine* came in 1998, a phantasmagoric look at glam centered around a Bowie-esque star (Jonathan Rhys Meyers). Bowie himself refused to let his music be used in the film.

For *I'm Not There*, Haynes did clear the use of Dylan's songs, but says he's never spoken with him directly. Dylan currently has the film's DVD on his tour bus but has yet to report back with a reaction. Haynes also has yet to hear from most of the Dylanologists, though brags that Greil Marcus, author of the beloved *Invisible Republic*, about *The Basement Tapes*, is a big supporter.

Says Haynes, "With Dylan in particular, there are tons of literate, poetic, philosophical or political passages in the music and the phrases that jump right out and speak to your life. But they're not necessarily coherent in the way a story is.

"I don't understand all the references in his lyrics," Haynes says. "But that doesn't keep me from feeling like I can fully partake of his music."

# From Underground to Multiplex:
# An Interview with Todd Haynes

Scott MacDonald / 2008

From *Film Quarterly* 63, no. 3 (2009). Reprinted by permission from the University of California Press.

Todd Haynes's roots are avant-garde and independent. *Superstar: The Karen Carpenter Story* (1987), which is no longer available because of legal action (as Haynes explains in the interview), uses Barbie dolls as characters in a highly experimental biopic, while his debut feature, *Poison* (1991), was inspired by Jean Genet.

More recently, Haynes has had a successful commercial career. His excellent update of Douglas Sirk weepies, *Far from Heaven* (2002), is especially notable. It earned Julianne Moore an Academy Award nomination for best actress and Haynes a nomination for best screenplay, and won Golden Globes for Haynes (screenplay), Moore (actress), Dennis Quaid (supporting actor), and Elmer Bernstein (original score).

Haynes is not, however, moving linearly from underground to mainstream. Another unconventional biopic, *I'm Not There* (2007), has much in common with avant-garde films, fracturing narrative and using other disorienting devices in its kaleidoscopic presentation of Bob Dylan's life and music. *I'm Not There* brings an avant-garde sensibility to bear on a commercial project as successfully as any recent film I know.

To what extent does Haynes regard his work as part of the avant-garde tradition? On October 15, 2008, I hosted an on-stage conversation at Oregon's Portland Art Museum, where I raised this question. In order to provide reference points for our discussion, I showed excerpts from *Superstar, Poison, Dottie Gets Spanked* (1993), and *Velvet Goldmine* (1998). After I had transcribed and edited the interview, I went back to Haynes for his further comments and, for the purposes of publication, asked follow-up questions about *I'm Not There*.

My thanks to Autumn Campbell and Jeremy Rossen, directors of the Portland microcinema, Cinema Project; they organized the event, which was the kick-off for "Expanded Frames," a five-day celebration of Cinema Project's fifth anniversary. The Haynes event was co-sponsored by the Northwest Film Center.

**Scott MacDonald:** I've been interested in talking with you about your awareness of avant-garde cinema for several years. My interest was piqued once again when I saw *I'm Not There* in a packed downtown Boston theater last fall. Early in the film a few people left—something that happens at most any screening of avant-garde films attended by more than avant-garde aficionados—but after that, as far as I could see, nobody left. And at the end, when the credits were rolling, I looked around and everybody was still sitting there, talking. I thought, "Wow! Todd Haynes has made an avant-garde feature film that has kept nearly this entire audience in their seats."

You earned a B.A. from Brown and then studied at Bard College, which has long been identified with avant-garde filmmaking. . . .

**Todd Haynes:** I never got a degree from Bard; I was there only briefly, during the first summer of their three-year MFA program offered at the Milton Avery Graduate School of the Arts, a cool MFA program that you can do in summers. I had the concept and the script for *Superstar* with me when I arrived at Bard.

My sense of being a filmmaker was modeled on the people I had met at Brown, where I had been an undergraduate, people like Leslie Thornton, an experimental filmmaker I greatly admired, who joined the staff during my last two years there. At the time, she was just beginning her amazing collection of "Peggy and Fred" films. Leslie, along with my film theory mentors Michael Silverman and Mary Ann Doane, advised and participated in my thesis film, *Assassins: A Film Concerning Rimbaud* [1985].

I looked at the work of the filmmakers at Brown and at the work of filmmakers I studied there, and felt sure that my sensibility and my interests were never going to put me into mainstream filmmaking. I figured I should get a degree and teach. That's what they had done, and they seemed able to balance their own filmmaking with their academic lives. So with that plan in mind, I went to Bard, where it was just me and one other filmmaker (Marcelle Pecot); at that point, the Bard program was mostly painters and sculptors.

I spent that summer in the sweaty, mosquito-ridden heat of

Annandale-on-Hudson making the sets and props for *Superstar*. At the very end of the summer I got my friends together and we shot the film there. Then I moved to New York and cut *Superstar* in my Brooklyn apartment that fall.

I was soon involved in a new venture, with my friend Barry Ellsworth, who I went to college with, and Christine Vachon, who has been the producer of all my feature films. Barry had received an endowment and wanted to form a nonprofit organization that helped emerging filmmakers, and together the three of us started Apparatus Productions in 1987–88. Apparatus was a reaction to what seemed to us to be happening around independent/experimental film at this time.

I had been exposed to classic experimental film, best exemplified by Stan Brakhage—that is, a basically non-narrative, abstract, and personal cinema—in high school and in college. A very influential high-school teacher and poet named Christina Adams first exposed me to films by Brakhage, Michael Snow, Ken Jacobs, James Benning, and others.

But during my college years, during the early 1980s, there started to be something of a shift in the kinds of subject matter and the approaches that were acceptable and considered interesting to experimental filmmakers. I remember Sally Potter's *Thriller* [1979] as a turning point (Sally went on to make *Orlando* [1992]); and I remember *Riddles of the Sphinx* [1977] by Laura Mulvey and Peter Wollen—feature-length, but experimental in every other way. We studied *Riddles*, and both Peter and Laura came to Brown at various times to discuss their work.

These films were beginning to work with commercial genres and to make direct references to popular culture using the experimental vernacular. Of course, to describe this moment as a shift is to overlook whole traditions of experimental film that preceded Potter and Mulvey-Wollen, including Warhol and the Kuchar brothers—and others who, earlier on, were also interested in referencing Hollywood and genre filmmaking. But in the late 1970s and early '80s this was happening in a specific way that interested me, and Christine and Barry, tremendously.

We three began to think of ourselves as experimental narrative filmmakers, and what was of particular interest to us, as Apparatus Productions, was a difference in the way in which experimental film was produced before and after the shift I've described. If you were in the tradition of Brakhage, you were making your films alone, experimenting on an individual level with the nature of image and cinematic time. You didn't need any help; you could make your films by yourself. But as soon as you were employing references to genre and commercial style in your work, you needed people to help you, and we figured that that's where our organization could come in.

We thought that people just coming out of college and moving to New York City had no chance of getting grants from the New York State Council on the Arts or the National Endowment for the Arts, and that Apparatus would provide production support and financing to emerging experimental narrative filmmakers during that delicate transition period. Christine had to teach Barry and me the hierarchy of film production practice, and we learned and experimented with this new way of working in the films that we were helping to get made. Apparatus was never going to be about our own work. We did have three years of some success in getting interesting work produced [Apparatus helped produce seven films: *Cause and Effect* (Susan Delson, 1988), *Muddy Hands* (Even Dunsky, 1988), *American Lunch* (Julian Dillon, 1988), *He Was Once* (Mary Hestand, 1989), *La Divina* (M. Brooke Dammkoehler, 1989), *Oreos with Attitude* (Larry Carty, 1990), and *Anemone Me* (Suzan-Lori Parks and Bruce Hainley, 1990)].

As *Superstar* started to take off and gain attention, our experience with Apparatus, with the hands-on, New York–based practice of working with small crews and local craftsmen and creative people, led to our collaborating on my first feature film, *Poison*.

**SM:** I think you're correct that there was a kind of pivot at the end of the 1970s and during the early '80s, from filmmakers whose films looked more or less the same from beginning to end, or expressed a certain very particular kind of structure from beginning to end, to films that started to mix things up. *Superstar* was made almost simultaneously with Su Friedrich's *Damned If You Don't* [1987] and a year or so before Marlon Riggs's *Tongues Untied* [1989], and each of these films combined approaches common to both documentary and fiction, plus performance, poetic experiment, found footage . . . into a single work.

**TH:** Yes, there was less focusing on formal questions and the material status of the image, and more commentary about cultural and political issues and on the debates that were occurring around us.

**SM:** There was also a striving for a larger audience; by the late 1970s it was clear that certain forms of avant-garde film were probably not going to have anything like a substantial audience, at least not any time soon.
**TH:** I guess that was true. But though *Superstar* certainly generated a

bigger audience than most experimental films, a larger audience wasn't something that I set out for, at least as I recall.

In my mind, *Superstar* was an experimental film, but unlike early films by Su Friedrich and Abigail Child and Marlon Riggs, and others—and maybe this is *not* true for all those filmmakers; I'm not sure—it wasn't immediately accepted into the venues for experimental film.

**SM:** I understand that the Collective for Living Cinema wouldn't show *Superstar*.

**TH:** The collective refused to show it. The Whitney and MoMA people didn't want to show it. Millennium refused to show it. We had to rent Millennium's theater ourselves for something like seventy bucks a night (which at that point felt like a lot), to show *Superstar* and *Assassins*. Karen Cooper at Film Forum loved *Superstar* and *wanted* to show it, but was worried about the legal issues.

With *Superstar* we had three years of freedom before the lawsuits came. And I knew they were coming; I knew our days were numbered. *Superstar* did have a robust life, mostly due to the good fortune of getting a *Village Voice* review: [J.] Hoberman singled it out in a lead review, which helped art museums and galleries and art centers and colleges around the country start booking it.

*Superstar* did show at the New Museum in a theme series on video (during that first year it was almost always shown as a video film in museums and galleries) and at clubs. It was part of "Karen Carpenter Night" at the Pyramid Club, following fantastic drag performances of Karen Carpenter songs. Pyramid was *packed* with people just standing around talking, and I was afraid that they wouldn't stop talking to watch the film, but once the film started, everybody was frozen watching it and drinking their beer—amazing. That was one of my all-time favorite screenings.

So, as experimental film has always done, *Superstar* occupied a hybrid position between the more traditional experimental film venues, which had rejected it, and other, broader arts and semi-theatrical venues. Then eventually it became a kind of coveted bootleg object that circulated illicitly. As a result of this circulation of the prints and video copies, the *texture* of the film changed, and *Superstar* bore the marks of that illicit circulation. One writer said that the disappearing image on the surface of the bootleg *Superstar* tapes was like the disappearing Karen Carpenter body in the movie [Lucas Hilderbrand, "Grainy Days and Mondays: *Superstar* and Bootleg Aesthetics," *Camera Obscura* 57 (2004)].

**SM:** Of course, the most unusual aspect of *Superstar* is the use of the Barbie dolls to do the leading roles. When I try to think of a cinematic predecessor to this approach, the only film I can think of is *A Town Called Tempest* [1963], an 8mm film by George and Mike Kuchar. It's about a tornado coming through a midwestern town, and as I remember (the film is no longer in circulation), some of the characters are little plastic people. What was fascinating about that film was that even though George and Mike were using obviously primitive means, the brothers knew enough about genre film to effectively mimic Hollywood visual grammar. On some crazy level, the sequence works.

Did you know their work before you began making films?

**TH:** I can't remember when I first saw Kuchar brothers' films. It's very likely that I did see some before making *Superstar*, but I was much more conscious of Laurie Simmons. She's a visual artist who was using dolls at the time. I'm sure there are others who preceded her, but she became known for that work and for her beautiful photographs of dolls. I don't know if she ever made films.

I've never felt that anything I've done was particularly original. My work is about appropriating and responding to cultural influences and stimuli and ideas, and recombining those elements in ways that make you think about them or see them differently.

The whole *Superstar* project started innocently and goofily, when, one day, Cynthia Schneider, my best pal from Brown, said, "Let's make a movie together!" *She* said, "Let's have it be with pets!" and *I* said, "No, let's have it be with dolls!" I had studied narrative theory in college and was very interested in doing a genre piece where I would carefully follow all the rules of narrative structure, but use dolls instead of live actors. Would an audience feel the same emotional connections with the story if it was performed with dolls, as they feel when it's Meryl Streep up there? I wanted to see if the form has as much to do with how we connect with a film, as the content does.

But at first, we didn't have a content. We just knew that we weren't going to work with real people. One day I was sitting at Café Dante in the West Village, where they were playing 1970s retro music, and I heard Karen Carpenter singing "every sha-na-na-na, every woewoewoe." Karen had died just three or four years earlier, and hearing that music and that voice, after the death and after the new insight into this popular figure the nature of her death had given us, was suddenly very powerful.

She had become a figure of ridicule, even cruel ridicule, in some circles (I'll never forget that Grammy Awards where Bette Midler introduced

Karen Carpenter and *had* to say some nasty thing about her). Earlier you'd make fun of that deep, lilting voice and think, "Ah, she's just a crock; what does *she* know about pain and suffering!" But now, when I listened to it again, the song had other levels. I called Cynthia, and I was like, "We gotta do the Karen Carpenter Story!" and she was like, "Okay, okay, we'll use dolls!"

**SM:** Were you sued first by the music people or by the Barbie people?

**TH:** The Barbie people were the first to emerge. They sniffed around at what we were doing, even to the degree that I received in the mail copies of their patents on the Barbie doll body. The patents were all for separate body parts! There was a page for just the torso; turn the page, an arm; turn the page, another arm—demonstrating, as if there were any question, their legal jurisdiction over Barbie's body, which, of course, echoes what the film is about!

We talked to a lawyer about how to defuse the issue, because Mattel had a long history of going after products that were mimicking their originals. Many of the dolls that we used in *Superstar* came from thrift stores and weren't Mattel products, but knock-offs, so there was already a blur to the actual Mattel product that was being used. Mattel backed off quickly; I think they saw that the music rights were a more severe legal obstruction heading my way fast, one that would also take care of their problem just fine. And it did.

**SM:** The use of montages, of course, is common to commercial film as well as avant-garde film, but the montages in Superstar remind me of avant-garde work, including certain Brakhage films and some of Bruce Conner's work, especially *Report* [various versions, 1963–67], his film about the assassination of JFK.

**TH:** I've seen some of Bruce Conner's films, but I'm not certain I was thinking about his work in particular at that time, though you're right, the montage work in that film comes out of experimental traditions. It *also* comes out of narrative and genre traditions, although I think I was taking it to some extremes: I use references that explode out of, or can't be contained within, a narrative explanation of Karen Carpenter's bad emotional state.

**SM:** That's what reminds me of *Report*: at the end of that film Conner moves away from the death of Kennedy into a kind of free-form montage of the commercial context within which all political events play out in this country.

How fully were you trying to be funny in *Superstar*? Aside from the Barbie dolls, it comes across as a relatively conventional documentary about a serious subject.

**TH:** At the time, there was always a question about the film's attitude toward Karen Carpenter. Was I being a little too ironic or campy or something like that. Of course, as soon as you deal with dolls as a vehicle for telling a story or with a character as overdetermined as Karen Carpenter—particularly if you're a gay filmmaker, identified with traditions of camp sensibility and humor—you're going to create those questions. And they were fair questions I thought. But in fact, Cynthia and I had an almost childishly earnest desire to understand this character *against* the grain of the criticism and the dismissal of her as a serious subject or singer. We thought of ourselves as trying to rescue Karen Carpenter from her family.

*Superstar* was also our way of trying to understand anorexic behavior, which, as we learned, often occurs within very controlling families, and in Karen Carpenter's case, was compounded by the extraordinary pressures on a young girl who was suddenly in the spotlight and whose every change in body fat was being discussed worldwide. Her desire to take back control over her life was something that we understood and tried to create some sympathy for.

**SM:** In the *Superstar* montages there are images of spanking. Spanking is a major motif in your work for a while, and I'm wondering what spanking means to you. The way it's positioned in the films leads me to think that, among other things, you see spanking as a re-direction of repressed sexual energy, maybe repressed male, gay sexual energy. Am I stretching here or . . .

**TH:** It has different meanings in the different films, though I don't think spanking has recurred all that often. It occurs in *Superstar*, and, of course, in *Dottie Gets Spanked* [1993]. . . .

**SM:** And in *Poison* and also in Mary Hestand's *He Was Once*, on Apparatus film that you performed in. . . .

**TH:** I guess it does recur quite a bit! There's a fantastic article by Freud called "A Child Is Being Beaten." It looks at mostly female subjects who told him about their fantasies or memories of witnessing little boys being spanked in the schoolyard, and how this event would create tremendous pleasure, sexual and otherwise, for them.

**SM:** You've included that idea in *Dottie Gets Spanked*; the sister clearly enjoys seeing a boy getting spanked.

**TH:** Absolutely. What I found so interesting, and useful in terms of anorexic behavior, is the tremendous pleasure some female subjects have in orchestrating a sadomasochistic spectacle for themselves, where they are basically controlling all aspects of the situation. Freud sees it as a clitoral stage where girls are empowered, and feel a freedom of expression and agency that they don't feel later when they're vaginally oriented.

I remember reading accounts that made clear that to an anorexic, control over the body brings great pleasure and is, in fact, part of the addiction. Anorexics would say, "I hear a voice telling me, don't eat, don't eat, and another voice, telling me, okay, okay, I won't." This suggests the double role of being victim and punisher at the same time: a miniature sadomasochistic drama is going on in the anorexic subject's head.

In *Superstar* the only time you see human hands is when hands make one doll spank another. There I was referring to the way kids play with dolls and play out their fantasies, sexual and otherwise. The spanking in *Dottie* is more personal, more weirdly rooted in my early childhood memories and in a dream that I had as a child, which is actually replicated in the film.

At one point I was back at my parents' house. They'd put aside a box of my childhood drawings for me, and as I was sorting through the images, I was reminded of how obsessed I was as a kid with Lucy, and Elizabeth Montgomery, and the Flying Nun and *Alice in Wonderland* and *Cinderella*—all that girl stuff. It started with *Mary Poppins* [1964], the first film I remember seeing. I would draw these women endlessly, and I especially remember loving to draw the eyeliner and the big nails and the lipstick; in my drawings the women all look like whores!

I grew up in Los Angeles, and I think my parents met Lucille Ball on a vacation somewhere, so I was able to go to her show as a kid. I visited during the run of *Here's Lucy* [1968–74]. As in *Dottie Gets Spanked*, I made her a book and handed it to her when we visited the set. We all know that the television "Lucy" she portrayed was a sort of child woman, so it was phenomenal to watch the real-life Lucille Ball controlling the entire production like a general. There was a sort of mock director standing to the side, but Lucille was clearly in charge of everything, and then suddenly she'd be back in character, crying "Waaaaaaa!"—the child woman again.

That duality was fascinating to me, partly because it mirrored a different duality in my life and my fantasy world.

At a certain point, PBS, through ITVS, was trying to get independent filmmakers and experimental filmmakers involved in television; they wanted to produce short films dealing with issues of family. I decided to work with my childhood fascination with Lucy and to focus on the spanking issue—even though my parents didn't believe in spanking.

**SM:** That's talked about in the film.

**TH:** Right, because the boy *doesn't* get spanked, and he notices that other kids *do*, and so it creates curiosity and desire around spanking.

Another part of this project came from that dream I had as a child. I must have been three or four—very young; the dream ended with a spanking that I received from the strongest man in my world: my Uncle Barry. At the time, my grandmother was studying art, and she had all these instructional books around that featured the musculature of the human body. In the dream, at the point of the spanking, I experienced a flood of images; I saw a rapid-fire montage of these drawings and experienced a kind of orgasm.

**SM:** This orgasmic moment expressed itself as a montage?

**TH:** A cinematic montage. Right out of Bruce Conner!

I find spanking a fantastic theatrical ritual in the family setting. There's something interesting about *desiring* spanking, *desiring* subjugation: it unseats the power dynamic, because you're not supposed to want to be spanked. To desire spanking is to undermine the father's control.

What's so interesting about *He Was Once*, Mary Hestand's evocation of the *Davey and Goliath Show*, is that it's almost *Superstar* in reverse. Mary wanted to have actors playing dolls, and so we shot the whole thing moving in half-speed motion, and under-cranked the camera so that our movements seemed to be in normal speed. We did a slow-motion pantomime to the prerecorded dialogue. I love that *He Was Once* ends with the *father* being spanked, being completely undermined in the power dynamic.

**SM:** At one point in the dream sequence from *Dottie Gets Spanked*, the father is standing behind the mother who is standing behind the boy who is sitting in front of the TV set watching Dottie. This brings back something in my own life. When I was the boy's age, my favorite television personality was Liberace, which made my parents nervous. I didn't get spanked for it and they didn't tell me to turn the show off, but when I was enjoying Liberace, I could always feel them behind me, worrying about what this might mean, or worrying whether they should be worried, and I always felt defiant of their concern.

**TH:** It's amazing how kids understand shame before they even understand the word! They *feel* it, and that's a lot of what *Dottie* is about. In the scene that directly follows the sequence you just mentioned, the boy carefully folds up his drawing of Dottie getting spanked, wraps it in tinfoil, and buries it in his backyard, and the film ends. It's as if he's preserving something for the future.

**SM:** You were born in 1961. I'm surprised of how well you seem to know the 1950s, and what it was like for my generation growing up, in *Dottie* and in *Far from Heaven*.

**TH:** Well, I learned about the 1950s from the *films* of the period. People who lived through the 1950s have told me, after seeing *Far from Heaven*, "It was *exactly* like that!" During the production of *Far from Heaven* I was very rigid about the idea that we were recreating a Hollywood sound stage experience from the time. In fact, when we were looking for extras, many of the people we considered looked too much like *real* people from the 1950s, not like the sort of patrician, handsome, blonde, *movie* people that you see in the background of those Sirk films. So everything about *Far from Heaven* was filtered through a very self-conscious, *cinematic* depiction of the period. It says a lot about the 1950s if my movie connects you to real memories and experiences.

**SM:** I remember going to see Sirk's *Imitation of Life* [1959] at the huge Fox Theater in St. Louis. The climactic scene is the mother's funeral, where the daughter returns full of regret that she disowned her mother for so long, and throws herself on the coffin. During this scene, the theater was in a paroxysm of crying, but for my friend and me, the scene seemed utterly preposterous, ridiculously over the top. Actually, my friend Jerry burst into laughter and I thought we might have to fight our way out of the theater! But as a result, I never took Sirk seriously, at least until you brought him back to me with *Far from Heaven*. For me your film is actually New Improved Sirk, Sirk made credible.

When you were first seeing Sirk, did you take the films seriously?

**TH:** I was first presented with Sirk in an entirely different context, an already elevated context—in college. I didn't have the experience of seeing the films when they first came out, or even of watching Sirk on late-night television like so many people did. My first experiences with Sirk were positioned as something of intellectual value—but I know exactly what you mean; even understanding the intellectual defense of Sirk, his films are difficult to watch. And for me *Imitation of Life* is one of the more accessible Sirk films emotionally.

There is something about melodrama that is unsatisfying, over-determined, and under-explained. The characters in melodrama do not come to knowledge about their predicament; they are pushed along by the forces and mores of their societies, and ultimately they crumble under the pressure, against their own desires. You're supposed to want them to comply, because you know that that's the way movies get resolved, but you also feel, "No! Wait a minute! I thought you were in *love* with this person!" For many people this is exactly what makes melodrama radical: melodramatic films are not about people who are free agents, who are in control of their destiny; they're not like the protagonists of Westerns or gangster films, more male-associated genres where men have a kind of infinite freedom. Often the female subjects in melodramas are trapped, and so, even though they live in these hyper-artificial-looking environments, the characters are more like real people, who don't, in the end, have the strength to be heroes.

**SM:** The characters in *Far from Heaven* do seem to learn and they do seem to change their lives.

**TH:** They do and they don't. All three of the central characters are suffering in one way or another. I felt that it was really interesting to compare different levels of oppression in a particularly codified, repressed era. And ironically it's the gay man, Frank Whitaker [Dennis Quaid], who has the most freedom, and who gets closest to satisfying his desires, through hiding. He's not as intensely visible as Raymond the gardener [Dennis Haysbert], who has to move. But Cathy [Julianne Moore] is at the bottom of the hierarchy; she gives up the love object, loses the husband, and is left with the responsibility for the children.

As I was getting ready to shoot *Far from Heaven*, I thought, "How the hell are these actors going to deal with these roles?" and I remember Julianne Moore saying that Cathy was easy to perform because everything about her *is* on the surface; she really has no deeper psychological dimension. There's no Aristotelian conflict in these characters, who are too innocent and ill-equipped to deal with the big issues they confront. Julianne found that freeing.

**SM:** You've made it clear, even in the opening credits, that *Poison* is based on three Jean Genet novels, but I can't help but see a connection to a Genet film, and one of the great avant-garde films: *Un chant d'amour* [1952].

**TH:** *Un chant d'amour* is just so amazing, so radical. It's from 1949, right?

**SM:** 1952.

**TH:** 1952—so it came *after* Kenneth Anger's *Fireworks* [1947]! Oh, *that's* amazing, too.

*Un chant d'amour* is Genet's one film, and uses a prison setting. It has one of the most erotic and understated moments in all of cinema, the scene of one inmate putting a reed through the stone wall dividing him from his neighboring inmate and blowing smoke through this narrow reed so that the smoke comes out in the other inmate's cell where the neighbor inhales it. It's very simple, but so beautiful and powerful. And the film is an incredible, frank depiction of nudity and homoerotic imagery. It's exquisite. So yeah, *Un chant d'amour* was a kind of ghost text that inspired me in *Poison*. I didn't want to reenact any of it; its influence needed to be implicit, not amplified.

**SM:** The scene of the men getting married in the "Homo" section of *Poison*, which I assume is a fantasy scene, evokes for me the fantasy sequence in *Un chant d'amour* where the men frolic in the woods.

**TH:** That scene in *Poison* isn't a fantasy, actually. All the scenes depicted in and around that rustic courtyard refer to Genet's depictions of Mettray, the penal colony he romanticizes in *Miracle of the Rose* and contrasts with the scenes of adult prison life at Fontenal—though Genet's romantic inversions have all the investment and desire of fantasy.

**SM:** One of the early screenings of *Un chant d'amour* in this country was in San Francisco; it was shut down by the police, who confiscated the film. Saul Landau, who later was involved with the San Francisco Mime Troupe, wrote a brilliant defense of the film. It was the first important essay to be published in what would become a key publication for those interested in avant-garde cinema from the mid-1960s into the '80s: the *Canyon Cinemanews*. Landau had courage; one of the first things he did after the brouhaha about the first screening was to show the film again, this time as a benefit for Kenneth Anger.

When did you first see *Fireworks* and also *Inauguration of the Pleasure*

*Dome* [1954], a film that is about identity being multifarious and composite, a theme in much of your work?

**TH:** I think I was first seeing Kenneth Anger films in college, or maybe even in high school. I forget which one I saw first, probably *Scorpio Rising* [1963]. The story behind *Fireworks* is so interesting. It was made in 1949, right?

**SM:** 1947.

**TH:** Unbelievable. His parents are gone for the weekend and he and his friends make this radical, homoerotic, crazy, *beautiful* film.

**SM:** It's the earliest openly gay film that I'm aware of. Kinsey was in the first public audience for the film, and, according to Anger, Kinsey bought the first print.

**TH:** Then that film traveled to Europe, and Genet and Jean Cocteau and all those dudes had their screening of this Los Angeles teenager's film. Pretty remarkable.

**SM:** Like *Scorpio Rising* and some other avant-garde films—Jack Smith's *Flaming Creatures* [1963] is a notable instance—*Poison* ran into trouble with "moral guardians," particularly because of its depiction of homosexuality.

**TH:** The production of *Poison* was given a $25,000 grant by the National Endowment for the Arts. After the film was finished and won the prize at Sundance, there was a review by the *Hollywood Reporter* that misdescribed the film. *Poison* is made up of three stories—"Homo," "Hero," and "Horror." The review described the whole movie as if it were "Homo," as if the entire film was about anal sex in prison. Somehow, Donald Wildman of the American Family Association heard about the film and took up the cause, and several senators got involved. This was not long after the "NEA Four": Karen Finley, Tim Miller, Holly Hughes, and John Fleck, performance artists who were given grants and then charged with inappropriate use of taxpayer money. In the end, their grants were rescinded.

    *Poison* became the next in line for that kind of fame. All of a sudden I was on *Larry King* and all these other shows; and *no* politicians were supporting my position. Sometimes it was me and Dick Armey, or later, me and Ralph Reed, the head of the Christian Coalition. Many of the people attacking *Poison* hadn't even seen the film; they were just arguing that money shouldn't be put into public art that might offend American sensibilities. It wasn't a fair discussion: I was just the artist who made the film with a grant; and they were opposing the whole notion of giving artists grants. If we were going to have a discussion about the *film*, I could have spoken to that, I suppose; but since the issue was public funding of the arts, it would have made more sense to have a politician in favor of public support for artists, defending that position.

The best thing was that they had to have special screenings of *Poison* wherever senators and congresspeople go to see movies, so they could see what the controversy was all about. In the *Washington Times* I was called "the Fellini of Fellatio"—a proud moment! One senator's wife said that watching *Poison* made her want to "bathe in Clorox" afterward. Pretty good press! I think this was the first time, or one of the first times, a *film* was the subject of questions about public support of the arts.

**SM:** The controversy over Marlon Riggs's *Tongues Untied* predates the flap over *Poison*.
**TH:** That's true. These controversies are almost always about gay-related stuff.

At some point during the flap over *Poison*, Robert Redford wrote a letter to John Frohnmayer, the head of the NEA, that went something like: "Hey, John, I just want to speak up in favor of this homo-y movie that you have such problems with. . . ." I think because of Redford's support and because *Poison* had the sanction of the Sundance Award, Frohnmayer finally had the nerve to stand up and defend the film.

That's been my only big controversy, and really I'm happy to be part of the tradition of controversial films like *Un chant d'amour*, *Scorpio Rising*, *Flaming Creatures*, and *Tongues Untied*.

**SM:** In *Velvet Goldmine* the character of Jack Fairy is pretty obviously an allusion to Jack Smith, who is increasingly considered not only an important avant-garde filmmaker (his *Flaming Creatures* is a crucial 1960s film), but the initiator of what's now called performance art, as well as a major influence on Warhol and so many others. Am I correct that you too see Smith that way?
**TH:** Oh, absolutely. I love the famous stories of his performance pieces that would go on for days. They were like eastern traditions where you watch a Nō play for twelve hours or whatever. And I love the way his performing was woven into his life; living and performance weren't separated by a curtain or a proscenium.

**SM:** I remember a Smith performance at the Times Square Show in 1980.

Smith arrives and seems to be getting things ready for his performance, putting things where they need to be. The audience waits for what's going to happen. Half an hour goes by, and he's still getting ready; then it's an hour. Finally we realize that this is the performance: the process of seeming to get ready to perform is the performance.

**TH:** Exactly—the line between life and art is erased. In so many ways that crazy intersection of experimental filmmaking, erotic film (it wasn't called porn in the mid-1960s), and feature filmmaking—that crazy commingling of all those traditions that produced a moment when people would line up around the block to see *Chelsea Girls* [1966]—reflected a desire in people to blur categories, including the separation between art and life, and "radical" and "mainstream." All the categories were in a state of flux. This produced not only extraordinary filmmakers, but active and essential audiences. We don't have audiences like that today.

**SM:** One major theme, if not the major theme of your work, has been the quest to be free of identity, or at least of a simplistic sense of what identity is. This is reflected in your quest to be free of cinematic identity, your refusal to be restricted to one genre, one kind of presentation—a tendency obvious as early as *Superstar*. *I'm Not There* may be the ultimate instance. I get the sense that *I'm Not There* was an attempt to pay homage not just to Dylan's career and to his defiance of simple definitions of identity, but to the expansion of the American sense of film history that took place during the 1960s and '70s. You evoke so many dimensions of the cinema scene of that era. *I'm Not There* is a brilliant synthesis of commercial and avant-garde attitudes and approaches.

**TH:** Well, thank you. I had an extraordinary period at my disposal for that film (even though, of course, Bob Dylan's career has gone way past the 1960s); there were *so* many formal and visual, cinematic and otherwise, experiments going on during that time, experiments that produced a remarkable array of work and so many possibilities.

The subject of Dylan was clearly an expansive one, and one that doesn't stop growing, given his profuse and unending output. In addition to this I was applying a structure that was expansive by design—the opposite, in my mind, of the traditional biopic's determination to reduce and simplify. So I knew from the start that I would need to impose some conceptual limits on the thing. And since most of the characters I'd developed had their roots in the 1960s, an era as seminal to Dylan as he was to it, I decided to take that as my conceptual and stylistic sourcebook—though as creative limits go, the 1960s provided anything but. At the very least I could be guaranteed distinct and contrasting cinematic references for each of the stories that would all, still, come out of a period defined by experimentation, in effect the Vietnam years: 1964 through 1973.

**SM:** How early in the process of conceiving *I'm Not There* did you know you would use a composite of many different kinds of filming, a weave of various cinematic approaches?
**TH:** From conception. The specific cinematic references—the visualization of the film—was something I felt needed to be considered from the start, and would determine not only how the film would look, but how the script would be written.

**SM:** During the Cate Blanchett story, you remind us of the Warhol Factory and the various forms of image-making that went on there. In other instances, you remind us of the hand-held, gestural 8mm and Super 8 filmmaking of that era. In still others, you show your awareness of breakthroughs in documentary work (Pennebaker's direct cinema work in *Don't Look Back* [1967], most obviously). How fully were you thinking of particular makers of one kind or another as you conceived the film? Or were you just channeling the general zeitgeist of that moment?
**TH:** All of the references you mention were influences, along with many others. In the end the guiding cinematic references were not necessarily those that Dylan himself was directly associated with (like Pennebaker), but those that, to me, most closely illustrated what Dylan's music was doing at the time. For instance, the Jude story—Cate Blanchett's section—I'd initially pictured like *Don't Look Back*, in verité black-and-white. But this story was about the electric Dylan of late 1965 and 1966, the Dylan of *Highway 61* and *Blonde on Blonde*—a period in his music that was about as far from "social realism" or verité as one could get. So Fellini—and particularly *8½* [1963], a film whose rich baroque and urban ironies became the perfect conduit to *Blonde on Blonde*—replaced Pennebaker as the leading stylistic reference for that story (with some Richard Lester, Pennebaker, and William Klein thrown in, as well). Elsewhere the references are nearly as specific: early Godard for the Robbie [Heath Ledger] story; the hippie Westerns of the late 1960s and early '70s for Billy [Richard Gere]; black-and-white experimental minimalism for Arthur [Ben Wishaw]; leftist studio filmmaking—from *Face in the Crowd* [Elia Kazan, 1957], to *Bound for Glory* [Hal Ashby, 1976] for Woody [Marcus Carl Franklin].

Of course, the ways in which one particular artist has dodged the fixing of identity that the culture always seems to demand (and that so many people still struggle to fulfill, feel they need to fulfill) is certainly not confined to that particular era. There was more of an audience for experimenting with identity in the 1960s, but the issue itself hasn't changed so much. Of course, I knew from the beginning that whatever happened to *I'm Not There* in today's world market couldn't be the same as what was happening then, couldn't be—and that was fine. But I also didn't want to limit the range of possibilities suggested by *I'm Not There* because of today's different audience; as fully as possible, I wanted to honor the exuberance of that time and make it accessible. *I'm Not There* had fantastic actors and that helped to root a lot of people within the narrative fracture of the film, and the music gives a lot of people access as well.

**SM:** *I'm Not There* didn't do as well as we might have hoped.
**TH:** I was completely satisfied with the reception. Critically it was really well-received, more than I would have thought, and that felt bizarre and exciting. All in all, it was a surprising year for American film, and *I'm Not There* was in the company of a lot of interesting work. If the film was going to get such generous critical reaction, it would probably have done better in a less exciting year. But I was happy to see great commercial films by interesting directors coming out for the first time in what seemed like a decade—and then look what happened! In one year four major independent film companies folded.

Also, the ancillary possibility for DVD sales is disappearing: people download now. This is a really curious time for independent filmmaking. I just bought the great Criterion edition of *Berlin Alexanderplatz* [1983]: I hadn't seen it since the late 1980s. Fassbinder's films have been hugely influential on me and they still amaze and exhaust me. *Berlin Alexanderplatz* has become interesting to me again in part because I'm just now thinking about doing something in an episodic format, a long, multiple-part piece for television.

# Interview with Todd Haynes

Sam Adams / 2011

From the *A.V. Club*, March 25, 2011. Reprinted by permission from the editor, the *A.V. Club*.

Cinephiles need no introduction to Todd Haynes, the Oscar-nominated, endlessly lauded director of *Far from Heaven*, *I'm Not There*, and *Poison*, elaborately layered works that double as introductory film studies texts. But *Mildred Pierce*, a five-part adaptation of James M. Cain's 1941 novel whose first two parts air back-to-back on HBO Sunday night, takes Haynes out of the art house and into the living room, an environment where viewers aren't used to mingling drama and deconstruction. If Haynes's naturalistic take, adapted with Kelly Reichardt's frequent collaborator Jon Raymond, owes anything to his knowledge of film history, it's in the way the movie—"miniseries," though accurate, seems wrong—inserts itself into the lineage of television melodrama, the lowest and least-observed corner of a historically disreputable medium, and one of few arenas where female protagonists dominate the board.

There's nothing soapy about *Mildred Pierce*, but it's an unabashed and enormously affecting weepie, devoted to the intricacies of mother-daughter relationships and staged in the female spaces of bedrooms and kitchens. In the midst of the Great Depression, iron-willed housewife Mildred (Kate Winslet) drives out her unfaithful failure of a husband and pledges to provide for her two daughters herself. The revelation that her mother is getting her hands dirty as a hash-house waitress scandalizes Mildred's elder daughter, Veda (Morgan Turner for the first three episodes, Evan Rachel Wood thereafter), an innately snobbish child whose hostility to her mother only softens when she begins dating society-page scion Monty Beragon (Guy Pearce).

The battles between Mildred and Veda take on the stature of Greek tragedy, but Haynes never loses track of the details that make the story so enthralling, like the minute efficiencies that turn Mildred's chicken-and-waffle restaurant into a Depression-era hit. One thing he pays little attention to is *Mildred*'s 1945 film version, a Joan Crawford tour de force that imports the noir trappings of Cain's hard-boiled novels. Haynes's version is flooded with Southern California sun, an ironic counterpart to its increasingly dark turns. A week before *Mildred*'s première, Haynes sat down with the *A.V. Club* in New York to talk about balancing contemporary concerns and period feel, and why he toned down his self-aware style to reach out to a new audience. Warning: minor *Mildred Pierce* spoilers ahead.

**The A.V. Club:** The natural expectation when word first surfaced that you'd be returning to the source of a classic melodrama was that Mildred Pierce would be a *Far from Heaven* redux. But Mildred's style is radically different from anything you've done before, in that it's far more naturalistic.

**Todd Haynes:** It was always the idea. This will become a redundant refrain, but I always took my cues from the book. The style of the book invariably affected aspects of the way we depicted it, although of course Cain uses this tough, minimal kind of language and one can extrapolate his hard-boiled, more classic first-person novels from *The Postman Always Rings Twice* and *Double Indemnity*. But [*Mildred*] is him trying hard to do something different and be omniscient and speak in the third person and observe this relationship with very selective moments of psychological and emotional description, which when they occur have all the greater impact. Jon Raymond said, "You should read *Mildred Pierce*, the book—it's really, really great." I said, "I've seen the film" and he said he'd never seen the film, so we kept it that way. He never watched the movie, and I stayed away from the movie during the making of the film.

I was reading the book during the summer and fall of the financial meltdown, and it made me feel like this was such a relevant story to tell. But how to tell it was the question. I looked to the films of the seventies as a point of reference, because my first curiosity was at the level of writing. I remember those films as feeling like they were taking American genres and bringing them to a contemporary audience, this new generation of filmmakers. But what exactly was it about them that made them feel contemporary and sophisticated and that they were always speaking about the times they were in? Was it at the level of the script? Was it something they had done differently with the genres of those scripts? And you realize no, it really isn't. They're fairly faithful to the generic traditions they take on. It's really more a manner of eschewing the strong visual styles and filmic language associated with the genres: noir gang-ster stories in *Chinatown* or horror films and *The Exorcist*. There's a kind of dressing-down of the strong studio language of those kinds of mov-ies and a more observational distance, a kind of restraint of cutting and angles. And a different kind of breed of actors, of course, and different kinds of locations. So those were the cues that we took in a way almost of tricking audiences into feeling that same relevance. That was my goal: to make it feel contemporary while being faithful to the time.

**AVC:** You come out of a background in semiotic film theory and radi-cal queer filmmaking, both of which involve in a sustained challenge of traditional storytelling modes. Did you have concerns about embracing a style that's more transparent, that camouflages what you've previously worked to expose?

**TH:** No. I still felt that kind of naturalism was a different set of codes, and another artificial language that could be used for specific means, and I wanted to experience and explore it. I was also aware that this was a very different audience that I'm talking to. I respect that and I like that. I like that it's coming into their living rooms directly through a piece of furniture that's in their house.

**AVC:** Whether they like it or not.

**TH:** Whether they like it or not. I didn't want to set up obstacles in how to read this story. To me, the social and political themes that interested me the most were within the narrative itself, or within the story that I was trying to tell. If anything, I wanted to make the themes of the sto-ries, the conflicts of the stories, feel as available to an audience as pos-sible, so that they could really enter into it with their own investment in the characters, and their dilemmas would be what the learning experi-ence would be about, or that's what the issues and conflicts would come out of. And that, in many ways, just meant paying close attention to Veda and making her feel as genuine and authentic a person as possible.

**AVC:** Veda's the great challenge. You've got this young middle-class woman who in the midst of the Great Depression conceives this morbid distaste for wage-earning, in a time when large numbers of people were desperate for work of any kind. In the 1945 version, Veda is positioned as an outgrowth of her mother's social-climbing snobbery, but it's not that simple here. There are moments when Veda feeds her mother's ambi-tion rather than the other way around; Veda is horrified her mother is working as a waitress, so Mildred makes up a lie about learning the business so she can start her own restaurant, and then she decides to follow through on it.

**TH:** Yeah. Absolutely true. I wanted to show much more of a kind of circular series of influences between these two women, and that there is a slippery slope from the classic hard-fought middle-class values of working hard and valuing labor and valuing hard work and valuing dedication to one's job and career and to one's family, to the kind of aspirational goals of any middle-class parent to give their kids everything they couldn't have, to ascend a social ladder generationally, to give them access to culture and the finer things in life. It's amazing to me how much that spectrum of middle-class expectations was established and solidified and considered absolute in one decade: the 1920s. By the end of the twenties, when the rug was pulled out from under middle-class American life, and every other aspect of American life, people were like, "No way, we're not giving that stuff up. That still holds firm. That's who we are." How deeply ingrained in American identity those ideals were is really interesting.

**AVC:** Is there a kind of conservatism embedded in that? The blueprints for her husband's failed development project, Pierce Homes, bear the slogan "Good enough for folks," which is a much more modest form of aspiration than Mildred embodies. Is there a sense in which she's punished for reaching too far beyond her station?

**TH:** I think there's a cautionary element in there. One can't help apply to the fact that this story comes right out of an excess of consumption in the twenties and the housing boom that collapsed, and that I re-encountered it at the end of our own much more brutal, or comparably brutal, boom and bust, and a much longer period of mindless consumption that was revved on by a conservative strain of middle-class values or whatever drumbeat. What it doesn't tell you is that there is a right way to do it. It doesn't show you the good example. It shows you that there are these potential dangers lurking in basic middle-class yearning and that there are extreme dangers embedded in maternal configurations and expectations, and the irresolvable conflicts between mother and child.

**AVC:** There are polls showing that Americans consistently place themselves higher in social class than they actually are; in one case, that 19 percent think they're in the top 1 percent. It brings to mind the poignant symbolism of Monty Beragon living in this enormous mansion that's been stripped to the bare walls, maintaining a single room as a vestige of his former wealth. There's a basic failure to face up to reality there.

**TH:** Exactly. Amazing. I know.

**AVC:** It's the Depression-era equivalent of driving a leased Lexus while defaulting on your mortgage.

**TH:** Well, it's one way that we can explain why so often American voters vote against their own interests and preserve whatever: deregulation and voting for big business and favoring the wealthy, and then going out to the Lotto every day and spending that dollar, hoping and thinking that might just be them, and you better not foreclose those freedoms at the top.

**AVC:** American movies aren't particularly interested in work, especially women's work. Men are identified with their jobs, even though we don't see much of them, women by their relationships, as mother or lover or friend. But in *Mildred Pierce*, some of the most loving sequences are devoted to the way the restaurant kitchen operates, and the refinements Mildred makes to the process over time. I felt a giddy kind of joy watching the plates changing hands.

**TH:** I agree. That's how I felt reading the book. That's what got me so excited about doing the film version and having the space enough to develop that and get into stuff that people would think is wasted time, or that you can condense it or you don't have to tell the whole story or show the whole process. At a certain point, the opening of the restaurant is almost like a backstage musical. The upstairs and downstairs are the wings and the audience, and I loved that about it. I think that's so exciting. You get completely invested in what it takes, and the small elements really matter. Watching her become skilled and train herself, and watching this sort of innate, almost unacknowledged talent that she has, starting with making pies and ending up being a sort of entrepreneur. Things she never knew she even had until she was forced to go out there.

**AVC:** The very first thing we see is Mildred's hands making pies, although it takes a couple of episodes to fully grasp its significance. Her fanatical emphasis on efficiency—"Never make a trip in or out without something in your hand"—makes her the Henry Ford of chicken and waffles, if not the Frederick Taylor.

**TH:** Yeah. A sense of economy. It really is about capitalism, this story, and I think in some ways how those themes or models invade domestic conflicts. There's this value that both women keep extracting from the other and each requires from the other. It motors a machine of with-holding and desire that propels them and fuels this engine that gets played out through themes of money and labor in the film.

**AVC:** Mildred's emphasis on hard work—"Do your duty and a little bit more"—contrasts with Veda's grotesque sense of entitlement, as well as her innate gifts. She practices piano for years, but has to confront the fact that she's only a "Glendale wunderkind," and then all of a sudden she finds out she's a natural operatic coloratura. The way that's glossed over is a little bit absurd, although there's the superficial explanation that she's simply built to sing.
**TH:** It is the explanation. Exactly. But it is something that she'd been in-tensely training and committed at. She had skills. It took a combination of something innate and something intensely practiced and procured over time.

**AVC:** She'd never admit that, of course, that the music training her mother paid for is integral to her eventual success. That's what's so in-furiating about her. The vicious and heartless way she treats her mother makes it difficult not to loathe her, but even though we're meant to iden-tify with Mildred's sorrow and her feelings of betrayal, we also need to understand what she loves in Veda, or else she's just a sap. How do you understand where Veda comes from?
**TH:** I find it easy to understand, up to the last episode where it takes certain turns. The aspects of her duping of the Forrester family, that is narratively excessive. But kids always have to push back against their parents, and when you have strong maternal investment in you—which I had, and even though I didn't have the kind of mother/daughter ex-tra stuff that often accompanies that, I still had to push back and create some space and become the executioner, almost, of that love. I witnessed stuff between my mother and my sister that only emerged when my sis-ter was in adolescence, an extra kind of scrutiny and pressure from the mother to the daughter that I may never completely understand. That's about the maternal projections onto the daughter and the difficulty of two women trying to forge distinct and separate lives, subjectivities, who are also objects in the world. And learning what that means and what their bodies represent and suggest and what sort of powers their bodies contain. The level at which Mildred invests in Veda means there is going to need to be extra pushback—I mean, an extraordinary amount of it.

When [Veda's younger sister] Ray dies, that sort of hysteria around loss is all the more unnatural.

Then there are these really key moments, very important ones narratively, like when Veda is first cast out of the music teacher's office, the first one, and she says, "Mother, I thought he wasn't going to take me and then he said that I was good and I had a mind." You realize her own self-doubt is exposed, and that façade of being completely intact and secure is shifted. Maybe even more importantly with the second one, when she really is rejected as a piano student by Treviso. Everything about her self-regard: The projections of Mildred's investment in her are just mortifying and horrifying to her, and it makes her feel even more of a failure because of all of the estimations that Mildred has been laying on her through her whole life. That's just pure teen self-hatred that you project onto your parent. These are all things I remember, and I came from nothing like this household. There was a sort of brutality that was required to exert your own voice.

# HBO: *Mildred Pierce*—The *Evening Class* Interview with Todd Haynes

Michael Guillén / 2011

From the *Evening Class*, March 26, 2011. Reprinted by permission of the *Evening Class*.

Even as I sit in good fortune conversing with Todd in the Sundance Kabuki's green room, anticipating the special San Francisco premiere of the first two episodes of his HBO miniseries *Mildred Pierce* (2011) co-presented with the San Francisco Film Society, I am aware that out there in the "real" world I have friends who have been out of work for two, sometimes three, years without being able to find another job, friends who are losing their homes due to predatory loans and subsequent foreclosures, friends who are losing their health because they can't afford health insurance, friends who have had to migrate out of San Francisco to continue living in the Bay Area, and—for those friends who have been able to find a job—that it's involved setting aside specialized skills and talents to wait tables, tend bars, or drive cabs. With few apparent options or remedies, I can't help but wonder how we as besieged Americans can retain vision when nothing seems to be left in plain sight?

This national dilemma is not lost on Todd Haynes who has skillfully analogized James M. Cain's classic 1941 novel *Mildred Pierce* to the current economic situation in which we now find ourselves. How he has accomplished this is his subversive genius. By staying true to its literary source, Haynes has revealed the relevance of this Depression narrative to our current lives through the long-form format of a cable miniseries, which has allowed the novel to unfold at its own pace. "*Mildred Pierce* is set during the Depression," explains Haynes, "but not the Depression of dustbowls and breadlines. The crises it explores are those of middle-class privilege—issues of pride and status, the struggle first to regain one's standing and then to persevere through hard work and ingenuity. This feels very much like the particular struggles of our current economic crisis, coming out of a period of unbridled consumption." It reminds me of what my friend Mike Black once characterized as facing up to "the ignobility of work" and how so many of us toil our lives away at jobs that feel "beneath" us. The class struggle here seems to be between those who lead authentic, creative, and productive lives and those who simply don't, and suffer for it.

Negotiating around the famous Oscar-winning performance by Joan Crawford in Michael Curtiz's 1945 "noir" classic *Mildred Pierce*—no mean feat, I might add!—Haynes astutely relies on Cain's novel to reveal the compelling narrative of the rise and fall of Mildred Pierce. Kate Winslet unflinchingly inhabits the role, making it all her own, by remaining faithful to the book's characterization. If mythologist Joseph Campbell's suggestion is true that an individual's brilliance shines through in the performance of their everyday tasks, then Kate Winslet's *Mildred Pierce* is radiant with a growth maneuvered task by task, step by step.

The miniseries debuts on HBO, Sunday, March 27. Check the official website for details. [This conversation is *not* for the spoiler-wary!]

**Q:** I'm of that demographic, Todd, that came to your films by way of *Far from Heaven* (2002) and then went back to visit your earlier work and I have to say that your films have the unnerving quality of making me bawl in public. [Haynes laughs.] If it weren't for the kind shoulder of the young woman sitting next to me at *Far from Heaven*, I don't think I would have made it through that film.
**A:** [Laughing.] That's sweet. Thank you.

**Q:** And, of course, your recent HBO film *Mildred Pierce* has its moments as well. The scene where Mildred (Kate Winslet) and Bert (Brían F. O'Byrne) agree to divorce is a heartbreaker.
**A:** I *know*! These powerful actors of mine.

**Q:** What is it in the specific catharsis you mine from the melodrama of these women's narratives that assists you in your filmmaking vision?
**A:** It's just the most fascinating form. In a way the term "melodrama" is so clumsy and imprecise unlike other genres that we might talk about— like westerns, film noir, gangster movies, or whatever—because it also incorporates a kind of pejorative attitude about emotional or sentimental excess. But it's almost because of that, that it makes me want to get in there and roll up my sleeves and figure out why? What is that? Why is it

dealt with derogatorily? Why do we dismiss melodramas and domestic drama as something second-class in preference for genres that are, first, more escapist and more associated with male protagonists? Genres that express more freedom in exploring frontiers (as in westerns) or investigating crimes (as in gangster films)?

Melodramas are stories about families, and women in houses, and relationships that don't always work out, and people making tough choices under the pressure of societal views and prejudices. Not only do melodramas have that brand because women are so central to them but it's really about our own lives; it's really about what we all experience in life. I like that about melodramas, although I've tried to do something quite different in the style of *Mildred Pierce* than what I did in *Far from Heaven*. In *Far from Heaven*—which was quoting from the most stylized period of the melodramas in the fifties and trying hard to be true to those cinematic styles—it was almost more an experiment. It was almost riskier. When people had strong emotional reactions to the material, it proved to me that this genre has incredible legs and really endures because—even though we were working through an artificial visual language and pushing it further than normal—people did have a strong emotional reaction to that film, which says a lot about the form. It says a lot about melodrama.

With *Mildred Pierce*, however, I was exploring naturalism. It's a more understated treatment of the material than what I did with *Far from Heaven*. The intensity, the drama, the extremes are all in the material and I didn't need to add to that an extreme visual language or an intense musical score. I wanted to give the audience room to find their way into the material and not overdetermine their emotions.

**Q:** Some of the immediate feedback I've read on *Mildred Pierce*, and what I experienced watching the first two episodes, has been exactly this measure of restraint. And as you've described it elsewhere, the film exhibits a "relatable" naturalism, which speaks exactly to how a genre can be resuscitated in such a way as to find relevance with modern audiences. Yet still I wonder why a genre that was so blithely dismissed in the 1950s as "women's weepers" has elevated into modern relevance? Would it have anything to do with the power politics in the film's male-female relationships? Your films give the yin and yang of relationship a postmodern flip of the coin. The yin is expressed through your earnest, enterprising women and the yang by your indolent but attractive men. What do you seek out in such gendered tension?

**A:** *Mildred Pierce* is different from traditional domestic dramas that usually explore women who are somewhat disempowered and who are more in a domestic space and don't usually trespass beyond that. A real line is drawn between the working world and the home world. *Children* are the ones who are ushered out to cross that boundary, such as in the more traditional classic mother-daughter stories like *Stella Dallas* (1937) where—and this is often true with these stories—the kid represents the tension. The mother doesn't want to let go of the child but she also wants the child to move up the social ladder. That usually ends up with the mother having to sacrifice greatly and sometimes even hand the kid over to the wealthier part of the family and let somebody else bring her up better than she could. That's how *Stella Dallas* ends, for instance, with her maternal sacrifice.

But what's so interesting in *Mildred Pierce* is that it's *women* who are running the show. The men are waylaid by the economic catastrophe of the 1930s that they're all trying to figure out; but, it seems like women just had to—by necessity—take action and become active in the work place. In Mildred's case, it starts with small steps as you've just seen in the first two episodes where she has to get a job and re-examine who she is in the world as a single mother and what her middle-class identity is really all about. So she has to take a job that she considers beneath her; but, through that experience, she learns a great deal, and discovers she has a lot of innate talents and skills that she keeps learning more about to see how far they can take her. Ultimately, they take her quite far indeed. But the men in *Mildred Pierce* are passive and I think that's so interesting. It's not the war years yet—it's not the time when the men are gone and women are running the factories—it's prior to that. In a way, all of the men in *Mildred Pierce* are passive failures, of various varieties in the story.

James M. Cain has said that one of his missions and what he set out to say by writing *Mildred Pierce* was to tell the story of a woman who uses men to get what she needs. What I think he probably meant is that she doesn't see what she's doing; she's doesn't do it knowingly; she does it instinctively. And then gets in trouble. And then discovers how it happened. Of course, what it *really* is all about is this mother and daughter relationship. Mildred finds men and puts them to the service of her ambitions that are all being fueled by the needs of the daughter. She is preoccupied with and over-invested in this one child. The men fall into service to that mission, with all sorts of various outcomes along the way.

**Q:** Elsewhere, you've referred to that intense mother-daughter relation-ship between Mildred and Veda as an unrequited love affair. And there's already some buzz about your having "queered" the narrative by imbu-ing an incestuous lesbian flourish to their dynamic. Do you agree with that?

**A:** Not if you read the book! It's even more startlingly pronounced in Cain's amazingly modern 1941 novel, on which the 1945 film version was based. More people are better familiar with the 1945 Crawford ve-hicle than even the novel, but that film took great liberties and changed a great deal of the novel. There was no murder element in the original story.

**Q:** They slapped some noir onto it?

**A:** Exactly. And to try to appeal to and bridge to the audience that they had established so well with Cain's crime novels. There is a scene—which you haven't come to yet if you've only seen the first two episodes, and I hope I don't give too much away—but, when Veda first confesses to Mildred that she has been seeing a boy and is pregnant as a result, in the book it literally describes Mildred as doubling-over with nausea out of utter jealousy. She doesn't react like, "Oh my poor daughter, she's going to have a kid! What are we going to do now? Her reputation is screwed." Or whatever the typical maternal reaction might be. Instead, she ex-periences utter jealousy that Veda has gone out with a boy and gotten knocked up without her knowing anything about it. It's intense. There's also a kiss you will see in Episode 5 between mother and daughter, but it's directly out of the book, this remarkable book, which is incredibly fearless about venturing into territory that challenges all traditional and acceptable ideas about mother and daughter and the limits of those relationships.

**Q:** Let's talk about the film's visual flourishes related to gesture. The ges-ture that specifically sticks in my mind as near-brilliant is when Mildred repossesses the car from Bert, arguing that she needs it because she's working. She drives him back to where he's staying, drops him off, and then you have that image of her right hand gripping the steering wheel, flexing its fingers. Her taking command is evident; but, it made me won-der how you direct a gesture like that? How do you know when you have the gesture right?

**A:** It's a really good question because it gets to the core of this specific character, this woman who functions by doing and by action; not by reflection and self-awareness. In fact, Mildred is someone who has big blind spots about what motivates her. But she muscles through life by doing things and by transforming frustration into productive work of all kinds: whether she's baking a pie, or repossessing the family car. But what's interesting is that's the way that many actors, including Kate, prepare their role: the externalization of the character through physical tasks and challenges. It's often just simply practical.

For example, Kate had to train how to separate chickens and look like a master doing it. She had to have waitress skills that were convincing for when she ultimately masters that task as a character. All of the physical tasks that define Mildred as a character and chart her growth and her rise as a business woman are activities the audience had to absolutely believe. This is true as well for Evan Rachel Wood who—as the grown Veda—becomes an opera singer who had to master arias in different languages. Evan had to learn how to sing them so that she looked like she was singing them properly. Morgan Turner—who plays the younger Veda—likewise had to learn how to appear that she could play the piano. For actors, the externalization of who they are through tasks is really helpful. It's concrete and helps them find the character through the act of doing something. It's specific.

But this is also interesting because it says a lot about how Mildred the character and Kate the actress share this as people. Kate really understood that about Mildred. Kate has self-awareness and the critical faculties that Mildred doesn't because she's an actress and an incredibly brilliant woman.

**Q:** So the actors come to you with gestural suggestions that either comport to your vision or not?
**A:** It's not even that deconstructed. It's just part of the meaning we're trying to convey in this particular scene or that particular scene. Unless it's literally her separating chickens because there are specific ways to separate chickens. Kate and I are both massive *Top Chef* freaks and we visited Tom Colicchio at his house and he gave her instruction on how to separate chickens. He came up to me at the party we just had a few days ago at the New York premiere and thanked me for thanking him at the end of the film. Whenever I see Tom Colicchio coming up to me, I always think that the smile's going to drop and he's going to ask me to do some really tough challenge. [Laughs.] He's actually really nice in person. He is to me. Tom was incredibly helpful and Kate was relentless

about mastering it and doing it right. Kate had to feel that she was doing it right and she approached everything she had to do as the character accordingly.

**Q:** Clearly, it's a given why you cast Kate Winslet in the title role and I'm aware that she was in your mind even as you were drafting the script, but I'd like to draw some attention to the supporting actresses in the series who—in the two episodes I've seen—are already revealing remarkable work. When a frequently-heard complaint is that there are few good roles for middle-aged actresses anymore, you have populated *Mildred Pierce* with nuanced performances by a variety of great supporting actresses, most notably Melissa Leo as Mildred's friend Lucy and Mare Winningham as Ida. Can you speak to casting?
**A:** It's an embarrassment of riches when you're picking actresses in that age bracket of who can play these roles because we have so many fine, great serious actors who don't get offered roles all the time who are in their forties, during their fifties, whenever it is, even late thirties and into their sixties. To me, that's the walking troupe of our finest actors, because they have the life experience at this point and the professional experience to bring to roles they may not have had twenty to thirty years ago when we first knew their work. No, it's disproportionate, there just *aren't* enough great roles for that brand of actor. For several of these roles it was hard to narrow it down to make an offer to one because they were all so great. There was a long list of really solid people.

**Q:** Shifting to your working relationship with your cinematographer— who's worked with you previously on *Far from Heaven* and *I'm Not There*—you mentioned earlier that your intention with *Mildred Pierce* was to shift away from the overblown melodrama you were quoting and subverting in *Far from Heaven*. Yet Richard Porton, in his recent column for *CinemaScope*, has observed: "Haynes's talent for balancing intimacy with a distancing mise en scène in which the actors are viewed through windows, bars, or mirrors is gloriously Fassbinderian." Which harkens, of course, to a notably different style of melodrama.
Restrained, "relatably naturalistic" as you put it, the scene of Mildred sitting in the café realizing that she has to swallow her pride and suffer the ignobility of work that is "beneath" her was rendered so heart-wrenching, all the more for being watched from the street through a dusty window. And then Lachman's camera seems set adrift, roving around the restaurant, observing just the women in this environment,

just what they're doing—listlessly counting money at the till, gossiping about Garbo, clearing off tables, picking up tips. There's a feeling of disenchantment in the camera, as if it's becoming aware of something disappointing revealing itself beneath the surface. Did you intend that? Am I reading too much into this?

**A:** No, I *like* that! That's interesting. You're right obviously about the tendency of the camera to hold back and observe. In a way I wanted to suggest that in houses—especially where there's a lot of overinvestment in members of a family—that everybody's always watching everybody else; that there's no place where you're completely alone. We hear this in the story. Veda is always snooping around Mildred's things and knows exactly when there's a uniform or a bottle of scotch stashed in a closet. She knows exactly when Bert her father leaves because his clothes are gone. So there are these third eyes that are always observing behavior and I just wanted to have enough distance to feel like you don't really know who's watching who all the time; but, there *is* a feeling of being watched and that adds a level of tension to the intense difficulty of a kid needing to separate from their parent and identify themselves as their own person. But there's such mutual contamination—of space, of investment, of desire, of love, of projection—onto this girl Veda and a lot returned. There are a lot of weird projections of Veda onto Mildred that the separation of mother and daughter becomes a much more fraught process. But, yeah, as you say, we play it out in scenes that go beyond the house and that happen in the world outside.

I started by watching the really great revisionist films of the seventies that would take classic genres and material and be faithful to the genre and tell the stories sincerely and passionately. But there was something about how they made audiences feel that there was something modern and contemporary about the way they were doing it that made me think it was somehow about today. When you look at those movies, what you see is a restrained camera that pulls back, that lets shots play out at length, and I think what that does is it makes the audience see things for themselves. You're not always cutting to what the audience is supposed to look at. You're not scoring it to tell them what to feel. By letting the shot play out, the audience feels like their own reading is important and there's room for them to find what's important in the frame and to navigate the frame themselves. It gives them room to apply what they're seeing to other contexts. That was the spirit of it.

# Daughter Dearest

Amy Taubin / 2011

Todd Haynes specializes in two kinds of movies: analytic music biopics (*Superstar: The Karen Carpenter Story* [1988], *Velvet Goldmine* [1998], *I'm Not There* [2007]) and revisions of the genre that Hollywood dubbed the "woman's picture" (*Safe* [1995], *Far from Heaven* [2002]). We can now add to the latter *Mildred Pierce*, a five-part miniseries that premieres this month on HBO. Fans of Michael Curtiz's 1945 movie starring Joan Crawford will be surprised to discover that in this new version—which faithfully adheres to the eponymous James M. Cain novel on which the earlier film, too, was based—there is no murder mystery. Cain's novel, an attempt by the author to break from the hard-boiled genre fiction with which he was identified by writing a serious piece of social realism in the mode of Theodore Dreiser, tells the story of a Depression-era mother struggling to give the daughter she loves beyond reason the life she never had for herself. It's the mother-daughter symbiosis (rather than some trumped-up murder plot) that fuels the narrative in both the novel and Haynes's miniseries. Hardworking, unimaginative Mildred hungers for the love of her talented but narcissistic and callous daughter Veda, who wants nothing more than to escape her clutches. Centered throughout on Mildred, the series starts slowly, gradually intensifying as the struggle between the two women becomes emotionally brutal. Carter Burwell's score, punctuated by some lively jazz recordings, and cinematographer Edward Lachman's lighting are expressive not only of the period but of underlying psychological dynamics. Perhaps the series' crowning achievement comes at the end of episode 4, when Mildred, who has been completely estranged from the now adult Veda for months, sits staring at a radio from which the glorious coloratura soprano of her daughter issues forth. Never has Veda been more distant from and more mysterious for Mildred than when this medium of mass communication makes her accessible to all. The sequence is stunning, not only in the way it signals an irrevocable divide between mother and daughter—they literally exist in different registers—but also in that it suggests the beginnings of the thoroughly mediated society in which we live today.

**Amy Taubin:** The obvious question: How did you get involved with adapting *Mildred Pierce*, and why?
**Todd Haynes:** I saw the movie first when I was in college at Brown, in Mary Ann Doane's feminist film class. And we read Pam Cook's article "Duplicity in *Mildred Pierce*." It was all about the hybrid noir-melodrama.

**AT:** I never thought it was a noir.
**TH:** Really?

**AT:** No, it has certain stylistic elements of noir in the framing story, but that's about it. I think of it as a murder mystery crossed with a woman's picture.
**TH:** Bifurcated. You know, the framing device of the murder and the detective inquiry, which was constructed by the studio, enabled Michael Curtiz to do nice, neat, tidy flashbacks, voice-over driven, that could supply all the backstory economically. But what I remember is the image of Joan Crawford with a shadow going across her face.

**AT:** Had you read the book back then?
**TH:** No, absolutely not. It was only fairly recently that my friend the writer Jon Raymond told me to read it. When I was working on *Far from Heaven* in New York, Jon was in a graduate program at the New School. I was meeting all of these "Yes, Mr. Haynes, I've seen all of your films" kind of assistants, and it just made me uncomfortable. I thought, "I'm going to ask Jon if he'd work with me on the movie," and he said yes. All of a sudden I had a peer as my assistant, somebody who could sort of laugh a little bit about the whole adventure with me and keep me grounded. Jon said, "You've got to read the Cain novel *Mildred Pierce*." He had never seen the movie. I had never read the book. This was during the *I'm Not There* period. So finally, in the summer of 2008, I did. The financial markets were starting to tumble and would reach their full collapse that fall, and there I was, reading this book set in the thirties, during the Depression. I don't remember the Depression even being referenced in the movie version of *Mildred Pierce*.

**AT:** No, they transposed the story to the World War II era, but the exact years are left pretty vague.

**TH:** I deliberately didn't look at the movie again. But of course, we all think of it as a glamorous sort of forties Curtiz production with all the trimmings of a Joan Crawford vehicle that ultimately takes her to a level of sophistication and glamour worthy of her status. And yet what I remember is the very last shot, when the police realize she's innocent, and she and her ex-husband walk out of the criminal-court building together, and the women are scrubbing the floor in the corner.

**AT:** When I teach the film, I always talk about how the studio had to re-enclose her in that marriage, and that is so different in tone from the ending of the book.

**TH:** When I began reading the novel, I discovered that it bears scant resemblance to the film version. The book felt so shockingly current. It reflected what was happening right now. And then, of course, Mildred's sexuality and the details of her erotic life are so frank and surprising and vivid and not at all what you expect—since we presume that there was no sex before the sixties, which is utter malarkey. And so you learn a lot more about the sexual politics of that time and about the contradictions and complexities of this female character and, maybe most important, about the nuanced, mutually projected relationship between mother and daughter. I would classify the Michael Curtiz version as a noir because it offers only two choices for the female characters—to be good or bad—and that hangs over the film as an enigma that it will ultimately solve: Who's innocent and who's guilty of the murder? Mildred or Veda? And you know that as soon as one is deemed guilty, the other is fully redeemed. There can't be any middle ground. But in Cain's book, the situation is just so much more interesting, multicolored, and complex. The novel may be even harsher on Mildred than we've been in our miniseries. In the book, when Mildred discovers that her estranged daughter has become a coloratura soprano on the radio, she decides she's going to get her back and that she's going to marry Monty Beragon [the charming playboy whose social status and disdain for middle-class pieties make Veda adore him] if that's what it takes. There's no sense of any chemistry remaining between Mildred and her former lover, just this ulterior motive to get Veda back, and Mildred goes for him like a shark. We changed that a little bit in our version, because I wanted there to be this genuine rapport between Mildred and Monty. Maybe it exists only in the bedroom, but it's something that can be retriggered and that complements these other goals. Which is what we do in life. We have multiple clusters of motivations for going out with people. Cain's impetus was to tell the story of a woman who uses men to get what she wants, and he was simultaneously tracing the formation of a coloratura soprano, the evolution of this very distinct character of Veda Pierce.

**AT:** So how did this project come about?

**TH:** Christine Vachon [who has produced all of Haynes's movies] had worked with HBO on two feature films. She suggested that there might be interest from cable in my doing a long-form dramatic piece. We were great consumers of television series like *The Wire* and *The Sopranos*. I'd get caught up in the serial nature of them. Nothing came to mind, though, until I read *Mildred Pierce*. Because the Curtiz film is such a classic, I knew that the book would need to be explored fresh. And so a long-form dramatic piece made sense.

**AT:** And when did Kate Winslet come into it?

**TH:** I pictured her from my first read of Cain's description of this woman, who has this intense work ethic and this driven physicality, this determination and force. Mildred is a young mother. She was seventeen when she had Veda, and her age span in the book is from twenty-eight to thirty-seven. Kate Winslet happened to be right in the middle of that span. She has this fierce workhorse aspect, and there's also an erotic side to her that we've seen in certain roles, and her fearlessness. I just felt that she was meant to play this role. And that she would bring something totally different to it than Joan Crawford did.

**AT:** Just sticking with the idea of serial television, were there any miniseries that you were addicted to—not ongoing like *The Wire*?

**TH:** As a kid in the seventies, I was into the BBC miniseries *The Six Wives of Henry VIII*, and then in the eighties, *Brideshead Revisited*. With *Mildred Pierce*, I wanted something that felt like a hybrid of the miniseries form and the revisionist feature filmmaking of the seventies, which brought a certain sophistication to classic genres, like the gangster film in *The Godfather* [1972], the detective film in *Chinatown* [1974], the horror movie in *The Exorcist* [1973]. It imbued those genres with a maturity and a political relevance that they hadn't necessarily had in the decades prior. But when I look at them today, no matter how stylistically and formally beautiful they are, they don't challenge the conventions of the genres. They comply with the generic forms. It was more the performances, the cinematography, the rhythms, and, in terms of period films, a kind of dressed-down idea of the costume drama that made them seem more modern.

**AT:** Doesn't it have more to do with codes of realism than genre?
**TH:** Absolutely. Realism is a constructed idea that's always changing. And that's why, looking back at films from the seventies that felt realistic at the time, I was surprised to see that they follow the generic conventions completely. The performances have more nuance, the actors aren't as glamorous, and there's no noir lighting in any of those films. They're using a sense of natural light, real locations, and different kinds of cues to establish their realism. But they still follow the generic tradition. And today those seventies stylistics don't connote realism any more than the thirties style does. Now, handheld camera and the constant showing of every detail are what pass for realistic filmmaking, for naturalism.

**AT:** It's what's called observational cinema, right? So where do you think your series falls in relation to seventies cinema and today's? It isn't handheld, . . .
**TH:** No, no, no. Actually, the term *observational* is funny in relation to what we did, because our camera is also very self-consciously observational—it pulls back from the action, it favors long shots, and it favors all kinds of shots through windows, through doorframes, through glass, through—you know, there's a kind of voyeuristic observational element, but with a completely classic, controlled, and restrained camera.

**AT:** I was also very much aware, as I always am in your work, of certain kinds of close-ups of process. The first episode opens with close-ups of Mildred's hands making a pie. It's exactly like the opening of the book. But did the amount of detail and tight framing have anything to do with television? Were you thinking about a small screen?
**TH:** It was more about conveying a sense of time and place through detail. When I made my image book of the film to use in discussing the look with the production designer, the cinematographer, the costume designer, and whichever actors were interested, I pretty much took historical photography of Los Angeles in the thirties and interlaced it with this new naturalism of seventies filmmaking. It was different from the stylized sort of language of thirites cinema vis-à-vis the fifties that I had explored in *Far from Heaven*. I was also looking closely at *Bound for Glory* [2004], a collection of the work of WPA-era photographers, and some

of it is color as early as the late thirties. The quality of the color is like nothing you see anywhere else—not in the early color films of the thirties or in late-forties or fifties color photography. It's totally distinct. It has a muted palette but still maintains its full spectrum. It doesn't look like hand-tinted photography or like early Technicolor. That was a real influence.

At the beginning of the project, Mark Friedberg, our designer, who was also the designer on *Far from Heaven*, became the most significant figure creatively. We were thinking about how to convey the 1930s when we didn't have the budget to construct thirties Los Angeles in LA or in New York—you know, to do whole street builds. Mark said, "You should look at this guy," and dropped a book of Saul Leiter's color photography on the table. All of a sudden we were looking at these unbelievably beautiful photographs that were riffing on some of the images that I already had in my production book but took it way further—refracted shots through precipitation on windows, and dirty bus windows looking out onto the street, and reflections and distortions. They conveyed much more of a sense of time and place than a panoramic view of the street would, and which we could never produce anyway. And that became a touchstone. I gave the book to Jon Raymond when we were being asked to cut the script down to a size we could afford to shoot. And the Saul Leiter visual language gave us a template for minimizing the plot and the writing on the page. It was influential in a lot of surprising ways.

**AT:** So now it becomes obvious why you shot on film. Ed Lachman said you used Super 16.

**TH:** Because Super 16 can accommodate the aspect ratio. I wanted 16 because I really wanted that grain. Stocks and lenses today are so fast, so high-speed, that you lose the grain. And when you look at these seventies films, the first thing you see is grain dancing on the surface of the screen.

**AT:** When I was talking to Lachman, he asked, "Why are so many gay men interested in *Mildred Pierce*?" And the film is also an icon of feminist studies. But, frankly, I can't see many heterosexual men being interested in the *Mildred Pierce* mother-daughter dyad.

**TH:** In fact, the movie had never been one of my favorite maternal melodramas, a form that has had a huge impact on me as a filmmaker.

**AT:** Which are your favorites?

**TH:** Well, [Douglas] Sirk's and many others. If you're talking about strong female actors from that period, I will take Bette Davis over Joan Crawford anytime. It's just my personal taste. And the Veda-versus-Mildred conflict in the original film just doesn't sustain my curiosity. Veda is cast as so venal and irredeemable, and Mildred is sort of proud and proper. It's so true to Joan Crawford's own life that it's like watching a documentary. But Cain's Mildred is contradictory, and these ambiguous aspects were harder for Crawford to convey because she was so invested in propriety, in attaining respectability. She really had a lower-middle-class upbringing and spent most of her life striving to gain status culturally, through marriages and through different relationships. It's very similar to Mildred's plight.

**AT:** What is it about the mother-daughter relationship in the book that drew you to it?
**TH:** The ways in which it relates to issues of identity. And, of course, identity and its pathologies have always been interests of mine. What an incredibly fraught process the separation of mother and daughter is, maybe even more so than of father and son. Because of the role as object that women are encouraged to play in society, the differentiation between mother and daughter is full of confusions and projections. I think that men, who are allowed to simply become subjects, have an easier time. Male aggression and competition help propel that division between father and son, through classical Oedipal terms.

In the book, the struggle for identity is all tangled up in the American dream of social ascension, the hope that your children can achieve goals that you yourself couldn't. Mildred gives Veda all these things that she didn't have growing up. She dreams her daughter will one day be a concert pianist. And Veda is striving to be something great, which for her entails rejecting—even looking down on—everything her mother stands for. It's amazing to me that the one consistent thing about the woman's film is the extent to which class plays into the mother-daughter dilemma, the way women and women's bodies are the displayers—almost the conductors—of class aspiration in the family. The mother is always the one who says, "No, we're *this* kind of a family, and these are the things we do, and this is how we dress, and this is how we behave." And that plays into the American desire to keep transcending class limitations generationally. And it's all the more fully played out here because Mildred is the provider. Mildred is this industrious figure who is the breadwinner, so she literally materializes the rise in social standing that she also projects onto Veda. What I discovered is how much those middle-class American expectations of ascension took shape in one decade: the 1920s. And today we're suffering from this psychic crisis of a crumbling economy after thirty years of unbridled consumption. We share the same crises of social identity after the crash that we see in *Mildred Pierce*, which is the story of middle-class identity crisis. Today it's not breadlines and dust bowls but the middle class worrying about who we are now that we're not making the money we once did. Those expectations and values took form in the twenties.

**AT:** So your *Mildred Pierce* is a contemporary update on the woman's film in the way, say, *Chinatown* breathed new relevance into the detective story during the Watergate era?

**TH:** I'm so proud to be telling this story right now, this tough-love morality tale that takes the innate pathologies of domestic life, in the mother-daughter relationship, and links them to the irreconcilable pathologies inherent in the American dream of social ascension and the psychological costs that underwrite it. There's a fine line between being a solid middle-class mother who wants the best for her daughter and the spoiling of those very values, just as there's a fine line between the rugged, can-do pluckiness that defines us as a culture—or so we'd like to think—and the contamination of that virtue. What you end up with is an unbridled character like Veda.

Working on *Mildred Pierce*, I came to love the way those two irreconcilable things are paralleled. And it's not sentimental. It's a woman's film—it's full of emotion and death and so on, but there's a dose of hard-boiled toughness from Cain and the kind of 1930s "buck up" sensibility that's just so lacking today. We're such an indulgent, whiny, self-pitying culture. So there's a lot to learn from that time. It's exciting to be putting it out there now. And I did TV. I didn't do *Berlin Alexanderplatz*, but come on, you can't have everything.

# Todd Haynes on *Mildred Pierce*: Too Racy for Indies, but Perfect for TV

Eric Kohn / 2011

From *Indiewire*, April 8–9, 2011. Reprinted by permission of Eric Kohn / *Indiewire*.

Todd Haynes began his career as a daring provocateur with his feature, *Poison*, twenty years ago. While he has continued to work against the grain in a handful of unconventional follow-ups, from *Safe* to *I'm Not There*, as Haynes's profile has grown, so has the visibility of his projects. There is no greater example than his latest effort, a sprawling five-part adaptation of James M. Cain's 1941 novel, *Mildred Pierce*. With Kate Winslet in the role that won an Oscar for Joan Crawford in 1945, the series has garnered some of the best notices—and cross-over potential—of Haynes's career. The epic melodrama follows Winslet's character, a single mother, through the harshest years of the Great Depression.

Although *Mildred Pierce* involves none of the cinematic trickery associated with the majority of Haynes's career, it still deals with the unnaturally dark, alluring themes of repression and desire found throughout the filmmaker's oeuvre. In the first installment of *indieWIRE*'s two-part interview with Haynes, he discusses the warm reception for the series, his initial interest in the material, and why he felt comfortable working in a commercial environment. Stay tuned for the next installment, where Haynes looks back at *Poison* and considers its relevance in today's climate.

**Q:** Some people who never got into your style of filmmaking before have said that *Mildred Pierce* is the first Todd Haynes movie that really worked for them. When you took this on, were you thinking about how you might be addressing a larger audience?
**A:** For sure. It was definitely conscious on my part. This was a different mode of connecting to audiences—on television and, more specifically,

in a long-form dramatic miniseries. That excited me. I liked that challenge. In a way, I felt like the narrative experiments that might characterize almost all of my feature filmmaking in one form or another were less germane for this. I wouldn't probably have felt as committed to the material if I didn't feel that the material itself and the feelings of class and domestic pathology weren't really pretty radical, but also really truthful in their own terms. I felt like the themes were really interesting and also particularly relevant right now, but it didn't need a challenging structure or style on top of it. This is coming into people's living rooms, and I respect that. I'm a consumer of popular entertainment as well and I think it has tremendous powers. I was happy to explore it.

Also, I liked the technical challenge of creating suspense over time. This novel of James M. Cain's is also a departure of his own from the kind of work he's associated with—crime-based, first-person-narrator-based. It's almost this dogged attempt to be classical in a way. What he attempted was a realistic portrait of a mother-daughter portrait. A woman who tries to get what she needs for herself and her daughter. And how doggedly he stays connected to Mildred as a character was something that John and I honored, so it's intensely linear. Nothing occurs in it that isn't witnessed by Mildred in this intense, forward momentum.

**Q:** While the story has been around for decades, this is very much a television project of the moment. You couldn't have made a miniseries in this fashion in the early nineties, when your career was just getting started.
**A:** That's absolutely true. The logistical experience of working with HBO, where they are today, what that offers independent filmmakers is really rare. I really appreciated it. It was a real surprise to find such intelligence at the top of that studio. They were invested in the complexity of the material. There's stuff in there that even at an independent studio, distributors would have been more skittish about.

**Q:** What do you mean by that?
**A:** I assume I just meant—not that material in *Mildred* would be too racy or challenging for the indie film world, but just that it's increasingly harder to find financing these days for serious dramas, domestic stories, female-driven narratives—everything we already know. The recent record profits of studio productions one would hope would have the effect of broadening, not narrowing, the possibilities—since they can afford

it—but, unfortunately, it's having the reverse effect, and that anxiety impacts independent financing as well.

**Q:** What was your motivation for taking on a project like this right now?
**A:** Christine Vachon, my producer after all these years, had just been moving increasingly towards working in television. She had been realizing that the practical opportunities were there for a lot of the projects she had been trying to get off the ground. She said I should really think about doing something for cable at some point. It would be a cool opportunity to do something for that format.

At the time I was going through stuff like *The Wire* and just being blown away. Of course, that's a different thing; it took place over the course of several years. That, along with *The Sopranos*, is some of the best serial television ever produced, just so complex and so socially and politically engaging and intelligent. There's a lot to respect and admire about what's been possible on HBO and other channels. *Mad Men*, on AMC, was sort of a revelation. People sort of bring up that it's very much within the spirit of what I was doing on *Far from Heaven*. I think there are similarities, but I also think they're doing something different.

So it was also serendipity of reading *Mildred Pierce* just as the financial markets were starting to tumble and not having known the book before then—I knew the film version, of course—but not the intense differences between the film and book, and how much more about the financial plight of Mildred is played out over time in the novel. It felt like a really topical and exciting thing to do right now. I had been hearing so much about how we were repeating the Depression years. I was like, fuck, I want to get into the Depression myself and study and learn and immerse myself in all of the details of the era. And it was a very different kind of maternal drama where issues of work and labor are so much more a part of the story because Mildred is this industrious character and all the more interestingly, one motivated by all these sort of unhealthy and misplaced desires based around her daughter. How she transforms that stuff into productivity.

**Q:** To a certain extent, the themes in the film mirror those of *Far from Heaven*. You're dealing with an era of American society in which certain norms resulted in a lot of repressed desires. Also, in both cases, you've adapted to existing conventions of melodrama.
**A:** *Far from Heaven* was going back to what seemed to be the most

apolitical climate of fantasy production—the melodramas of the fifties, a la Douglas Sirk—at the time, although people have been studying those movies and finding all kinds of latent radicality and embedded critical perspectives of modern life, like Fassbinder and others. It's the least likely place to find social political critique, and I think that's all the more reason it's there in such interesting forms.

For *Mildred Pierce*, I looked at it as an opportunity to use a different reference point. There was a time of consciousness about using classical forms and genres and reconfiguring them for a modern audience, and that was the seventies, when traditional genre was being returned to by that film school generation of filmmakers. Those films, while technically honoring those traditions, embodied the sense of the modern, the contemporary. It seemed like they were speaking very overtly about the political and cultural climates of their time. I really liked that. I felt like that was my sort of ambition with taking this on when I did, to talk about now through that framing device. So I was really looking at the way that changed those genres and took them into something relatable and using a very heavy cinematic language.

**Q:** I heard someone speculate the other day that more people saw the first few episodes of *Mildred Pierce* than the entire number of ticket-paying audiences who saw *Far from Heaven* during its initial theatrical run. And that was your biggest box office hit!
**A:** Even still, I heard that the ratings for *Mildred Pierce* were disappointing for a television drama with a major star. I mean, they're not comparable and I never set out to reach the biggest number of people in my work. That's not what motivates me as a filmmaker. And yet *Far from Heaven* might have been my biggest onscreen crossover film, and that was gratifying for me at the time but definitely not something I set out to do. It was really surprising because I wasn't being squeamish or tailoring those codes of storytelling for a contemporary audience.

To me, it was a real statement that the melodrama, that form, really still works and there's something incredibly primal about those stories and using the abstract language of cinema to tell that story. I was even really pleased with how well *I'm Not There* was received—a really difficult, complicated movie. It's full of visual and visceral pleasures. I think it's a fun movie to watch, but it's not a simple structure for today's audiences. I feel like we're becoming less curious as mainstream viewers of film, less open and excited by deviations and experiments. People really want to feel in control of their narrative experiences. That just wasn't the spirit of cultural connoisseurship that I got into during my coming of age, during college. It's a little more conservative culture now. So to get a supportive critical reaction and a passionate following—I definitely don't take that for granted.

### Todd Haynes, Part II: "There's no way I could make *Poison* now"

In the first installment of *indieWIRE*'s two-part interview with Todd Haynes, the director discussed his new miniseries adaptation of *Mildred Pierce* for HBO, which will air its final two episodes Sunday. Here, the director talks about his controversial first feature, *Poison*, which Zeitgeist will re-release on DVD June 21 to commemorate its twentieth anniversary.

Boldly repurposing the writings of Jean Genet to reflect the concerns of an AIDS-afflicted gay community, *Poison* emerged as one of the definitive works of New Queer Cinema, toying with genre and identity and announcing Haynes's arrival as a major film artist. The director spoke to *indieWIRE* about the particular climate surrounding the release of the film, why it couldn't happen today, and the way his original filmmaking community has evolved.

**Q:** Zeitgeist will rerelease *Poison* on DVD in June. Based on what you're saying, it sounds like you wouldn't have been able to make that movie today.
**A:** There's just no way, man. Oh my god. It's sad but true. In some ways, it's because the need to make a movie like that, coming out of the AIDS crisis when it did, there was a whole different regard about the lives of people who were gay that we felt at that time. That was the determination for me to make that movie and also for a lot of other filmmakers to produce work that was loosely characterized as New Queer Cinema. It's because of that necessity, the feeling that this was a means of expression that could be made really pertinent to what was going on in our lives, made me part of that camp. That doesn't happen all the time and creative media don't usually have that extra fire motivating them.

**Q:** The gay relationship story *Weekend*, which premiered at SXSW, was a huge hit. But a lot of people said they were just happy to see a gay movie that was actually good. Why do you think the momentum of New Queer Cinema went away?
**A:** Well, that's interesting to hear. I have to check this film out. It's just such a different culture today. The kind of things associated with gay

people are belonging to mainstream culture, like being gay in the military. I guess, on the most basic level, that's what New Queer Cinema was all about—legitimately feeling like this epidemic was targeted, this minority was not being seen as a priority. Very basic life-or-death issues were at stake. Along with that, there was a questionable discussion about what it means to be gay and look at the world from an outsider perspective. There's a value in that. All of us felt this tremendous power in that marginalization. [Jean] Genet, whose work inspired me to make *Poison*, I don't think he would have had any interest in these exclusion-based politics of contemporary gay culture.

**Q:** Do you think the original inspiration for *Poison* is still alive in the world today?
**A:** I feel like it was a different time, and I was certainly a different person, because the person who was different had more to do with the critical or experimental influences that felt more validated back then. Now, it's not simple for me to watch *Poison* because of all the people we lost as we made it. There was great emotion and tenderness in *Poison*. It was sort of this love poem to Jim Lyons, who was becoming my boyfriend during that time, and was this romantic object in the film, and was my coeditor—he passed away four years ago. That just makes it so much more intense for me to watch. But he's so alive in it, almost unbearably alive. But that's just my own perspective. Certainly, *Poison* meant something specific to that time. I don't know what it would be like for younger people to see today. I'm really interested in finding out what that would be like, but I would totally understand if the connection were difficult.

**Q:** There was a documentary at Sundance about the initial AIDS outbreak in San Francisco called *We Were Here*—
**A:** Oh, that's David Weissman's doc. I just saw him really briefly in San Francisco. We had a little premiere of *Mildred* at the San Francisco Film Society. I'm dying to see his film. I hear it's getting a really great reaction, and it's so simple, just the testimonies of a few people. It's exciting to have it directed at people who need the context and the accessibility. That's awesome.

**Q:** With *Poison* coming out on DVD, do you want the discussion of the film to revolve around AIDS perceptions then and now?
**A:** It's maybe the hardest movie I've made to separate from my own experience of making it, and from its time and place. My films back then

were inspired by social or cultural issues, but they were also experimental narratives, and *Poison* is an extension of things I started looking at with *Superstar*. It's a different style of storytelling from the standard biopic. I was just excited that it reached a certain level of discussion with all the restrictions around it. It also engaged people emotionally, so they could get past the intellectual experiments, and have discussions about how it's being told with dolls. People were talking about the narrative perspective. That excited me. With *Poison* I tried it again by taking three different stories and looking at what the different social attitudes or prejudices of them are. I don't know how people relate to those kinds of narrative experiments today. I'm just happy that it turned into this beautiful new transfer on DVD.

**Q:** Speaking of *Superstar*, I'm watching it right now on YouTube. The clip that I was able to pull up currently has more than 231,000 views. How do you feel about the life this movie, which could not be released due to music rights issues, continues to have?
**A:** That's awesome. That will always be my most famous movie. [laughs] All you have to do is ban something to make sure it's still out there. The desire for it is exponentially increased.

**Q:** The *Poison* DVD includes behind-the-scenes Polaroids shot by Kelly Reichardt. That was before she had even made her first feature, *River of Grass*. Do you think she could make a similar jump to the television arena?
**A:** You know, it's funny, I saw a trailer for *Cinema Verité* the other day, that miniseries about the shooting of *An American Family*. These projects are things she herself would be interested in doing. She was an amazing creative consultant on this project, just so engaged with it. I was calling her constantly. She watched all the auditions and listened to the audiotapes of the novel. So maybe there are more surprises in Kelly's future.

**Q:** It sounds like you've kept the same community of filmmakers close to you over the years.
**A:** Yeah, Jon Raymond was my friend in Portland who I just met socially before I started to read his work. I met Kelly there as well, and she did *Old Joy* based on his story. Then I introduced her to Michelle Williams after we did *I'm Not There* and they did *Wendy and Lucy*. That was a real positive turn for everybody involved. The Jon-Kelly relationship is very close to me.

**Q:** What else are you working on?
**A:** I have some things in my head that I've started to think about, stuff to read over that people have handed me. It's too fresh to talk about. *Mildred* was hard, a real physical endurance test.

# "Something That Is Dangerous and Arousing and Transgressive": An Interview with Todd Haynes

Julia Leyda / 2012

From *Bright Lights Film Journal* 78 (November 2012). Reprinted by permission.

In the process of compiling and editing this collection of interviews with Todd Haynes, I took the opportunity to meet with him myself and ask him some questions of my own. I sat down with Todd Haynes in Portland on March 29, 2012.

**JL:** You've done several movies that are very clearly woman's films, but the movie that I am most fascinated with in terms of gender is *Velvet Goldmine*, which is not usually interpreted in that context.
**TH:** No, except it's probably gotten the strongest female fan base of any of my films. And what's wonderful for me is to see new generations of young women, even as we think we progress as a society and there are new options available to each new generation that seem to be catering to that market more acutely, still *Velvet Goldmine* offers that market something that they're not getting elsewhere. I always love it when girls come up to me at festivals and that's the one, that's the movie that really turned them around.

**JL:** I'm interested in the trope of playing with dolls in *Superstar* and *Velvet Goldmine* as a way to figure gender, embodiment, desire, identification. You said in an interview that playing with dolls is what you're doing in *Velvet Goldmine*, as a metaphor for the filmmaking process. So what about the female characters in *Velvet Goldmine*? Fans, rock and roll girls like Mandy—talk a bit about them.
**TH:** Interesting question. The character of Mandy was probably one of

the hardest roles I've ever had to cast. We did a really thorough, international search for who could play Mandy. When I look back on the experience, I'm amazed at how many actresses agreed to read for the role who don't often do so. I think what was difficult about Mandy was that she, and the Angela Bowie template for that character, harkened back to a kind of performative femininity of which there are very few contemporary examples anymore. I see it as the Patti Smith divide in terms of rock and roll and public depictions of femininity, whose image emerged finally, after so many variations on the codified mannerisms that were available to women in midcentury American film, for instance, and popular music (although there have always been interesting deviations from this). I think over time a lot of the affectations associated with performing femininity had fallen away, to the point where you came to this iconic figure of Patti Smith, whom I see as similar in a way to the Jude figure in *I'm Not There*, a very androgynous, more masculine-identified figure. For young actresses reading the role of Mandy it became clear that recent examples of that kind of almost camp presentation of an affected, theatrical persona were very hard to locate; I think of Liza Minnelli, and maybe Parker Posey was one of the later examples, of almost a gay male idea of femininity.

One thing that was very interesting about Angela Bowie is the way she navigated the English and American influences and her accent would come and go, and that was one of the things we wanted to incorporate into the performance, but that's very tough on an actor. We wanted to make it understood that it's a mutable way of fixing into each culture with some fluidity. I mean, there's no question that Angela Bowie was a central driving engine—her autobiography is amazing, and it's supported by most of the documentation and oral histories of those years—in the transformation of David Bowie, who was experimenting with different kinds of feminine representations but ultimately fixed on this Warhol-infused figure of the Ziggy Stardust character. It was really Angela Bowie who championed these kinds of characters, part of the second-generation Warhol clan, who made their way to the UK and appeared in this play *Pork* in 1971. They just loved her and she loved them, and in a weird way Bowie was sort of a spectator, an observer of this love and energy. And I think, based on what she wrote in her book and other documentation, she was very interested in the gay liberation movement that was burgeoning at the time and she wanted to appropriate it, take it on, and become the spokesperson in a rock and roll vernacular for those ideas.

I don't know if this relates directly to doll-playing except that it really might be the last time that you see an active female figure freely utilizing artificial terms of self-expression and persona in an unembarrassed, unabashed, almost radical way. That was in a way the fascinating counterpart to the more aloof, silent, objectified figure that Bowie assumed as Ziggy Stardust. Of course, there was also that hardcore influence from the American music that he loved—the Stooges, the MC5, and the Velvet Underground and Lou Reed—as the final ingredient to give it that kind of duality, the cross between English musical traditions and this American hardcore, a direct assault. He needed both of those, but there was still a kind of passivity and object-ness of that figure that seemed more quiet, and more comfortable being an image, an idealized beautiful façade that people could project onto; whereas Angela Bowie was active, pulling the strings and moving the levers—in that way, I think, making him up so that he was the doll that she was playing with. So a lot of that energy and that fire and fearlessness I think could be attributed to her.

**JL:** That is how I see the character of Mandy in the film, and the way that she gets shunted aside, because he's moving on to a different persona.
**TH:** Exactly. After first embracing bisexuality in the free flow and openness of that marriage and the flexible terms of their sexual dalliances, she is ultimately excluded by this little romance, pushed to the side and becomes the spectator in the wings. I think of that one scene where they all gather in the wings watching Curt Wild perform a kind of apocalyptic ultimate expression of himself, she's this melancholy observer of what she's had a hand in fostering and then been excluded from.

**JL:** In the doll-playing scene in *Velvet Goldmine*, the girls are like Mandy, manipulating them and fantasizing about them. So that trope of little girls playing with dolls scene really gets at the way the movie is about bisexuality and a kind of less bordered sexual identity, that is based in play, in fantasy—
**TH:** —is fluid, is mutable, is conducive to all kinds of voices and all kinds of players pulling the strings. But one thing that *Velvet Goldmine* kind of misses is how strongly and passionately young women were the driving desiring consumers of this very unique moment in popular culture history. That has continued, too: the androgynous male object is something that still attracts a really passionate, active female spectatorship. That's so fascinating to me, and you can see it played out in so many

different ways: the tradition of the Japanese comics of the seventies, what's it called again?

**JL:** The subgenre of manga with the boy lovers and its girl fans, yaoi.
**TH:** Exactly. The boy lovers and the girl fans, really directed at girl consumers and it's this androgynous, starry-eyed princes and pretty boys who have sparkly eyes for each other.

**JL:** I wondered if you were aware of yaoi or not. When I was working on a conference paper about the girl fans in *Velvet Goldmine* some of my colleagues said, Hey that's just like yaoi! And I said, Wow, it really is.
**TH:** It was a tangent that I learned about in the process of research, but I don't remember when exactly. I was certainly aware of how there was a particular Japanese following with a passionate attachment to the Bowie phenomenon, glam rock, T. Rex; Japan made up a major part of their market. But I think it's an interesting counter-argument to the classic Laura Mulvey idea of a limited female spectatorship and if anything it only further underscores—although I think this is all embedded in that, and though I haven't read those articles in some years—that marginalized subjects, such as gay subjects and women, have to find a more dexterous and nuanced way of reading culture and finding their way into all kinds of content that is not designed for them. I think there's this ability to transform and to enter into all kinds of different subject positions of which this is one amazing and fascinating example: the glam rock thing with young girls' driving interest in it.

**JL:** When I was a teenaged Bowie fan, my mother would say, "You're attracted to him, you have a crush on him, why do you want to look like him? When I was younger I loved Jean-Paul Belmondo, but I didn't want to look like him." But in the seventies, and in my case the eighties, and still today I think, girls of all sexual orientations experience that overlapping between desire and identification—it's there in the Arthur character, too, but I'm thinking of in the opening sequence with the glam girls rampaging.
**TH:** Right, they're absolutely rampaging, terrorizing the town in utter desire. And we all know that the passion that we see displayed there, the intensely sexual display of female spectatorship probably started with Valentino, Sinatra, the Beatles, and Elvis.

**JL:** It's almost hysterical.

**TH:** Yes. There was in these cases an androgynous, feminine element to the actual performance; in a way, just for the star to be up on stage, just to be objectified, is to arguably be feminized. These artists in their unique and shaded ways capitalized on that and the result among female spectators is something that society is still startled by: that radical emotional response that it engenders.

**JL:** Similarly with the British band the Libertines, there was a great deal of sexual ambiguity between the two male performers and it wasn't clear whether they were lovers or just close and demonstrative in ways that we aren't used to seeing among men, but female fans went crazy for that. I think that plays right into this glam dynamic as well—a sort of punk, hard-edged rock and roll, but with a homoerotic side that plays to the girl fans in particular.

**TH:** This *Twilight* phenomenon too—it doesn't really end. Each generation has its own variant on that. It does call into question all sorts of assumptions about opposites attracting, the whole simplistic reductive ideas of what drives desire—

**JL:** —and the borders of identity.

**TH:** Yes, and the female subjects, spectators, consumers, maybe because they've had to learn how to occupy different subject positions in dominant patriarchal culture, have revealed the ways that desiring has narcissistic or self-reflexive aspects. On the other hand maybe male spectatorship has just been so much more catered to and delineated in solid terms, and thus hasn't been able to explore the margins as thoroughly, but women and gay people and African Americans, for example, all have to find different ways of entering mainstream cultural production.

**JL:** I love that the girls with the dolls in *Velvet Goldmine* are storytellers, they are controlling the narrative, in a sense, and that you say that that's what you were doing as a director.

**TH:** I think that's how we all begin to externalize our desires: through storytelling. Dolls are a tool that lends itself to that; they are supposedly made for little girls, and I loved dolls when I was a kid. The Barbie doll became a multiply useful subject in the Karen Carpenter film and that was the internal nod that I was making in *Velvet Goldmine*, but it was so relevant it didn't feel like a detour or a private joke—it felt like it was getting to the core of the intense affect that is felt by these kinds of characters in popular culture. That free-floating desire in the little boy romance that the little girls are constructing is about as sweet and tender as anything in the film.

**JL:** That kind of storytelling, the freedom in play, helps the characters, but also the rest of us, decide who we are and how we want to tell our own stories.

**TH:** It's the story and the engine of the film. It is really the fan's point of view—the Arthur character, obviously—but it's really the theme and the whole motor of it. I always knew I wasn't really interested in getting inside the closed doors of these famous subjects and that's why a fictionalization of this unique period made sense. We all already fictionalize and fill in and fantasize. And we see it too in the whole slash fiction phenomenon, which I didn't even know about until *Velvet Goldmine*, and in which *Velvet Goldmine* has itself become a category.

**JL:** That's the cool thing about *Velvet Goldmine*—it is itself a sort of slash fiction, and there's this ongoing spinoff slash fiction community carrying the stories forward—it's a perfect loop.

**TH:** Yes. To ignite that little flame that makes people want to respond actively and creatively and participate. It reminds me of a girl. . . . I was scared of Bowie when I was in junior high school, and I remember I was aware of him but it was all just too freaky. There was a girl in a lip sync show in seventh grade who picked his song "Changes." She was this beautiful girl and she imitated him, as many girls did, right, because he was so pretty.

**JL:** It was easy for girls to look like him because he was so pretty.

**TH:** And he was mastering makeup, cosmetics, clothes, style, and posing, in every stage of himself, in his evolution: things that girls maybe do a little more in the mirror than boys? But maybe not much more.

**JL:** At that age, with makeup, yes.

**TH:** Exactly. And she just did the perfect lightning bolt like Aladdin Sane, and she got her hair just right—I forgot if she wore a wig. But she performed "Changes" and I remember hearing and thinking, "Oh, this isn't so scary . . ." because I expected it to be really hardcore music and I would be put off by it. But it was so pretty.

**JL:** So she turned you on to Bowie.

**TH:** She really helped. Jean Sagal, I think that's her name.

**JL:** I wonder if she's related to Katey Sagal—[*Married with Children's*] Peggy Bundy.
**TH:** I actually think she is.

**JL:** That would be cool.
**TH:** That would be cool. I think she actually might have been the sister of Katey Sagal.

**JL:** I'm trying not to let my brain explode with that idea! I remember that scene in *Velvet Goldmine* where they're reporting on the news, saying something like, "Girls everywhere are wearing glitter makeup" and that conveyed the society's sense of fear, of what are all those girls up to? The idea that they're going to need to be controlled again somehow because they're getting a little too weird or too powerful.
**TH:** The glitter girls, as they were sometimes called, especially the LA version of the glitter girls, that's another thing I really remember from junior high. As I read later when I studied this period, they were a force to be reckoned with—extremely precocious, among some of the youngest, most adventurous and not violent, but persevering, fearless, active fans. They peopled the Rodney Bingenheimer English Club on Sunset Boulevard—

**JL:** Like the Runaways.
**TH:** Yes, they gave birth to the Runaways. I think it was one of those girls who ended up in Roman Polanski's house, who was fifteen or however old she was, but that's why it's very hard to examine that infringement outside of its cultural context and what was happening at the time in Los Angeles. Glitter girls scared the shit out of me when I was a kid—they were tough, and girls were already ahead of boys at that age, but they were miles ahead. It was intense. I can absolutely picture those kinds of girls and they were intense, in their platform shoes and glitter makeup.

**JL:** With Arthur, I thought you did such a great job developing that character as a kind of giddy, exuberant, awkward young guy. You've said that *Velvet Goldmine* was your most affirmative film, even though the eighties scenes are so dark, it provides the character of Arthur with this memory to cherish even in the middle of the awful eighties.
**TH:** Totally. I don't know if there's a more joyful moment in any of my movies than that little passage that I've been showing as a clip in a couple of festivals and retrospectives of Arthur getting the record, and making

his brother agree to lend him the money, taking it home, opening it up, and that cherished—

**JL:** Fetishized!

**TH:** —fetishized record. And then he leaves the house, stashing his coat and just prancing proudly with his badges down the street with the song playing, and yet still being met with this higher echelon of socially superior kids who look down on him, and the pretty boy who scowls at him for his presumption to even be in their company. But still I think every kid has some version of that: his awkwardness, his passion, his vulnerability, and his strength, too, are all embodied in that ability to fall in love.

That beautiful sequence ends with him turning the page one more time to the page with the image of Curt and Brian kissing. And I remember feeling that, a kind of recoiling, confusion—like it's tapping something exact, absolutely precise, but just too many membranes down to be able to be freed up, able to be voiced or affirmed. But it's something you're bookmarking for the future, that feeling you're going to return to when you have a little more strength, a little more perspective. It's touching something that you know you're going have to get back to because it's something that is dangerous and arousing and transgressive. Christian's performance is so amazing because that sequence starts with him in the classroom, where he really looks all of a sudden like he's fourteen years old, with his ruddy cheeks—

**JL:** —and his really bad bangs. I identified with him utterly and painfully in that scene. And his flailing dancing scene. My God, that character is so beautiful.

**TH:** He did such a beautiful job. He really was so committed and so profoundly inside that guy. I remember when we wrapped and he put away the Arthur clothes and he came back and said, "I just put away the Arthur clothes and cried a little bit." And I don't know if I cried but I sure felt like I could've. I think despite all the beautiful, fancy guys in that movie, I think my heart belonged to Arthur.

**JL:** Of course, because Arthur's us.

**TH:** He is.

**JL:** When he takes that coat off and starts walking down the street it's just: yes! We were all there. I like the way that film gives a few different

positions over to that kind of fandom: audience member, fan, young person who's still working things out, still trying to figure out who they are, and who they want, and who they want to be. The girls as well as Arthur.
**TH:** It's also why the whole package of bisexuality, a kind of performative, made-up, dressed-up sense of identity and self, and coupled with this sense of being extraterrestrial, speaks so directly to adolescent instability and to that moment of uncertainty. It couldn't have been a more total package for the mutability of that time, touching all the nerves and also the freedoms that dressing up allows you, and imagining different kinds of love objects that aren't necessarily the ones you're supposed to have. But even that is blurry, unfixed.

**JL:** Tommy Stone's star image shows the other side of that dressing-up, right? If you can change yourself that radically, you can also change yourself into a horrible, plastic thing.
**TH:** Right, and a kind of converse example. The female fan who comes up to Arthur in that final scene at the bar who is so ecstatic about Tommy Stone because that's all that generation has. That's what they got—it's not their fault that the same desire, the same need for something special is expressed, but it's just not radical, or progressive, or culture-changing. But it's what they've got and I didn't want to blame them because they are part of a culture that had to clamp down around categories once again, resume control of those categories that were seeping into each other so surprisingly for a brief time.

**JL:** Exactly. That limited world that she inhabits and Arthur's wistful smile as he gives her the press pass, seeing her giddiness.
**TH:** Just as the emerald pin is the ultimate token of passing on heritages and opportunities or insights or ways of radically inverting a person's destined experience. That's how that scene is framed with him passing on the press pass to her and Curt passing on the pin to Arthur. There's a nice sense of camaraderie among generations and different stations.

**JL:** Today we're living in what's being called a postfeminist era, meaning that there is the sense among much of the general public that feminism is a kind of done deal, we don't need it anymore, we've achieved gender equality. So many people feel that gender is no longer a required or relevant category for analysis, or for politics. But the women in your films, struggle with their embodiment, their identity, their social positions. *Superstar* and *Far from Heaven* work within those kinds of very limited social roles, but how did you see *Mildred Pierce* departing from that and/ or fitting in with them? For me, Mildred is able to work and to express such eroticism, her embodiedness or physicality comes through more strongly than in your other woman's film characters.

**TH:** So much of the material is full of so many fascinating contradictions. On the one hand, I was startled when I read the original novel at the complexity of this female subject, given the period and the way that we today clumsily impose a sort of pre-sixties idea of what sexual options were available to women in those days.

I mean this as a preface to answering your question—it's evident from the political discourse that's going on right now in this country on the right that we are hardly postfeminist and these are hardly settled issues. It's stunning to think of how recklessly, shockingly honest the conservative right has become. Joe Biden recently said something about how startled he was, because in all of his years in politics, the Republicans have always had to hide the ball. And all of a sudden in this new era they don't have to hide the ball anymore, and they are so unbelievably blatant and vocal about it now. It's clearly backfiring, and let's just pray that there's a price be paid for it.

But what's so fascinating about Mildred as a character is the way she has all of this potential for incredible productive and sexual success: a willfulness and a sense that she deserves it. Of course, there are all kinds of things she has to overcome initially, the sense of pride, before she can go out and get a job and work her way up the ladder and discover her innate talents and, similarly, to venture into areas of sexual exploration that it seems evident that she had never experienced with her husband, while at the same time being so thoroughly harnessed to a whole other set of terms that have everything to do with feminine identification and subjectivity, and mothering, and class. She is just this fascinating contradiction. I found that so relevant and useful to discuss today.

So yes, unlike most domestic dramas, she occupies both the domestic space and the world of work, labor, commerce. And, in this narrative microcosm, the world of work and labor is almost solely manned by women, so to speak. It's all women, and men are casualties to the economic crisis, and to the shifting social and class definitions and aspirations of a radically challenging moment in American social and economic history.

But I don't think I would have been interested in telling that story were Mildred not imbued with all of these strengths and abilities and possibilities, countered by a serious pathology around her daughter, and based also around middle-class aspirations around mobility and excess and all the things that we're told we should be giving our kids. So it all came from an economic and social idea of what middle-class life is about, even while she's seemingly breaking those rules, or expanding or disregarding the limitations that they suggest. Then she turns around and is just completely immobilized and all of her power and confidence and good instincts are undermined by this other issue.

On some basic level, it's about misplaced love or misplaced desire; it's the way that Mildred has invested a kind of romantic love and satisfaction in her maternal role, and how effective withholding love can be, on the part of Veda. She's learned how powerful that is.

**JL:** Right. It's interesting too because Mildred has managed to kind of convert her domestic skills into a corporate success, doing all the motherly, housewifely things cooking and serving home-style meals, but doing them in the market instead of in the private home. But she's unable to make a similar kind of conversion in the other areas of her life.

**TH:** Exactly. And literally converting homes into restaurants. It's all about a conversion of domestic skills and domestic knowledge into an effective business model that is successfully addressing a certain need. In the zeal to give her daughter everything, so much more than she has had, it's so intensely—in the James M. Cain novel, which we're pretty faithful to—and rigorously about class. I just find that to be such a brilliant, critical point of view that counters all of the genuine admirable qualities and successes that she displays. It's a smart, tough, unsentimental criticism of America. It's great.

**JL:** It is. In the original novel there's the whole part about how she loves to drive fast, which is a powerful metaphor for her desire for excitement, power, control, and mobility. In my dissertation I used a quotation from the novel, toward the end of Chapter Four, just after she's dropped Bert off at Mrs. Biederhof's and zooms away in the car:

> She gave the car the gun, excitedly watching the needle swing past 30, 40, and 50. . . . Then she eased off a little on the gas, breathed a long, tremulous sigh. The car was pumping something into her veins, something of pride, of arrogance, of regained self-respect, that no talk, no liquor, no love, could possibly give.

She's so energized, independent, satisfied. So in a way this character makes me think about how much farther she gets to go than Karen

Carpenter or Carol White or Cathy Whittaker, and yet she's still totally frustrated in what she sees as the central relationship in her life. In a way, she seems to break out of some of the woman's film conventions of domesticity, but even though she breaks out of some of that, it's not what she needs.

**TH:** No. I guess I'm just always interested in the ways in which we are not free agents, that our desires, our instincts, our anger, our determination, our survival instincts all butt against social constraints and social learning that are really deep. It's not just a matter of changing your job or your lover. So, in the Depression, the whole way we were looking at how we were going to rebuild this country and retain and preserve certain values that had been learned in a relatively short amount of time, in the 1920s, showed this ability and courage and great examples of human endeavor, but was ultimately still curtailed and limited by patterned behavior about worth and value and rooted in ideals of wealth and success.

**JL:** The women in those films are dealing with so much, particularly related to embodiment: illness, pathology like eating disorders or environmental illness or hysteria, but in Mildred's case also just hard work and the drive that her character seems to physically embody. That drive is part of her physicality, her sexuality.

**TH:** Yes, she's literally a worker in ways I don't think I've explored in a female-driven story. And that performance by Kate Winslet is so remarkable because I think I must have picked up on this in other roles that she's played, but I don't think I've seen it so thoroughly explored as in Mildred: how you see her working and just stomping through life. Even in her sexual life with Monty, she allows herself to go places that are also transgressive. In a weird way it's almost the only place she does seem to feel comfortable being demeaned: in a sexual context where roles are being played in the bedroom and there's a surprising pleasure in enacting different kinds of more denigrated positions, which I think her character and her pride would protect her from in her life outside the bedroom.

Another sense of that appears in the play-acting of class, the performing of class, which it always is at some level and which we learn when we see that Monty has actually lost his money and she's propping it up and underwriting it. This whole idea of a privileged blue-blood, the closest we come to an aristocratic tradition, who is being constructed and supported by middle-class labor.

**JL:** Chicken shacks.

**TH:** Exactly. Because we need the image of it. We see it performed in a questionable way in the world and then performed in a way that can provide surprising and unexpected pleasure in a sexual context in the bedroom. But in both cases it's performative. There's something so funny about how, when Americans are asked what their class affiliation is, it's always wrong. It's always a put-on.

**JL:** That self-misrecognition.
**TH:** Exactly. Rich people always claim they're middle-class, and poor people always claim they're middle-class, and so everybody's middle-class. Such a fascinating way of not knowing ourselves and projecting our wishes, and denying our differences.

**JL:** That fits today obviously, as you said, and with the thirties context with the way that the characters who are most invested in upper-class identity like Veda and Monty are both such horrible, wretched human beings. Also Mrs. Forrester, who tries to hire Mildred as a maid, and tells her she has to come in the back entrance. What Cain was going for and you were able to convey there was the unflinchingly anti-rich sentiment of the time.
**TH:** Right. It's that post-Crash, Depression-era America, quite unlike our recent economic meltdown in which somehow the rich have not been as fully indicted as one would expect. And yet, what is so brilliant is that we see so many people we are supposed to respect and admire, like Mildred, who are so enamored of wealth and those values associated with it. Even just classical music is a marker of ascent, of high-brow culture and of upward mobility; it's something that you proudly allow your children to explore while you can't quite pronounce the words yourself. In a weird way you are guaranteeing your loss of, or disconnection from, your own offspring and that relationship, by propelling them upward.

**JL:** *Stella Dallas*! Exactly the same thing. The working-class mother pushing her daughter to achieve upward class mobility beyond where she herself was able to go, so that they leave their mothers behind.
**TH:** Exactly. The maternal sacrifice.

**JL:** I think that fits in the thirties, but I also wonder if that image of the wealthy from the twenties can also speak to us today. I'm thinking of Fitzgerald's early work, *The Beautiful and Damned*, which is a slightly sympathetic satire of a young upper-class couple who are waiting for him to come into his inheritance, but there are little moments of pathos amid the drunkenness and decadence, because the novel shows how they've been conditioned into their class identity so thoroughly—and it destroys them. It's a drama and a critique all mixed together, which in a way reminds me of *Mildred Pierce* but the other side of it, maybe, and pre-Crash.

**TH:** I haven't read that novel, actually. But I find it very interesting how much *Downton Abbey* has become such a fascination for Americans right now, definitely took some of the wind out of the attention for *Mildred Pierce*, when we were literally competing for prizes. I just said, "Yep, that's who we Americans are. That says it all." Intense worship of wealth, privilege, and the moneyed classes—that persistent and irksome insistence that it's available ultimately to any of us, that you don't want to end the Bush tax cuts because maybe someday that might be me! That little nagging Lotto desire—you have to admire that sort of optimism. All the things we believe about social mobility unfortunately are not supported by statistics anymore, but are still stubbornly rooted in our sense of who we are and who we could be.

**JL:** That was an ironic moment for the awards, sadly perfect. It really does show where the American people are right now.

**TH:** And we know even in the thirties the movies provided escapism, although most of those Fred Astaire / Ginger Rogers movies were about some level of counterfeit assumption of wealth, where he was usually a regular guy who found his way into the top hat, as in the song. A kind of appropriation of those styles, a regular guy could enter into the shoes of the wealthy and be as dashing and graceful as any of them. But those images were profound and provided an imaginary escape from what was happening. It shouldn't totally surprise us, I guess.

**JL:** No. *The Beautiful and Damned.* I want you to make that movie.
**TH:** All right. I will. Good, I'll read it.

**JL:** Here's a Fassbinder quotation about Sirk's *Imitation of Life*: "The cruelty is that we can understand both of them [Sarah Jane and Annie]. Both are right and no one will be able to help them, unless we change the world. At this point, all of us in the cinema cried, because changing the world is so difficult." Every time I read that quote I cry—it gets at the power of melodrama to make people political, not through intellect but through affect. It seems to me that that's something that runs through Sirk and Fassbinder and also a lot of your films. What do you think?

**TH:** That's one of my very favorite passages. With *Far from Heaven* I was trying to devise a sort of diagrammatic narrative without a villain—many melodramas originally featured a dastardly villain tying the heroine to the railroad tracks—but the sophisticated midcentury period of melodrama, which has its roots in the thirties with John Stahl's films that were often directly adapted by Sirk—

**JL:** And *Stella Dallas*.

**TH:** Oh, exactly. In those movies, the rigid social environment is described and basic, relatable human desire emerges and that's all it takes for certain decisions to be made that put inordinate pressure on the subjects. What's really touching about melodrama, as Thomas Elsaesser has written, that these films are about people who are not up to the challenges that they face, they are not heroes. And while they seem to be about as glossy and gorgeous and perfect as any hero in any other kind of movie, they really are like us that way. So they cave in.

I love that moment in *All That Heaven Allows* after she's broken up with the Rock Hudson character due to the pressure of her kids, and then she calls them up and they're like, oh, mom, I'm going to sell the house, and I'm going to marry this guy, and all of a sudden, everything she just sacrificed to satisfy them, and to stop the tears from the daughter in that insane scene in the daughter's bedroom with the stained glass window, all of that comes to nothing. Life has these sudden absurd turns where we're left behind and no one even knows it, it's not intentional; it's just life. It moves forward and leaves you and your sacrifices behind. So melodrama shows the ways that we give in to the social pressures that we see as futile and meaningless, and we wish that that person could have stood up and said no, and when they do it's just too late for other reasons and there's a twist of fate or timing that makes it all feel so fragile, so fickle, and so out of their determination. *Imitation of Life* is the one that makes us all cry in ways few other Sirk films do—they are all Brechtian in so many fascinating ways, they do bring you in and push you out at the same time, and push you to consider these subjects against the social forces. But in that one there's something so innately bare and exposed about Annie's pain and the daughter who just wants to have a life, and more options and choices. She didn't plan to be light-skinned; it's just what she is and so she's afforded certain movement in society that her mother wasn't. You do understand all the sides, and it kills you.

In *Far from Heaven*, I tried to put everybody in a kind of tangle so that when one person makes a step toward their desire, it ricochets around everybody and everybody suffers accordingly. But you can't really blame or isolate any individual for that. In *Safe* it was a bit more tricky, in that I was following the logic and the narrative expectations that we come to have in the tradition of disease movies, and the way a kind of self-realization is afforded these subjects in these kinds of movies by the end of the film. We followed those narrative steps while laying evidence of the values attributed to that self-knowledge, that growth, that realization, against the viewer. So you have to weigh the evidence, and feel the narrative closure that usually makes you feel relief, but in this case you had collected too many cues to question whether these values are really beneficial to this character. I had that young person's slight nastiness in misleading you, like making Peter Dunning a sufferer of AIDS, which we knew was a kind of plus—you have to trust him because he has AIDS, so what he says to his gathering of followers has got to be reliable. It's a little trick to hook you into thinking.

**JL:** So at the end of *Safe*, when she says, "I love you" to the mirror: I always saw that as a dark moment where she's mouthing the words of the other character from earlier in the film, in her desperation. But I just watched it again last week, with a friend who argued that Carol is getting better, because in the last part of the movie she actually laughs more, she's finding something new in her life. I thought, wow, you are so much more of an optimistic person than I am.
**TH:** Right. It's complicated. It plays into what we are all told, these universalized ideas about self-reliance and about feeling empowered by assuming responsibility for what happens to us in the world. That's very much what the conservative model is when it's played out in political terms. A notion of liberty gets construed with that, and when a government tries to create safety measures and ways of intervening imbalances and fates that seem to be beyond the individual's control, you're depriving them of their own liberty, mobility, freedom, and responsibility.

Yet I saw that same idea being played out in more leftist recovery theories. And we all are subject to them, we all play that game when we get sick, saying "What did I do to make myself get sick?" Even in the smallest ways, and in the biggest ways. Culpability makes us feel like we can control things that are bigger than us; it's a profound and fascinating part of human nature. I think in that way it's not an absolute; you see somebody following the rules and being told that they're in control, and it feels good to be told you're in control even when you may not win in the end. I think that's why people can have both points of view about it. But I always find that middle section of *Safe* to be the most optimistic or hopeful, where everything is falling apart and she doesn't even know who she is anymore, and she starts to go to the discussion group and she's taking an active role in questioning the terms of her life and illness in ways that she never had before. Maybe she's not laughing but there's some potential there; she's not being told what to think. There's a sense of the unknown and the indeterminate, that each subject has to figure it out for themselves.

**JL:** I see that, the way she's trying to investigate her illness and contradicts her doctor.
**TH:** Right, and standing up to her husband.

**JL:** That is a particularly American desire for control. That's the way you have talked in earlier interviews about the Louise Hay books—and there is a similar rhetoric in cancer self-help literature; even as we know that the immune system is influenced by things like stress, that doesn't give you cancer. There is that imposed causality and self-blame that the sick person ends up with. That movie perfectly illustrates that dynamic.
**TH:** I just wonder when people say, everything happens for a reason, that idea—does that translate to European cultures in the same way? Cultures that have social safety nets in place and where the individual is liberated a bit from their own part in everything that happens to them. Is there at least an acknowledgment by governments that things happen that we don't necessarily control, determine, and should be held responsible for? There was a fascinating article recently in the *New York Times* about how certain districts in the United States that receive the most support from Medicare and Medicaid are often also the most Republican. They have a contradictory way, at best, of understanding their dependency and their entitlement to those programs. They speak sometimes within the same sentence on both sides of the discussion, but ultimately, in their gut, they resent the government social welfare programs even when they are recipients. They don't realize how much a fading middle class has forced Medicare to be something that pays out so much more than we paid into it, it's had to grow and prop up a waning middle class when it's never had that burden before. It's so interesting and complicated and stubborn.

**JL:** I was talking to a German insurance agent about health insurance there, and I asked about pre-existing conditions. He said, that's so ridiculous. If you're sick, you definitely need insurance—why wouldn't we give it to you? I wonder if it's related to the cliché that European thinking is more fatalistic, so that they accept that you're going to get sick—it's not a question of personal responsibility or blame. You can't bootstraps yourself out of a serious illness.

**TH:** Bad things are going to happen, we're all going to get sick, we're all going to die.

**JL:** Right—death is definitely something Americans don't want to think about. So you're working on something about conservative American politics now.

**TH:** Yes. It's still early on, but it definitely engages all of these economic ideas and in my own way, similar to my process of making *Safe*, I'm trying to understand things that I might initially have resistance to or prejudice against or even dismissal toward. In this case, it's about a populist, conservative way of thinking, and a contempt for government that has been so effective for the right. How that relates to working and rural Americans and some less educated populations, and how it has been so effective and enduring. The far right's policies don't really seem to be interested in the specific needs of those constituencies, and yet they've had a way of speaking to them. It clues into these exact ideas and instigating positions that we're talking about.

**JL:** The narratives of personal responsibility, the bootstraps rhetoric.

**TH:** Exactly. And the feeling that other people are getting benefits, gaming the system—the old "welfare queen" idea that really hasn't died. Sadly, it's just so disheartening to see, after an economic crisis that was so much the result of an unfettered, unregulated financial culture run wild, wreaking such havoc on these exact communities and lives, that it hasn't engendered a fellow feeling for other people. That seemed to be the case in the 1930s, where you just see more of a politics of resentment, and hate at its worst, far too many examples of it. And it's coincidental with a shifting majority in this country, with, obviously, the first black president—a kind of panic over what it means to be a white American looking forward in time, and asking who's looking out for the white American man today. That's unfortunate because it just feeds into similar kinds of resentments toward otherness of all kinds, that there are too many ways of expressing.

**JL:** That reminds me of Huey Long. I'm from Louisiana, just a disclaimer, but he branded a form of populism in the thirties that scared the hell out of the rich. He could have been president if he wasn't—
**TH:** —a maniac!

**JL:** Right, a maniac, and from Louisiana, and deeply corrupt. But his rhetoric tapped into something and caught on fire and scared a lot of people in power.
**TH:** Oh, definitely.

**JL:** So when I saw *Mildred Pierce* and started thinking about the things that the thirties and today share and don't share, that's one of the big ones. A real respect for working people, and some kind of left populist political movement. Melissa Harris Perry just said something like that about Long on her show, and I thought, bingo.
**TH:** Yes, what's so funny is so many people now who consider themselves conservatives, were part of the counter-culture of the sixties and the Baby Boomers: a lot of people who voted for McGovern in '72 and identified with the anti-war movement, which was also an anti-government movement.

**JL:** And anti-authoritarian, which today's anti-government movements don't share.
**TH:** Exactly. The same anti-government instincts, resentments, suspicions of so many things: the draft, Watergate.

**JL:** So that slots into the seventies.
**TH:** Right. The seventies economic challenges created a kind of hocus pocus where the very same people who hated the LBJ government because of Vietnam in the early seventies and carried those resentments and applied them to the Nixonian corruption of the mid- seventies, ended up voting for Reagan in 1980. It's the same people. The only through-line is a sense of "get off my back," whether it was the left or the right, and the party affiliation becomes a more mobile flexible afterthought almost. It was the brilliance of the Reagan culture to tap right into that, and also what we don't see today, to filigree it with optimism and a benign future, and that American exceptionalism, again, the idea that we can overcome our problems and rise up the economic ladder. The same promises to working people that they have the ability to ascend. It was a newly

glamorous era as well, which when you lived through it was disturbing, but it worked.

**JL:** I just taught a "US Film in the Seventies" course and my students were amazed by that seventies-era, across-the-board rejection of authority: that suspicion of government, of parents, of traditional middle-class sexuality. Anti-authoritarianism was such a given at that time and then there's just a wall that comes up in the eighties with Reagan and Thatcher. *Velvet Goldmine* positions that really well too.

**TH:** Yes, it was a radical shift. When you look at the policy positions of Republicans in the seventies, like Nixon, it's stunning to see how far out of the mainstream they would be today. How far we have diverted to the right, while at the same time, certain social values have progressed in positive ways: views about gays in this country, for example. You can see a society literally learning, the way you did in the civil rights era, and actually exceeding the positions of politicians, moving faster than them. That's an amazing thing to see amid so many other kinds of resentments.

**JL:** In the nineties, in the context of multiculturalism, different liberation movements were concerned about the politics of representation: is visibility the ticket to equality? Or is it just another kind of tokenism, where people can say, "Well, there's a black character on this sitcom, so we're not racist anymore." Especially with a growing number of queer characters—mainly white, male, middle-class—more and more visible on television, and the "It Gets Better" movement. I saw a really interesting YouTube comeback to that by a working-class lesbian of color, who said, basically, "It doesn't actually get better if you live in my neighborhood, but you get stronger. Don't give up, and live strong."

**TH:** That's cool—that's interesting.

**JL:** She was putting a powerful class spin on what I previously had seen as a great grassroots movement, but suddenly she reminded everybody—

**TH:** —where that might be coming from. Right. I read something recently about southern gay marriages and couples in the South, how there's a growing number of women getting together with other women in the South, often in interracial relationships, where in terms of regional social and economic factors you would least expect it. It also seemed to make a lot of sense. I think the changes in attitudes about gay issues is just a result of the fact that it does happen everywhere—it's not determined by socio-economic or racial or regional factors. Because people have more opportunity to speak about it, they're recognizing that they know gay people in their lives all over the place. What determined Jesse Helms, in the very last years of his life, all of a sudden reversing his positions about gay issues? My only explanation is that there was a kid, a nephew or somebody in the family who emerged, like in the Cheney family. It's unavoidable now.

But I do think there's been a retreat from complex issues of representation around gay subjects, and minority subjects. New Queer Cinema in the 1990s was really a pivotal moment not just because it was fueled by a socio-economic crisis and imperative to speak about gay themes, but it produced complex work that didn't simply create new gay heroes as subjects. It dealt with the politics of representation, it ventured into transgressive themes, whether it was a film like *Poison* or *Swoon*, challenged simple ideas about victimhood and subjugation. It's really hard to find examples of that surviving today. Although clearly the increasing number of gay characters inhabiting television shows, like *Will and Grace* and *Glee*, is positive. One hopes that that makes the experience of gay teens coming out a slightly less lonesome, fearful experience, although I've heard so many stories over the years: it's always hard. It's hard to be a teenager, period. It's hard to confront your difference from others, period. And we all have them no matter who we are and what we are. And it's just hard times and you feel alone. We see the examples of that to this day, even when we think that we have a much more benign and accepting culture, surrounding us. But it's still tough—it's tough just at an individual level.

And that's why melodrama is so powerful still—I was so surprised to see how effective it was, sticking so rigorously to the artificial language of fifties American melodramatic tropes a la Sirk, almost as a kind of academic exercise or an experiment in how that would communicate with a contemporary audience. And because we were so rigorous about that, I felt like I was making as experimental a film as I made in any of my other works. To see that film get a larger reception was rewarding, and it really worked for people, those forms really work. That was reassuring in so many ways. It took a careful appropriation of them with the very best actors possible obviously, but it was not something I would have expected; other genres, I can see how they endure and keep finding relevant and new audiences that speak more directly to their allure. But melodrama is kind of a closed system, as movies they're not as pleasurable—even the very best ones leave you feeling kind of frustrated and uncertain at the end.

**JL:** Yes, exactly. The exquisite pain of melodrama where you're feeling so emotionally devastated by what's happening on the screen at the same time that you know it's a story, it's not real. True, Sirkian melodrama is systematic, but I'm thinking of maybe a bigger category such as the woman's film. Recently, not only *Far from Heaven* but *Black Swan*—as a hybrid of body horror and woman's film—and some interesting foreign films like Almodóvar's *The Skin I Live In*, where he's playing with the mad scientist horror genre (a nod to *Poison*?), but it's a woman's film although it turns out the character was originally not a woman. And more conventional woman's films are still being made abroad as well: in *When We Leave*, a young Turkish woman in Berlin struggles with her family's conservatism and her own bicultural subject position. So I think you're right that *Far from Heaven*, even working within the very fifties-based signification system, touched something in American audiences that maybe they didn't know still worked; and of course some of these other woman's films can still do that in a more modern style.

**TH:** Oh, definitely. I think there's a message about difference in a lot of them, too. I mean *The Help* is another example of a recent crossover story—but they're supported by these excesses of self-awareness or self-knowledge: that way that we expect characters to come to an understanding of their circumstances and that we learn as they're learning. And yes, Almodovar, who constitutes his own brilliant tradition of playing with humor and camp excess coupled with incredibly poignant depictions of women across his films. But with room for a pleasurable interaction where you can enter and exit the confines of the story with a little bit more self-awareness.

I think the tricky thing about melodrama is that the characters don't really come to profound knowledge—they don't have that element of tragedy that has a cathartic payoff, where your suffering is made overt, externalized, and then they come to see the truth. And that's tough, because then you're only left with a sadness. In many ways, *Far from Heaven* had a bit of a tragic ending, an ending of mourning and loss, that the more traditional Sirk films don't provide you—they more often provide false happy endings or little trick catastrophes at the end that are somehow sustained in an irrational way. They leave you feeling uncertain about how things can change—I think they don't make you feel that things can change. They reify the social constraints that the characters struggle through all along and you're watching them move into a dire circumstance and you want to help them, but you can't and they can't really help themselves. So there's no real fun in it.

**JL:** No, no. But it's a weird masochistic pleasure.

**TH:** It is. And that they're ultimately socially indicting—that's for many of us the ultimate pleasure, and a rarity. That in the most popular, gorgeous, art-directed melodramas, which are seemingly full of really prescriptive examples of the way we are supposed to live and supposed to look, society is not let off the hook, that it is finally the intractable villain.

**JL:** Yes, right. That's almost the opposite of what some of the criticism you hear about *Mad Men*, that we see how sexist and racist people used to be and how great everything is now. I think that's a huge oversimplification of what that show's doing—

**TH:** Yes, I agree.

**JL:** —but with the Banana Republic tie-ins and the smart phone apps and that PR side of it, there is a whole corporate, entertainment industry project that has to be mobilized to create what *Mad Men* is—it's not just what we watch on the screen. Whereas in something like *Far from Heaven* you absolutely shut down the possibility of that kind of condescending attitude. We can clearly see that her world is much worse than ours, but it doesn't make us happy about our world necessarily or cause that self-congratulatory sense that at least some audiences of *Mad Men* experience it.

**TH:** I think also the complexity of so many of the characters of *Mad Men*, who we live with now, they are kind of our companions—I think that immediate sense of superiority that it first espoused, snickering about smoking in front of your baby or putting cellophane over your kid's face, doesn't keep working when you live with these people over time. I just watched the first episode [of season five] and I don't know what to make of it, I'm still adjusting to it again—it's been a while since I've seen it. Don is so erotically and seemingly romantically directed toward the new wife, Megan: I'm confused by it. I mean, he still seems like a complicated character who's hard to totally condone, but I find this troubling—he's troublingly healthy!

**JL:** Right—we want him to get better, but we don't. We love his pathology!

**TH:** We don't! That's right.

**JL:** I haven't watched it yet. But I didn't want to stop you because I wanted to hear your take on him.

**TH:** Oh, sorry! I don't think I gave anything away. He's still with her.

**JL:** I think all of your work has balanced on that knife edge of nostalgia— *Velvet Goldmine* clearly, even *Superstar*, in which you shut down the potential for smug irony almost immediately, because it is so surprisingly but instantly compelling and so easy to sympathize with the dolls. In *Far from Heaven*, too, it's impossible to feel a distance from those characters. That gets back to what the Fassbinder quote, the idea that the social or political critiques that we get from those films are only effective because they're inside us, they've moved us emotionally, not only convinced us of an intellectual argument.

**TH:** Yes, I think that's true. But I do think there's a dance around being outside and inside, with that film and wondering what the filmmaker is really doing with these conventions.

**JL:** *Superstar*, you mean?

**TH:** Both. I guess I was thinking of *Far from Heaven* but it's definitely true for *Superstar*. It has a more seemingly gleeful or initially pernicious, campy play, that in a weird way disarms you so that I think you become exposed to the emotional impact of it precisely because it seems to be devoid of that. I think with *Far from Heaven* there's probably something comparable going on, but we're more thinking, ah, okay he's doing these things with these conventions; where is it going? As opposed to the relief of those conventions as in a movie like *Pleasantville*, where the black and white becomes color and the past becomes sophisticated and it's very much a kind of *Mad Men*, retro, superior take, updating and painting in the past to give it the sophistication of the present. You're not afforded that privilege or superiority in *Far from Heaven*, and I think at a certain point the content really sneaks up on you, and the performances and the music and the language of the medium actually work. But I suspect that some of that is because of the "I'm not expecting it to do so" equation—

**JL:** Because some people will see it and think it's going to be really fake—

**TH:** Yes, and it's a play on the past styles and storytelling of the past, using those kinds of retro midcentury American clichés against our allegedly more sophisticated perspective of today. I think that might disarm you from resistance to its emotional impact, in a weird way. This wasn't necessarily strategic on my part—I just wanted it to be beautiful, and beautifully artificial, and make a visual impact with that magnificence of cinematic artifice, all the elements including the music, the color, the clothes, that are kind of a pure, non-cognitive perception.

There was a little three-year-old child who watched *Far from Heaven* with her mom on her lap. She just figured the kid would go to sleep while she watched the DVD, and watched the whole movie and at the end of the movie the little kid started to cry. She looked down at the kid and she said, honey, what's the matter? And the kid said, Mommy, how come that nice lady can't be with that nice man? And that's where I felt that there's something about that classical language that we had so humbled ourselves toward, reappointing and re-summoning and learning from and trying to bring to a contemporary film. I felt it works, and that's the kind of movie that I've always loved. I was kind of shocked because I never really thought that I could ever do that, because I have too many ideas and authorial interference, but, at that level, I thought that was cool. That speaks to the form and to these traditions that go beyond critical apparatus and really communicate at the most basic level of what cinema can convey.

**JL:** I would love to experience that movie as an innocent—it's impossible. I already know Sirk, so when I watched it I was just cheering it along.
**TH:** Do you know the movie *The Reckless Moment*? Because it's hard to find.

**JL:** Yes! The scene on the bed, and in the car when they're talking, oh yes!
**TH:** It's fantastic. I love that movie so much. It's another one I group with the Sirk films that inspired *Far from Heaven*.

**JL:** Which is such a guilty pleasure for people who know, but I love that it obviously appealed to people who didn't.
**TH:** Yes, probably more so than any other film I've made. *Mildred*'s the hard one to gauge, because I know that more people saw it than anything I've made, but it's TV. The process is different, so it's like this crazy void that you throw your work out into. Of course, you never really know what people's experiences are, but you use those few examples of being in screenings of your films as little indicators of the experience, so there was a lot less of that with *Mildred*.

**JL:** I guess so. So you didn't get to watch people watch it—that's too bad. So are you doing other things for television?
**TH:** I'd like to—there are some things I think would be appropriate for a multi-episode scale.

**JL:** Are you doing something with the novel *Dope* by Sarah Gran?
**TH:** That's a project that Julianne Moore brought to HBO and wanted to turn into a series, I believe. Do you know the book?

**JL:** Yes, I liked it a lot and could envision it as movie or miniseries immediately.
**TH:** Yes, it's really interesting. But it didn't come from me; she asked if I would do the pilot of it for HBO. I think they're still figuring out if they want to do it, and she's still figuring out about the timing of doing a regular series, whether it would be a good idea. But I love the time and place of it, it's so unusual. And the central character.

**JL:** Yes, and what it's doing with that hard-boiled genre is so freaky and great.
**TH:** I know! I could picture it when I read it.

**JL:** I could see you doing that. That would be another adaptation—you've previously written all your own movies up until *Mildred*.
**TH:** And this isn't something I originated; she just asked me if I would do the pilot. I don't even know what that entails—I think to some degree you set up the style for the ongoing series, but I don't think I would be the showrunner or the regular person on it. All this is sort of new to me, this whole TV thing.

**JL:** Well, the paradigm of quality television is still being created, right? Filmmakers like Scorsese working on *Boardwalk Empire*. Shows with well-known directors to initially—
**TH:** —launch them, right. And then move on. It was a great experience working with HBO in the end. I really admired their intelligence, expertise, and conscientiousness about it and it felt finally for the first time maybe ever that we were—well, we were working with a studio! On intensely solid ground, and I don't think I've ever felt that before—I don't think Christine [Vachon] has ever felt that before. Even just for her, I was thinking, you have so earned this, man! You have just earned this in spades, to feel supported where there are other people worrying about every cent and you can be there for the creative experience, like she was on *Poison* and other stuff at the very beginning. But she was often dueling with the dragons and slaying the beasts on most of the films we've made together since.

# Key Resources

This book of interviews is necessarily partial and incomplete, reflecting editorial decisions, access to material and to permissions, and, of course, the still vibrant career of Todd Haynes as he continues to make movies. This list offers some of the interviews that aren't reprinted here, along with other published works of interest to students and scholars of Todd Haynes.

### Interviews Not Included

Demby, Eric. "Wylde in the Streets." *Ray Gun* 62 (1998). Print.

DiStefano, Blase. "An Interview with Director Todd Haynes." *OutSmart*, November 1998. Web.

———. "Heavenly Haynes." *OutSmart*, June 2004. Web.

Kennedy, Lisa. "Doll Boy." *Village Voice*, November 24, 1987: 68. Print.

Klinger, Gabriel. "A Velvet Goldmine's Worth of Good Press in an Interview with Glam's Screen Author." *24FPS Movie Fanzine*, 1998. Web.

Krach, Aaron. "Stardust Memories: Todd Haynes Recreates the Velvet Revolution." *Independent Film & Video Monthly*, December 1998. Web.

Kugler, Ryan. "Life Affirmed: An Interview with *Far from Heaven* Director Todd Haynes." *Cinemaspeak.com*, November 4, 2002. Web.

Lally, Kevin. "Far from Hollywood: Todd Haynes Breaks Convention with Sirk-Inspired Melodrama." *Film Journal International* 105.11 (2002): 12–14.

Levy, Shawn. "Interview: Todd Haynes on *I'm Not There*." *Oregonian*, November 18, 2007. Web.

Marcus, Greil. "Dylan Times Six." *Rolling Stone*, November 29, 2007: 73–77. Print.

Michael, David. "Todd Haynes: *Far from Heaven*." *BBC Films*, November 2004. Web.

Moverman, Oren. "Human Haynes." *Interview*, February 1997, 60+. Print.

———. "Superstardust: Talking Glam with Todd Haynes." *Velvet*

*Goldmine: A Screenplay*. Todd Haynes. New York: Miramax-Hyperion, 1998. ix-xxxi. Print.

Nelson, Rob. "All that Glitter Allows." *Citypages*, November 4, 1998. Web.

Painter, Jamie. "Dottie Gets Spanked." *Film Threat* 15 (April 1994): 53. Print.

Polito, Robert. "Todd Haynes." *The Believer*, March / April 2008. Web.

Radish, Christina. "Kate Winslet and Director Todd Haynes Interview: *Mildred Pierce*." *Collider*, February 2, 2011. Web.

Romney, Jonathan. "Interview: Todd Haynes." *Sight and Sound* 18.1 (January 2008): 21+. Print.

Schaefer, Stephen. "Gold Miner." *Advocate*, September 15, 1998: 43–47. Print.

Sprott, Stephen. "Ground Control to Major Todd." *Index*, June/July 1998. Web.

Stephens, Chuck. "Gentlemen Prefer Haynes: Of Dolls, Dioramas, and Disease: Todd Haynes' *Safe* Passage." *Film Comment* 31 (July/August 1995): 76+. Print.

Taubin, Amy. "Nowhere to Hide." *Sight and Sound*, May 1996, 32–34. Print.

Thompson, Ben. "Stop! Glamour Time." *Neon*, 1998. Web.

"Todd Haynes: From Karen Carpenter to *Poison*." *Film Threat Video Guide* 7 (1993). Print.

Winslet, Kate. "Todd Haynes." *Interview*, March 2011. Web.

### Written by Todd Haynes

Haynes, Todd. "Early Cinematic Influences." *Cinema Papers* (1998). Print.

———. Far from Heaven, Safe, *and* Superstar: The Karen Carpenter Story: *Three Screenplays*. New York: Grove, 2003. Print.

———. Foreword. *Glam! Bowie, Bolan and the Glitter Rock Revolution*. Barney Hoskyns. London: Faber and Faber, 1998. Print.

———. "Homoaesthetics and *Querelle*." *Subjects / Objects* 3 (1985): 70–100. Print.

———. "Kelly Reichardt." *BOMB* 53 (1995). Web.

———. *Velvet Goldmine: A Screenplay by Todd Haynes*. New York: Miramax-Hyperion, 1998. Print.

Haynes, Todd, Julianne Moore, and Christine Vachon. ". . . And All Is Well in Our World: Making *Safe*." *Projections: Film-makers on*

*Film-making.* Ed. John Boorman and Walter Donohue. London: Faber, 1996. 198–234. Print.

### Video Sources

"Discussion of *Far from Heaven.*" *Jerome Hill Centennial: A Filmmaker and His Legacy.* Walker Art Center, Minneapolis. November 19, 2005. Web.

Dyer, Richard. "Double Indemnity: Todd Haynes / Edward Hopper." Tate Modern, London. June 4, 2004. Web.

"Filmmakers Live: Todd Haynes in der Black Box." Filmfest München. July 4, 2012. *YouTube.* Web.

"Infinite Pleasure: Todd Haynes on Max Ophuls." *Le Plaisir.* Max Ophuls. Criterion Special Edition. 2008. DVD.

Interview. *Reel Report.* CNETTV.co.uk. December 7 and 18, 2007. Web.

*Superstar: The Karen Carpenter Story. Google Video.* Web.

"Todd Haynes: From Fassbinder to Sirk and Back." *Ali: Fear Eats the Soul.* Rainer Werner Fassbinder. Criterion Special Edition. 2003. DVD.

"Todd Haynes Master Class: Conversation with Boyd Van Hoeij." XIIth Queer Film Festival Mezipatra, Prague. November 12, 2011. *YouTube.* Web.

### Books

Davis, Glyn. *Far from Heaven.* Edinburgh: Edinburgh UP, 2011.
———. *Superstar: The Karen Carpenter Story.* London: Wallflower, 2008.
Hastie, Amelie, ed. *Todd Haynes: A Magnificent Obsession.* Special Issue. *Camera Obscura* 57 (2004): 1–219.
Morrison, James, ed. *The Cinema of Todd Haynes: All That Heaven Allows.* London: Wallflower, 2007. Print.
Vachon, Christine. *Shooting to Kill: How an Independent Producer Blasts Through the Barriers to Make Movies That Matter.* London: Bloomsbury, 1998. Print.

### Book Chapters

Andrew, Geoff. "Todd Haynes." *Stranger than Paradise: Maverick Filmmakers in Recent American Cinema.* New York: Limelight, 1999. 233–56. Print.
Cook, Pam. "Rethinking Nostalgia: *In the Mood for Love* and *Far from Heaven.*" *Screening Nostalgia: Memory and Nostalgia in Cinema.* London: Routledge, 2005. 1–19. Print.
DeAngelis, Michael. "The Characteristics of New Queer Filmmaking:

Case Study—Todd Haynes." *New Queer Cinema: A Critical Reader*. Ed.
and introd. Michele Aaron. New Brunswick, NJ: Rutgers UP, 2004.
41–52. Print.

———. "Todd Haynes and Queer Authorship." *Auteurs and Authorship: A
Film Reader*. Ed. Barry Keith Grant. Oxford: Blackwell, 2008. 292–303.
Print.

Dyer, Richard. "The Point of Pastiche." *Pastiche*. London: Routledge,
2007. 137–85. Print.

Hawkins, Joan. "The Sleazy Pedigree of Todd Haynes." *Sleaze Artists:
Cinema at the Margins of Taste, Style, and Politics*. Ed. Jeffrey Sconce.
Durham: Duke UP, 2007. 189–218. Print.

Luciano, Dana. "Nostalgia for an Age Yet to Come: *Velvet Goldmine*'s
Queer Archive." *Queer Times, Queer Becomings*. Ed. E. L. McCallum
and Mikko Tuhkanen. Albany: State U of New York P, 2011. 121–55.
Print.

Shahani, Nishant. "The Surface of Things in *Far from Heaven*." *Queer
Retrosexualities: The Politics of Reparative Return*. Lanham: Lehigh UP-
Rowman and Littlefield, 2012. 67–90. Print.

Wyatt, Justin. "Todd Haynes." *Fifty Contemporary Film Directors*. Ed.
Yvonne Tasker. London: Routledge, 2002. 186–95. Print.

### Articles

Bennett, Chad. "Flaming the Fans: Shame and the Aesthetics of Queer
Fandom in Todd Haynes's *Velvet Goldmine*." *Cinema Journal* 49.2
(2010): 17–39. Print.

Bouchard, Danielle, and Jigna Desai. "'There's Nothing More Debilitat-
ing than Travel': Locating US Empire in Todd Haynes' *Safe*." *Quarterly
Review of Film and Video* 22.4 (2005): 359–70. Print.

Bryson, Norman. "Todd Haynes's *Poison* and Queer Cinema." *Invisible
Culture: An Electronic Journal for Visual Culture* 1 (1999). Web.

Bullock, Marcus. "Treasures of the Earth and Screen: Todd Haynes's
Film *Velvet Goldmine*." *Discourse* 24.3 (2002): 3–26. Print.

Burdette, K. "Queer Readings / Queer Cinema: An Examination of the
Early Work of Todd Haynes." *Velvet Light Trap* 41 (1998): 68–80. Print.

DeFalco, Amelia. "A Double-Edged Longing: Nostalgia, Melodrama,
and Todd Haynes's *Far from Heaven*." *Iowa Journal of Cultural Studies* 5
(2004). Web.

Grossman, Julie. "The Trouble with Carol: The Costs of Feeling Good
in Todd Haynes's *Safe* and the American Cultural Landscape." *Other
Voices* 2.3 (2005). Web.

Hastie, Amelie. "Sundays with Mildred." *Film Quarterly* 65.1 (2011): 25–33. Print.

Jacobs, Amber, and Rob White. "Todd Haynes's *Mildred Pierce*: A Discussion." *Film Quarterly*, 2012. Web.

Landy, Marcia. "'The Dream of the Gesture': The Body of / in Todd Haynes's Films." *boundary 2* 30.3 (2003): 123–40. *Academic Search Premiere*. Print.

Luciano, Dana. "Coming Around Again: The Queer Momentum of *Far from Heaven*." *GLQ: A Journal of Lesbian and Gay Studies* 12.2–3 (2007): 249–72. Print.

Reid, Roddey. "Unsafe at Any Distance: Todd Haynes' Visual Culture of Health and Risk." *Film Quarterly* 51.3 (1998): 32–44. Print.

Richardson, Niall. "*Poison* in the Sirkian System: The Political Agenda of Todd Haynes's *Far from Heaven*." *Scope* 6 (2006). Web.

Skvirsky, Salomé Aguilera. "The Price of Heaven: Remaking Politics in *All That Heaven Allows*, *Ali: Fear Eats the Soul*, and *Far from Heaven*." *Cinema Journal* 47.3 (2008): 90–121. Print.

Tougaw, Jason. "We're Still Vulnerable: Todd Haynes's *Safe* in 2011." *WSQ: Women's Studies Quarterly* 39.1–2 (2011): 43–47. Print.

Willis, Sharon. "The Politics of Disappointment: Todd Haynes Rewrites Douglas Sirk." *Camera Obscura* 54 (2003): 131–46. Print.

# Index